POSTHUMAN FOLKLORE

POSTHUMAN FOLKLORE

TOK THOMPSON

UNIVERSITY PRESS OF MISSISSIPPI / JACKSON

The University Press of Mississippi is the scholarly publishing agency of
the Mississippi Institutions of Higher Learning: Alcorn State University,
Delta State University, Jackson State University, Mississippi State University,
Mississippi University for Women, Mississippi Valley State University,
University of Mississippi, and University of Southern Mississippi.

www.upress.state.ms.us

The University Press of Mississippi is a member
of the Association of University Presses.

First printing 2019
∞

Library of Congress Cataloging-in-Publication Data available

ISBN 9781496825087 (hardcover)
ISBN 9781496825094 (paperback)
ISBN 9781496825100 (epub single)
ISBN 9781496825117 (epub institutional)
ISBN 9781496825124 (pdf single)
ISBN 9781496825131 (pdf institutional)

British Library Cataloging-in-Publication Data available

CONTENTS

PROLOGUE

It is often considered a bit *de rigueur* these days to offer up to the reader some personal perspectives of the author on the topic at hand. This reflexivity, it is hoped, helps the reader to understand the author's standpoint, interests, and any potential biases. Accordingly, I offer a brief account of my own personal connection to the topic at hand, as best I can, in this brief prologue.

My own personal views have been influenced not only by Western science, but also by my own experiences growing up in the backwoods in Alaska, where wild, unhabituated animals frequently interacted with my family's world. As I came to recognize the animals as unique individuals, each with their own concerns and personalities, I developed a notion of animals and humans as engaged in largely the same life experiences: growing up, playing with siblings under the watchful care of the parents, setting off on one's own and competing for a mate, acquiring food and shelter, and in turn producing and training the next generation. And, hopefully, having a bit of fun somewhere in all of that. My view of animals was also influenced by Native viewpoints, particularly that of the local Dena'ina tribe. As in much of Native North America, animals were acknowledged as "elder brothers" (a remarkable understanding of the basics of evolution, dating from long before it was acknowledged by Western discourse). In the Dena'ina stories, the animals referred to people as the "Campfire People" (both hominid and non-hominid animals being covered under the term "people"). In these stories, we humans were the people that made campfires, while the other people, our elder brothers, were the ones who first helped form much of what the world as we know it. Both these experiences provided me with a strong interest in animal intelligence studies, and I followed the growing scientific acknowledgment of the mental abilities and personalities of non-hominids with a certain sense of relief: what had always seemed obvious to me based on my own experiences was now becoming much more accepted within the scientific community.

I was also born on the cusp of a new era in human culture, the digital realm. As a member of the computer science group in high school, I witnessed the computer revolution revamp how culture was produced, reproduced, and disseminated. By the time I was in college at Harvard in 1984, personal computers were beginning to become widespread, mostly used as word processors. I have a sneaking hunch that I may have been one of the last students at Harvard turning in papers produced on a typewriter. By the time I entered graduate school in 1997, in the master's program in folklore at University of California, Berkeley, under the legendary Alan Dundes, the internet sensation was sweeping the nation. By 2000, most American households had access to the internet, a watershed date in human history. That same year, marking the new millennium, I co-founded along with compatriots in the folklore program, *Cultural Analysis: An Interdisciplinary Forum on Folklore and Popular Culture*, one of the first fully peer-reviewed academic journals distributed freely online. Folklorists were quick to note the explosion of folklore on the internet, in the form of jokes, contemporary legends, and many other genres. Much of the communication on the internet seemed very folkloric, being passed from person to person, changing and adapting, and often without an attributed author. Suddenly, the entire discipline of folklore became relevant towards understanding a whole new arena of cultural production. I entered graduate school in what was increasingly viewed as an antiquated discipline, and I emerged from graduate school in what was increasingly viewed as a cutting-edge discipline. It was not the discipline that changed: rather, the world around it had.

All the while, a wholesale collapse of the Earth's environmental ecosystem increasingly pointed towards upcoming catastrophes, and the ongoing decimation of Earth-based life. Wholesale extinctions became increasingly common. Minority cultures, particularly the indigenous, with their close awareness of our relationship to the Earth, were also continuing to be under assault. Culturally, the rapid loss of indigenous languages points once again to loss of biodiversity, and cultural diversity: a loss of remembrance of our connectedness with life on Earth, and a loss of balance against the anthropocentrism of much of contemporary world cultures.

These processes have not stopped, nor even slowed. The digital realm is vastly more complex and omnipresent than just a few years before, increasingly blending our everyday lived lives into the cyber realm. Contemporaneously, the ongoing climate devastation has continued to worsen, bringing with it a scholarly awareness of dangers of the Anthropocene, and the ongoing destruction of biologically based life on Earth.

These two processes must be seen as linked: the idea of the virtual is necessarily viewed along with the ideas of the biological. These rapid changes have brought wholesale changes to our cultures, politics, technologies, laws, economies, ecosystems, and, at the very base, our ontologies: our thoughts of what it is to be us. The philosophical impact of rethinking our ontologies, both in terms of the digital realm and the biological realm, are covered under the umbrella term of "posthumanism," which is to say, rethinking what we mean when we say "human." As an anthropologist, and a folklorist, my own investigation into posthumanism has close ties to my personal experiences, and to my interests in vernacular culture, in how people themselves perform these philosophical stances in the everyday lived lives. I invite the reader to consider these questions throughout some of the case studies I have assembled into this work. This book is not meant to be a comprehensive overview, but rather a sampling of some of the ways that posthumanism is increasingly influencing how we think of ourselves, and the world around us.

ACKNOWLEDGMENTS

First and foremost, I would like to extend a thanks to my late mentor, Alan Dundes, who always encouraged an engaged, rigorous, and fearless approach to scholarship. My work is in many ways continually indebted to his teachings. I would also like to thank my undergraduate mentor Charles Lindholm for setting me on this career path so long ago, and my high school mentor Keith Tanaka, who encouraged my academic pretensions from an early age. My parents, Stanley and Donnis Thompson, are ultimately the most responsible for my intellectual development, and I am forever indebted to all their hard work in providing for a wonderful childhood, exposed both to civilization and to wilderness. I have been extraordinarily blessed by having many mentors, teachers, and inspirations over the course of my life, and acknowledgments are due to all of them.

Thanks are also due to the wonderful colleagues with whom I have intensively discussed the work over many years: Anthony Bak Buccitelli, Regina Bendix, Anne Benvenuti, Gregory Schrempp, Alison Renteln, Jenny Cool, Henry Jenkins, Trevor Blank, Robert Glenn Howard, Sabina Magliocco, Robert Barron, Ray Cashman, Jay Mechling, Elliott Oring, Simon Bronner, Tim Tangherlini, Francisco Vaz da Silva, Jonathan Gratch, Leah Lowthorp, London Brickley, Stephen Winick, John Lindow, Robert Guyker, Robert Dobler, Terry Gunnell, Stephen Winick, Michael Dylan Foster, Kimberly Lau, Daniel Wojcik, Mirjam Mencej, Ülo Valk, Martha Norkunas, among many others. I extend a special acknowledgment and thanks to Valdimar Tr. Hafstein, who has been my constant friend and intellectual companion since our days in graduate school. I also want to extend a heartfelt thanks to the good work of the many anonymous peer reviewers who have helped refine my research. They made an invaluable contribution to this volume.

Slightly different versions of the following chapters were previously published in peer-reviewed journals as follows: chapter 1 as "Folklore Beyond the Human: Towards a Trans-Special Understanding of Culture, Communication, and Aesthetics" in *Journal of Folklore Research* 55; chapter 2 as "The Ape that Captured Time: Folklore, Narrative, and the Human-Animal Divide" in *Western Folklore* 69; chapter 3 as "Listening to the Elder Brothers: Animals, Agents, and Posthumanism in Native versus non-Native American Myths and Worldviews" in *Folklore* (Tartu) 75; chapter 5 as "Beatboxing, Mashups, and More: Folk Music for the 21st Century" in *Western Folklore* 70; chapter 7 as "Ghost Stories from the Uncanny Valley: Androids, Souls, and the Future of Being Haunted" in *Western Folklore* 78; chapter 8 as "What Does it Mean to Be a Human? Green-Skinned Troublemakers and Us" in *Narrative Culture* 4. Some of the material in chapter 6 was previously published in "Netizens, Revolutionaries, and the Inalienable Right to the Internet" in *Folk Culture in the Digital Age: The Emergent Dynamics of Human Interaction,* edited by Trevor J. Blank. I am grateful to these publications for their assistance in shaping the work, and for their permission to reprint.

Finally, a very special note of thanks to my wife, Cecilia Marie Thompson, and my sons, Oscar and Jasper, for their patience and understanding during all the long hours that I was not able to spend with them. This book is dedicated to them.

INTRODUCTION

Posthumans and Us

Posthuman Folklore is a book on posthumanism, and a book on folklore. More clearly, it is a book on the intersections between the two. Following this dyadic model, "posthuman folklore" refers to two connected things: the folklore regarding posthumanism, and folklore from beyond the human. On the one hand, I will be looking at folklore that does not stem from the human, challenging the commonly held notion that folklore is a human-only enterprise. And on the other hand, this is also a book about people's everyday expressions, showing how posthumanism is not mere academic sophistry, but rather that it is increasingly being recognized and enacted by widespread vernacular performances by everyday people in their everyday lives.

In a sense, both ideas are contained in the word *folklore*: folklore can refer to both the stuff itself (the folklore), and the study of the stuff (the discipline of studying folklore). What makes this work unique is the emphasis on posthuman folklore. Posthumanism is an important theoretical corrective sweeping the many disciplines in the academy. Posthumanist approaches include cyborg studies, artificial intelligence studies, human-animal continuum studies, and epistemological and phenomenological studies in questions regarding identity, agency, and action.[1]

Though longstanding in the humanities, posthumanism as a philosophical corrective has caused re-evaluations of major categorical distinctions, and provided new avenues for research.[2] Such moves are not isolated from society, but rather reflect the increased interest in artificial intelligence and cyborg human-machine interfaces. At the same time, developments in animal and plant studies have also increasingly impacted assumptions of "humaniqueness," and have documented the strong overlap between intelligence and life itself.

In considering the advances in artificial intelligence and cyborg culture, and the remarkable cultural and mental worlds of nonhumans, posthumanism complicates longstanding views about the uniqueness of human intelligence and culture. What makes us *us* has suddenly become a pressing question.

The book begins with the thread of animal studies: ethology (the study of animal thoughts and behaviors) recognizes that nonhuman animals have abilities and traits that were previously assumed by Western science to be uniquely human. Such posthuman moves challenge the categories of Western academic knowledge, which have long reinforced the binary of "human" versus "animal," as in the separation of the "sciences" from the "humanities" or the separate of "anthropology," the study of the *Homo sapiens sapiens,* from disciplines that study the behavior of nonhuman animals. Faced with new data, these categories increasingly appear problematic. Animal research has revealed that capuchin monkeys have a sense of fairness, and an expectation of equal rewards for equal labor[3] while octopi, more closely related to snails than to humans, are playful and intelligent creatures, and can learn how to solve puzzles by watching other octopi, resulting in "octopi cultures" of shared behaviors and traits[4]. Fish use tools.[5] Plants remember, and forests communicate experiences and memories in vast floral webs, including cooperation with other species, and the use of spores for communication.[6] Animal—and "animistic" per Graham Harvey's work[7]—studies have had a profound impact on reorienting scholarly discourse towards acknowledge other intelligences in the world. In turn, humans are becoming much more aware of their own animality—or perhaps of animals' humanity, and of all biological beings' inherent relationship with Earth.

The advances in animal studies sparked what became an epochal event in the rethinking of basic ontologies. The "animal turn" of posthumanism has witnessed a flourishing of new philosophical works from a variety of disciplines, representing a profound paradigm shift in not just one but in many different disciplines, even entire fields, an excellent example of a "scientific revolution," as per Kuhn 1962. For example, the entire field of "the humanities" seems based on categorical exclusions of non-hominids from studies of culture, language, emotions, and aesthetics. In anthropology ("the study of humankind"), Ruth Benedict famously proclaimed humans "the culture-bearing animal" (1934: 9–10), a title we now know to be non-distinctive. Beginning perhaps with Jane Goodall's documentation of tool use and complex social behaviors in chimps (Tonutti 2011; Peterson 2008), many of the previous assertions of absolute qualitative distinctions, the old hallmarks of "humaniqueness" were questioned and, increasingly, discarded as false.[8] The turn of the millennium has witnessed an explosion in animal studies and philosophy documenting and dealing with the implications of the growing awareness of our close kinship with nonhuman animals in many areas.[9]

Posthumanism's other main strand centers on the introduction of digital technologies, and has several diverse lines of inquiry, ranging from computer-mediated communication to artificial intelligences. One well-known early approach is the "cyborg feminism," which grew out of Donna Haraway's pioneering work "A Cyborg Manifesto."[10] Haraway explores the possibilities and implications of increasing human-machine linkages, particularly in the roles of identity and culture. Increasingly, scholars are recognizing the epochal impact of the introduction of digital communications, artificial intelligences, and the cyber realm.

Beyond viewing the implications of cyberspace as a cultural arena within which to fashion and perform identities, the notion of artificial intelligence has quickly moved from the realm of science fiction to the realm of the everyday. Already human-acting interfaces (bots) are a regular feature of internet communications, and the quest to build self-aware artificial intelligence has made great technological strides. Combined with developments in AI are related developments in robotics, and the emergence of the intelligent, humanoid robots known as the android.[11]

Posthumanism's two main branches, therefore, are interesting in their respective differences: ethology is largely studying intelligences whose origins predate the human, while digital studies emphasize newer, cutting-edge technological developments. One is based on questioning our relationship to the carbon-based life forms to which we are kin, while the other strand focuses on our relations to our own technological developments. Both can be used to help inform the other, and the wider question of basic human ontology: what is it to be human, and how do we perform our humanity?

Much of posthumanism is decidedly futuristic in its influences and theorizing, with ideas of the cyborg, and collective intelligences. Newness and multiplicity abound. Yet the future is also connected with environmental degradation, wholesale extinctions of species and widespread loss of nonhuman life on Earth: life in the Anthropocene. The central question of what is to be human relies on both topics of inquiry, and neither can be fully separated from each other.

As a folklorist, I am also interested in documenting the vernacular philosophical shifts, as our everyday culture continues to perform the posthuman. What the future of the posthuman age will be makes for interesting speculation: all that seems certain currently is that we are undergoing an era of profound change. For example, 2015 marks the first year that a writ of *habeas corpus* was issued for a nonhuman animal (two chimpanzees) in the United States, categorically challenging the definition of "person" as "human" (Feltman 2015). In 2018, the android Sofia was granted citizenship by Saudi Arabia. Questioning the new, virtual aspects of self leads us to looking at our non-virtual, biological selves. Yet our biology also leads in turn to our animality, and our kinship with the rest of biological life on Earth. The two ends of posthumanism are, at the end, tied back together in evolving notions of what it means to be human: what *are* we?

Such basic ontological cultural questions can have diverse influences, but two of the most prominent stem from science and myth. In this book, I investigate both, as well as the complex dance between them. The emergence of posthumanism is tied into other newer philosophical shifts as well, such as postnationalism and postcolonialism, which are also closely tied to the development of the cyber realm, and which detail the social, cultural, and political implications of the digital era. Philosophy is never truly divorced from the *zeitgeist*: rather, philosophy can be seen as an adaption of thought to the realities and concerns of the different epochs. If, as Antonnen (2005) asserted, the concept of folklore was created by modernity in order to establish a separate, modern identity, then posthuman folklore can be viewed as modernity in hindsight: the recalibration of expressive culture in the postmodern age. This recalibration occurs in the academy, to be sure, but also, and even more importantly, in the everyday world of the everyday person. Folklore, as always, reflects the culture that performs it: in examining folklore, we always find cues to cultural worldviews, belief systems, and senses of identity. In this sense, posthuman folklore is no different: it, too, reveals vernacular ideas of worldviews, beliefs, and identities. It's just that all these have shifted in remarkable, epochal, and revolutionary ways: the world, and ourselves, are not what we thought some few short years ago. Sorting all this out, making sense of this, and integrating these new realities into our current worldview is the realm of posthumanism. How this is all expressed in everyday culture is the realm of folklore.

PART 1

THE CONSCIOUS PLANET

Part one takes as its starting point the remarkable recent developments in ethology, which increasingly confirm our close ontological links with other life forms on Earth. The first chapter sets out the implications for such developments for our understanding of culture, communication, and consciousness, with a particular focus on the role of *aesthetics* as a possible touchstone. It makes the case, following developments in ethology, that folklore (and, indeed, culture in general) can no longer be considered the sole domain of *Homo sapiens,* but rather must be viewed as shared inheritances with much of life on Earth.

The second chapter, *The Ape that Captured Time,* focuses on what may be a significant disjuncture between the folklore of human and nonhuman animals, that being the *story.* The story is perhaps the single most significant factor of what it is to be human, and the story's strong relationship with folklore studies reveals this ongoing significance. Tracing the story of the story back in time may therefore tell us a good deal about human evolution, showing both what we have in common with other animals, and what we may claim as unique to our own species. The story is a fundamental part of nearly all aspects of being human, from the stories of nations, creation, fiction, to our own autobiographies, our very sense of self.

The following two chapters investigate some of the implications of posthumanism in how cultures envision their relations to animals. If animals are much like people, should they be considered persons? "Somewhat" persons? To approach vernacular attitudes of "animal personhood," I investigate the idea of souls: which cultures believe that animals have souls, and which do not? What are the foundations, and implications, of such beliefs?

The last chapter looks at vernacular ways of considering relationships, particularly the notion of sexuality. Sexuality proclaims, disclaims, and establishes relations. Sexuality is also highly culturally encoded, and in the case of Western cultures, integrated with the notion of souls, personhood, and culture. Why is it that animals have come to represent our "wild" instincts? Such thoughts tell us a great deal more about our own cultural views than they do of the wild itself, and, as such, provide resources for understanding vernacular thoughts of ontology.

Part one of this book sets the stage for thinking about our ontology, particularly in terms of a biological ontology: what is it to be an animal, and why are we so often uncomfortable with that label? Our kinship to our carbon-based kin is fraught with cultural signification. Looking at cultures comparatively can give some glimpses as to the contours of this signification.

Such investigations emerge from the "shadow side" of the other main strand of posthumanism, investigated in parts two and three, the increasingly cyborg quality of human life. If we wish to know what it is to be a cyborg, then we must become well aware of what it is *not* to be one: that is to say, to understand our virtual lives and thoughts, we are led back to examining our biological lives and thoughts, and, to do so, led back to examining our animality, and our kinship with life on Earth.

Investigations into our biological ontology are also important in understanding our current situation and potential futures: as we enter the Anthropocene, where life on Earth itself is being radically transformed (and attenuated) by humankind, such philosophical inquiries carry profound pragmatic consequences. Our biology dictates a need for our kin: without the rest of life, we will surely perish, not only as a culture but as a species. Philosophical investigations into our posthuman ontology are therefore no longer a luxury. Increasingly, such investigations are a necessity, in order to be able to provide for a future for our descendants.

To begin the inquiry, let us turn to how we came to be: an origin story, to be sure, but, like all good origin stories, one with radical implications on how to live our lives.

1

FOLKLORE BEYOND THE HUMAN

Toward a Trans-Special Understanding of
Culture, Communication, and Aesthetics

The scientific study of animal behavior (ethology) is increasingly employing the concept of culture to explain nonhuman animal behaviors and, largely stemming from this, the category of nonhuman culture is increasingly influencing the work of many scholars in the humanities and social sciences as well. This remarkable line of inquiry across diverse fields and disciplines has opened up new questions and avenues for research, in what many have called the "animal turn" in general philosophical discourse.[1]

My question in this chapter is how humanities scholars and social scientists, and particularly folklorists, may now approach the study of nonhuman culture, and what may be some of the theoretical implications of such approaches. Since folklore is a discipline focusing on the very topic of collectively shaped, traditional, expressive culture, it would seem to be in an ideal position to take the lead in this newly emerging realm of the study of culture beyond the human.[2] That nonhuman animals have folklore has already been proposed in folklore studies by Jay Mechling, in his work "'Banana Cannon' and Other Folk Traditions Between Human and Nonhuman Animals" (1989), which I reified in 2010 as the "banana canon"—the general recognition that nonhumans have folklore (see chapter 2). Somewhat contemporaneously, animal studies have

3

increasingly documented behavior among nonhumans that may be interpreted productively as cultural, traditional performances. How, then, may folklorists use these revelations in ongoing studies of nonhuman culture, increasingly noted and studied by biologists, and subsume them into the discipline? How can we bring the "animal turn" to folkloristics?

One of the necessary steps in such an approach is to try to destabilize the false human-animal binary (humans *are* animals)—and with that, the false binary between "social sciences and humanities" that study humans and "physical and biological sciences" that study (mostly) nonhumans—and to try to open up ways that scholarship can engage with animal thoughts without focusing on what people think of animals. There are difficulties, of course; folklorists are not accustomed to nonhuman informants and are not used to examining nonhuman cultural expressions. Our very vocabulary tends toward the anthropocentric (we often work in "humanities" departments, or perhaps "anthropology"). This chapter attempts to lay some groundwork in the other direction, in allowing folklore studies to productively study nonhuman cultures—analogous, perhaps, to how psychology has moved successfully toward allowing "animal psychology" as a valid subfield, which aids in the study of the evolution of psychological abilities and processes.

Perhaps the largest advantage in avoiding entrenched anthropocentrism is that this allows us to view cultural expressions in their evolutionary and biological framework.[3] Unless we believe that artistic and aesthetic impulses were gifted to humans in a transcendent moment, we must acknowledge that they have emerged firmly embedded in the development of life on Earth, displaying our close kinship with the rest of Earth-based life. Such a move attempts to shift from an anthropocentric view of consciousness and culture (with analogues to creationist Abrahamic mythology) toward one that is more in harmony with current scientific discourses of the evolution of life.[4]

In this chapter, I focus on the notion of aesthetics as a touchstone. I attempt to show how an evolutionary look at aesthetics not only helps cross the human-animal divide, but also how it can help bridge the entrenched notion of a mind-body split, by examining the evolution of consciousness as well. This chapter attempts to ground my calls for the study of nonhuman expressive culture in a philosophical framework.

EXTRA-SPECIAL AESTHETICS

To begin, what do I mean when I say that animals have a sense of aesthetics? Let me offer some examples of recent scientific discoveries.

Example 1: Songbirds Change their Styles

Songbirds change their songs over time, and females tend to be more interested in the latest trends and styles (Williams et al. 2013). Such journals as *Animal Behaviour* are now filled with references to nonhuman "culture," "tradition," and "innovation." How can ethnomusicologists help examine such trends? What can ethnomusicology contribute to animal studies noticing such phenomena? *Why* do birds change their tunes; are their tunes getting better and better? More or less diverse? Is there a weight of tradition, or is it more of a faddish, pop star of the moment sort of thing? What is the role of singing, and listening to songs, in the wider realm of avian culture? There are indications that birds, like people, change their repertoires in part depending on where they live: in the cities, the songs tend to be louder and faster—for both (see e.g., Slabbekoorn and den Boer-Visser 2006; Brumm 2006; Briefer et al. 2010; Nemeth and Brumm 2009).

Example 2: Nonhumans, Languages, and Dialects

Demonstrations of nonhuman languages (defined here as socially learned symbolic communications) have been steadily increasing in the scientific literature.[5] Perhaps one of the more interesting aspects of this is the existence of dialectical, as well as linguistic, differences. Examples include the sperm whale, the highly intelligent leviathans of the deep, who travel across the world's oceans in closely bonded, interrelated social groups. They communicate with each other at great lengths, displaying not only individual identity in their communications, but also displaying regional varieties of varying degrees (Antunes et al. 2011). We know next to nothing of what they are saying, yet it seems to be important to them. As highly intelligent and highly social mammals, they are also nomadic, which intensifies the importance of their social relations. What is sperm whale linguistic culture like? How many languages and dialects are there? What are the "verbal arts of performance" (see Bauman 1975, 1977) of sperm whales?[6] Note that sperm whales are not alone in displaying dialectical differences in their languages—far from it; other documented examples include orcas (Dayton 1990), the small furry hyrax (Kershenbaum et al. 2012), chimpanzees (Crockford et al. 2004), prairie dogs (Slobodchikoff and Coast 1980), and even goats (Briefer and McElligott 2012). Orcas have been observed learning new dialects (Deecke, Ford, and Spong 2000), and even learning to speak "dolphin" in captivity (Musser et al. 2014). The interesting interplay of dialects and social identity in aesthetic performances captures the complexity and beauty of communication. The discipline of folklore has long been involved with understanding the plurality of cultural expressions, in their variegated degrees of relatedness (and often in direct contrast to nationalist ideologies or the ideals of a standard national language).[7] What, then, could folklorists say about various dialectical differences in nonhuman cultures?

Example 3: "Madam, I'm Adam": Dolphins Give Themselves Names

Dolphins have personal names (King and Janik 2013). Not only do dolphins give each other, and go by, personal names, but they also seem to remember names of individuals for decades between reunions (Bruck 2013). Absent writing technologies, names are, of course, folklore. Are the dolphin's names nicknames, referring to some attribute of the individual? Or, if not, purely arbitrary? Family names? Is there a naming ceremony? If not, how *are* names arrived at socially; or, if there is, what is a dolphin naming ceremony? The questions far outweigh the answers.

These above examples reveal that aesthetic behavior, and, yes, artistic communication in small groups (as per Ben-Amos's famous 1971 definition of "folklore") have been increasingly documented in the animal studies literature. The pertinent questions then become: *Why* do organisms engage in aesthetic behaviors and reactions, and *how* did this evolve? How might different types of life have developed this differently?

Folklore performances are all deeply involved with aesthetics: what motivates a singer to sing a song (and an audience to listen), if not aesthetics? Does it matter whether the singer is human? Although there is no lack of work on aesthetics from all sorts of angles, there is precious little that looks at the aesthetics of nonhumans. Folklorists would seem to have much to offer in this regard: frameworks, perspectives, theories, concepts, and notions of "prior art" that could help elucidate performance and aesthetic behavior among nonhuman as well as human animals.

SURVIVAL OF THE FITTEST THEORY? SOCIOBIOLOGY AND FREUD

An approach from the discipline of folklore would likely be somewhat different than the ones offered by sociobiology, which is the only field up until now to hypothesize on the development of human aesthetics. Sociobiology has contributed several major works on the topic, but, as with all sociobiological arguments, causation is notoriously difficult to prove, troubled by the teleology implicit in such arguments; we are such-and-such way because of such-and-such thing in the distant past, which can never be revisited. Proposed correlations abound, enabling various hypotheses to be proposed as to why, sociobiologically speaking, we are who we are.

In terms of aesthetics, the explanations in sociobiology are usually derived from Darwinian ideas of survival of the fittest, relying on our survival (personal and reproductive) skills of natural selection. Many sociobiologists use a combination of Darwinian evolutionary theory with Freud's theory of repression and sublimation to explain human aesthetics. Freud's idea, explored particularly in *Civilization and Its Discontents* ([1930] 1962), was that humans developed civilization by the repression of incest. That repression of sexuality supposedly helps to form human societies through marriage and alliance groups, and is expressed in various dreams, fantasies, and cultural mythologies.[8] This move toward "civilization" required the elemental repression of individual desires. This repression of individual desires (sexual but also aggressive) in turn gave rise to the symbolic expression of these individual, tabooed thoughts and feelings in art. For Freud, the energy of "civilized" aesthetics comes about primarily from the repression of sexual urges. However, most sociobiologists focus on aesthetics as deriving not so much from the *repression* of sexual desires as from the *expression* of them—an interestingly opposite supposition. This may be the effect of Darwinian ideas in sociobiology, which tend to emphasize the individual choices involved in natural (including sexual) selection, yet the net result still suggests a sudden creationist moment, when aesthetics as an expression of sexuality became aesthetics as repressed sexuality, giving us, once again, an absolute split between *Homo* and all other life forms.

While Freud's theory may be attractive, there is of course no way to go back in time to see if this was indeed the case. And even if social repression of individual desires is at the root of aesthetics, what to make of the fact that sexual and/or aggressive desires are also strongly curtailed in many nonhuman cultures? Repression is not confined to *Homo sapiens sapiens* (see e.g., the classic *Chimpanzee Politics* [de Waal 1982]). Could this same Freudian principal then be applied to nonhuman cultures? Do their aesthetic activities also derive from social repression (and if so, what to make of the fact that our closest relatives, the bonobos, develop deep social bonds while engaging in a great deal of unrestrained sexual activity)? Further research in actual animal studies may illuminate this question, bringing a sense of testability to the Freudian theory on the evolution of civilization and aesthetics, rather than the common implicit assumption that aesthetics are another marker of "humaniqueness."

Most sociobiological works implicitly assume that only humans have aesthetics, whatever the evolutionary antecedents might have been. One influential book was even entitled *Homo Aestheticus* (Dissanayake 1995). Another more recent, and more influential, work is Stephen Davies's *The Artful Species* (2012) (the species to which he refers is, of course, humans). Such works underline the position that aesthetics is the realm of the human alone. Such a position is in line with Abrahamic mythological discourses that emphasize the absolute categorical difference between humans and all other forms of life ("God made man in His image"), but it is decidedly out of line with other mythological discourses, and current developments in Western science.[9]

While very often sociobiologists rely on the behavior of our relatives (particularly the close ones) to try to understand the biological roots of human behavior, this has not been well explored in the case of aesthetics. Instead, it is generally assumed that only humans have aesthetics, so there is no point of comparison between a human singer (aesthetically aware) and a nonhuman one (acting out of pure instinct). The relative lack of comparative animal studies of sociobiological theories of aesthetics is odd: most topics covered by sociobiology include a great deal of animal studies, while ideas of *Homo aestheticus* still seem predominant. Bereft of any useful comparisons from current data, sociobiological explanations of aesthetics are therefore even more hypothetical in nature than many other sociobiological theories. For example, one recent high-profile work, Denis Dutton's *The Art Instinct: Beauty, Pleasure, and Human Evolution* (2009), claims that people enjoyed a painting of a nice British landscape because it was like the savannah, in which we had evolved, implying that our sense of aesthetics derives ultimately from a survival need, as well as a long-standing environmental niche. There are problems with such approaches—why would aesthetic preference be for the savannah rather than the tropics, where we evolved for millions of years? Or the edges of glaciers that many hominids followed for much of the Paleolithic? Or the steppes and waving fields of grain of the thousands of years of the Neolithic?[10] Where, exactly, are such Lamarckian memories stored, let alone how? The book itself is aware of such issues, and prevaricates between the claims of "aesthetics by evolutionary design" and "aesthetics as a byproduct of evolution," while giving relatively short shrift to the influences of culture. In a review of the work, Justine Kingsbury (2011) also notes that biological claims of "functions" tend to imply a normativity, of what *should* be, a claim that anthropologists, trained in cross-cultural differences, are keenly suspicious of, with good reason. The "instinctual" factor is also misleading, since, for a book all about the evolution of aesthetics, there is almost nothing in the work on anything aesthetic except for *Homo sapiens sapiens*, a black hole from which aesthetics seems to suddenly emerge. In spite of its claim of a revolutionary way of seeing aesthetics through sociobiology, such a work still relies on a sudden creationist moment, this time gifted by "evolution" rather than "God."

In much of sociobiology, aesthetics is tied directly to mate choice. Stephen Pinker has famously espoused the idea of aesthetics as an evolutionary "mistake" or some sort of accidental byproduct of our mating strategies, in what he called his "Baywatch" theory of art (1992). One of the most well-known examples is the theoretical framing of symmetry: people often find symmetry attractive, and this is held to derive from seeing symmetry in a potential mating partner's body, since these are in general indicative of healthy genes (a common line of research in sociobiology; for an overview, see Rhodes et al. 1998). A more complex argument on the role of sexual selection can be seen in such works as Geoffrey Miller's *The Mating Mind* (2000), in which the role of the mind, and intelligence, is considered in increasing reproductive success. Which is to say, for humans, and doubtless others, being smart (including witty, funny, entertaining, etc.) has been highly selected for a long, long time, allowing for a sort of stepping stone between sexual selection and aesthetics generally.[11]

THE ROOTS OF AESTHETICS

But it seems to me that there is likely much more to aesthetics than mate choice alone. What appears as a beautiful sunset, or a lovely waterfall, might be hard to translate into mate choice strategies (or other natural selection strategies). Rather, I suggest that the roots of aesthetics go much deeper, to a kind of "fuzzy logic" approximation that all sensate beings have of the universe surrounding them. Such a view might include the use of aesthetics in courtship and reproductive success, but without limiting aesthetics to an evolutionary mistake arising from sexual desire. Certainly some examples point toward courtship; the songbird studies suggests that one of the main social uses of their singing is for courtship and establishing reproductive relationships, but courtship does not always seem to be the central focus of the activity. In addition to direct uses in courtship, a good display of aesthetics may also imply that the organism has other fit, reproductively healthy attributes—perhaps intelligence in particular—and therefore might make an attractive mate. Intelligence has been strongly selected throughout the evolution of life on Earth, not only for hominids, as in Miller's *The Mating Mind*, but for much, if not all, of life on Earth. Aesthetics therefore has been strongly selected throughout its evolution. While it may be an "evolutionary mistake" as per Pinker, it is not clear that this is so; aesthetics could well be an important part of the evolution of life, and consciousness, on Earth, allowing organisms to better interact with the universe surrounding them.

Consider, for example, colors. No humans have aesthetic reactions to ultra-violet light, because we do not see that part of the light spectrum—although assuredly some other species do. Red seems to have special aesthetic reactions in many human cultures, perhaps particularly due to red being the color of blood. Schematic studies have indicated that if human languages have a word for color (besides "light/dark"), then it will be for "red" before any other color (Berlin and Kay 1969). Colors are not "set" (there is no true Irish-Gaelic equivalent for the English word "green," for example) but seem to reflect our sensorial interactions with the physical world: an interplay of rods and cones, light waves, and linguistic, cognitive categories. In this example, we can view aesthetics as ultimately deriving from the surrounding natural world, as well as reflecting it, in varied cultural constructions.

We can observe this in music, too. Aesthetics are intrinsically a part of music, emotional links between the "performative act" and the perception of aesthetic forms. There is some sort of math behind music, of course, and this is expressed in rhythm and in harmonic soundwaves. Other animals also recognize harmonics, and seem to find the expression of their regularities pleasing. The easiest example is the octave. All people can recognize an octave, which is when a pitch's sound wave is exactly double that of the original. We might slice up the octave differently—the pentatonic, or five-note scale, being perhaps the most common for folk music—but all traditions agree on the octave. Similarly, researchers have noted that the octave seems recognized in other species as well, including birds, rhesus monkeys (Wright et al. 2000), and dolphins (Ralston and Herman 1995). As Josh McDermott and Marc Hauser put it:

> Perhaps unsurprisingly, a case can also be made for the biological basis of the octave, which seems predisposed to have a central role in music; it is both prevalent in musical systems worldwide and perceptually privileged, at least in some cases, in nonhuman primates. (2005: 51)

So when animals (including *Homo sapiens sapiens*) sing or dance, there is an interaction in "perfect" forms—the regularity of soundwaves (an octave really *is* an octave, and the perception of it reflects this). Thus, aesthetics is a way for an organism to involve itself in the mathematical regularities of the universe—things like rhythms (cycles of the seasons), notes (soundwaves), cadences, movements (dance) in the case of music.

Then there are also material designs of many species. Might not all these organisms have a "feel" for "good-looking" material constructions? The impressive constructions of bowerbirds inspired a provocative, if short, article by John Endler in *Communicative and Integrative Biology* (2012), entitled "Bowerbirds,

Art and Aesthetics: Are Bowerbirds Artists and Do They Have an Aesthetic Sense?" The idea of symmetry is mathematically powerful, and useful in consciously made designs—not just in assessing a potential mate's reproductive possibilities. Such approximations of mathematical regularities help develop the idea of "ideal" forms, somewhat like the Platonic *eidos*, for cognate organisms, based on their sensory and synesthetic relation to the actual, not-so-ideal world.

These can further be applied and expressed socially, helping to develop socially shared "ideal aesthetics." In many complex life forms, the role of *socially shared* aesthetics helps to create what seems to be a group mind of collective intelligence, or social knowledge, which presents an interesting quandary: although intelligence can be held collectively, the subjective experience is only experienced on the individual level. This tension, between the individual organism and the social group, has a very long history on planet Earth. To understand all this, we need to take a deeper look at the root notions of *aesthetics as a motivating force of life*. I further propose that folklore is well situated for this study. After all, the communication of aesthetics—and/or the aesthetics of communication—is a *sine qua non* of folklore. To be sure, not all aesthetic communication is folklore, but all folklore *is* aesthetic communication. Further, this is a very deeply rooted part of life. Living organisms are rewarded with pleasure in expressing symmetries of nature, the math underlying the physical universe, with which the cognate must interact, and, to better its own position, better understand.

This also connects the age-old problem of the "mind" and the body. The body is the device through which the sensate being interacts with its surroundings, which is to say, the universe. Hence, the regularities of the body (two ears for stereo sounds, two eyes for depth perception, etc.) shape the interactive potentials. Yet the body is not divorced from the surrounding reality, but has instead been intensively shaped in response to the surrounding physical environment. Consciousness has therefore come to be at this intersection of replicating material forms—organized matter, if you will—and the physical reality that surrounds, nurtures, and ultimately destroys them. The "mind" is shaped by the experience of stimuli and the perception of a surrounding reality from which such stimuli flow—this leads to the experience of agency; whether an amoebae, a fish, or a fisherman, one must *decide* what to do.

In the more complex beings, "meta" levels are recognized. For example, play behavior is a very "meta" activity. It requires the understanding of symbolic behavior, and the recognition of symbolic behavior in others. ("This is not a real bite, but a play bite.") Play behavior reveals not only a sense of aesthetics (defined here as the enjoyment of symbolic representations), but also recognition of the consciousness of others, of other wills and volitions (sometime called the "theory of mind" in the literature). Although playing does seem to be a fairly risk-free way to learn, the organism is rewarded by feelings of pleasure in engaging in this symbolic behavior: playing is fun. Playing has been observed throughout an impressive range of the animal kingdom (see, for an overview, Fagen 1981; for an extended discussion, Bekoff and Byers 1998). That is to say, most animals are sensate beings, capable of understanding symbolic action and behavior, and finely tuned to the aesthetics of fun. This is not a particularly new point—in his *Homo Ludens* ([1938] 1955), the Dutch cultural historian Johan Huizinga claimed that play was an important part of our evolutionary development. Although he claimed that humans should be called *Homo ludens* in honor of the importance of play for humanity, Huizinga recognized that humans are by no means the only animals to enjoy play behavior, and explored the topic of nonhuman play at considerable length.

In the next chapter, I discuss the importance of "play" by asking what folklorists can say about games like "tag." The game has been documented among many mammals, and is clearly far, far older than *Homo sapiens*. What makes for a good game of tag, versus the not so memorable? What can we say about the feelings of pleasure that play provides? How could folklorists, who often study games like tag, comment on non(and pre)hominid varieties? To even broach such questions may require a substantial reevaluation of our notions of agents, personhood, and culture.

POSTHUMANISM, THE ANIMAL TURN, AND FOLKLORE STUDIES

"Posthumanism" is the term applied to the general approach of questioning previously held notions of "personhood" in Western academic discourse, which tended to unproblematically assume a categorical link between "person" and "individual *Homo sapiens sapiens.*" Posthumanism has enormous societal, ethical, and legal implications; witness the growing sense of legal rights of nonhuman animals in such cases as two chimps being granted *habeas corpus* (relief from unlawful imprisonment) in the US, the declaration in India that dolphins are "nonhuman persons," and the general growing acceptance of "animal rights" in legislation around the world.

In the scientific world, most "animal studies" are now having to grapple with the enormity of the task, for which they have not been prepared. Animal studies are usually located in departments such as biology, reflecting the longstanding view of animals as biological (rather than moral or philosophical) agents, driven by "instinct" rather than thoughtful consideration, and linked to us only in our shared physiological features. Wildlife management, for example, does not generally take into account the disturbance of animal cultures; these are assumed to be "living in nature," and "wild and free," instead of cultured beings. How can environmental protection protect not just animal lives, but also animal cultures? What animal cultures have been destroyed already, unknowingly?

The confluence of human studies and animal studies stumbles across rocky ground; even much of the language that we use is ill-suited for understanding animal thoughts, feelings, and culture. If an animal acts altruistically, we may say it was a "humane" thing to do, while if humans kill each other, we may describe the participants as "beastly" or "acting like animals." Nondomesticated animals are called "wild," which problematically implies a freedom from societal constraints. Perhaps the largest stumbling ground lies in the words we use for ourselves: "folks," "people," "person," "souls," and "agents" are all often held to be coterminous with *Homo sapiens sapiens*. This has led to discussing animal behavior without discussing animal mentality. The songbird is often described as singing due to "instinct," yet few scholars would feel comfortable ascribing this same rubric to our own species. One initial step toward understanding folklore beyond the human seems to be to recast the definition of these terms to be able to include agents of other species.

The idea of understanding other species as aesthetic, communicative agents ("persons" by many definitions) is neither new nor novel as many cultures have long held such views. As Marc Brightman, Vanessa Grotti, and Olga Ulturgasheva put it in their "Animism and Invisible Worlds: The Place of Non-humans in Indigenous Ontologies," "Animism is, by definition, the attribution of human(-like) subjectivity, agency and emotion to non-humans: in short, non-humans seem to be endowed with personhood" (2012: 14).

Nor is this idea limited to humans. Several studies from biology have described various species learning the communications of other species, in order to derive pertinent information—and even, in some cases, lying to deceive their eavesdroppers (Wheeler 2009)!

It *is*, however, relatively new in western academic discourse, which has long been dominated by an anthropocentric view of a categorical split between humans and other animals. The dismissive charge of "anthropocentrism" (imagining that animals were like people) may be seen as diametrically opposed to these viewpoints. Rather than seeing animals "as if they were people," what happens when we view people "as if they were animals" (which, of course, they are)? The discovery of trans-special cultural studies is an intriguing one, with potentially important contributions.

Posthumanism and the animal turn have affected many disciplines. The widespread influence of this rises to the level of a "paradigm shift" as per Thomas Kuhn (1962). Anthropology alone has witnessed a host of recent works on the topics. For more on the idea of "multispecies ethnography" and the implications of posthumanism and the animal turn in anthropology, one could see particularly Eben Kirksey and Steffan Helmreich's "The Emergence of Multispecies Ethnography" (2010), discussing the *Cultural Anthropology* special issue dedicated to this topic, as well as Alan Smart's "Critical Perspectives on Multi Species Ethnography" (2014), similarly. An important contribution to this discourse is also Tim Ingold's "Anthropology Beyond Humanity" (2013).

In one compelling example, Eduardo Kohn explored how his hosts, the Amazonian Runa people, thought of nonhuman personhood, frequently commenting on the mental states of nonhuman "people." He says that Runa animism "is grounded in an ontological fact: there exist other kinds of thinking selves beyond the human" (2013: 94). Kohn's research causes him to reflect that "lives and thoughts are not distinct kinds of things" (2013: 99). He concludes with a note supportive of the consideration of animism within a philosophical framework, stating, "The world is animate, whether or not we are animists. It is filled with selves—I dare say souls—human and otherwise" (2013: 217). These considerations, stemming from both his experiences with the Runa, and the general trends of posthumanism, are important in the way that the nonhuman agent is considered.

Yet while Kohn maintains that symbolic reference (and, hence, morality) only occurs among humans (2013: 217),[12] I would venture a bit further to propose nonhuman agents as fully symbolic beings, since it seems that the notion of performative aesthetics is inherently symbolic, interacting with the apparent regularities of the universe (such as the octave example, discussed above, or the color spectrum, or time). The degrees of symbolic reference may be seen as quantitatively, but not qualitatively, different: a spectrum instead of a dichotomy.

While posthumanism has seen a flurry of works within anthropology, it has been much less in evidence in folklore studies, even as many discussions of internet folklore touch on the general contours of posthumanism. As posthumanism is also the theoretical bridge between animal studies and cultural studies, this lack of engagement inhibits the recognition and discussion of nonhuman cultural studies in the discipline. Unlike many disciplines, folklore has yet to come fully to terms with the implications of the "animal turn." With a few exceptions[13], there has been a conspicuous silence on the topic. Folklorists, for the most part, have continued as if nothing has changed, as if aesthetic performances and appreciations remain the sole domain of *Homo sapiens sapiens*. Yet, in many ways, folklore would appear to be an ideal discipline from which to engage with the animal turn. Folklorists, like ethologists, study performances.

"Who are the folk? (Among others) we are!" famously exclaimed Alan Dundes. (1980: 19). Following Dundes's reformulation of the "folk," we should ask anew: what is this "we," and who are the "others"? Can animals be "folk" as well? If performers and audience members, and members of folk groups, are also nonhumans, then how can folklore studies productively come together with animal studies in an effort to study culture in its trans-special context? What could folklorists offer to the vast study of nonhuman life on Earth?

Not surprisingly, I would assert that there is much that folklore could offer. For example, folklore studies has long noted the importance of accurate collections of performances, and perhaps particularly the role of archives. Recent moves in open access provide excellent models for how vast quantities of data collected from a variety of researchers can be stored, shared, and compared.[14] Classical theoretical developments in the field, such as the historic-geographic method and typology systems, have greatly aided folkloric research. Is there a way to type nonhuman songs, for example, so as better to compare them across time and space? Further, folklorists have also come to understand a great deal about how tradition works; it is always performed at some present moment, yet represents the past performances at the same time. It consists of a semiotic circle of meanings, with its own rhetorical weight.

Importantly, folklorists have emphasized the respect for the views and cultures of our informants. Very often, folklorists have found themselves working with minority peoples, many of whom have been viewed disparagingly by members of dominant cultures. The word "folklore" itself is perceived as problematic, due to pejorative notions attributed to the rural dwellers of Europe after the heyday of industrialization and modernity. Nonhuman animals, likewise, have had their personhood and culture denied by members of the dominant society—more even than most minority human groups, animal cultures lack a voice of their own in the academy.

Finally, the central importance of cultural performances in social relations lies at the base of folklore studies,[15] and this conviction seems applicable across the species divide as well. With aesthetic performances taken in the wide view as part and parcel of life on Earth, folklore studies seems to have a vast new frontier opening up, a new mission not only to understand the role of aesthetic performance among humans but its role in life on Earth. Such a quest shifts the focus from understanding human societies and psychologies in terms of aesthetic performances toward understanding nonhuman cultures and psychologies as well—indeed, even toward understanding the underlying basis of aesthetics itself.

CONCLUSIONS AND FURTHER QUESTIONS

How deeply rooted is all this? Although it may be tempting to start with the animals "nearest and dearest" to us—the domesticates, or extinct hominid species such as Neanderthals and Denovisans—what do we make of culture "in the wild" or among the more divergent life forms? The octopus, for example, has been observed engaging in social learning via observation and clear play behaviors (see e.g., Kuba et al. 2006). Octopi enjoy learning tricks. They seem to be very creative, intelligent creatures, yet they are *Mollusca,* closer to a snail than to *Homo.* How long have octopi, or their relatives, been engaging in such playful behavior? Surely for millions of years before humans!

Not to be forgotten is the rather remarkable recent research on plant intelligence. Plants have been shown to have memory and complex systems of communications.[16] Plants alert other plants of danger, sometimes specifically. While we know next to nothing of plant communication, the recent evidence points toward a great deal of lively communication taking place, in chemical and other signals, of which we have been nearly completely ignorant in our scientific discourse. If plants communicate, then do they also have social learning? Which is to say, is there a plant culture or cultures? If so, what sort of form might it take? What might be the aesthetics of the floral world?

Or what of the "hive mind" of ants and bees? Perhaps these are even strangest still to contemplate. Karl von Frisch noted that honeybees can communicate complex information to their hive mates with complex dances seeming to indicate the location of good food (1967). Is there an aesthetic component to this dance as well? To even begin to answer these questions, I believe we may benefit from this new, very broad view of aesthetics as experiences that bring feelings of pleasure or displeasure (in myriad forms), and that this is rooted in the basic properties of life, life as organized matter responding to stimuli from the outside environment.

An evolutionary understanding of aesthetics may also help dissolve the "mind-body" divide that has so long plagued Western philosophers. This "situated body" follows epistemological and phenomenological moves in philosophy that acknowledge biologically mediated experience (e.g., Husserl [1952] 1989; Merleau-Ponty [1945] 2012) and comports with many recent studies of the "embodied mind" (e.g., Francisco Varela, Evan Thompson, and Eleanor Rosch's *The Embodied Mind* [1991], Shaun Gallagher's *How the Body Shapes the Mind* [2005], Antonio Damasio's *Descartes' Error: Emotion, Reason, and the Human Brain* [1994], and Evan Thompson's *Mind in Life: Biology, Phenomenology, and the Sciences of Mind* [2007]). Unlike the "soul-like" image of consciousness (as in Descartes's "homunculus" view, predicating the "mind-body" split),[17] the "embodied mind," with its view of the necessary links between thought and the physical world, does not need homunculi nor souls. This approach has proved useful in posthumanist views of the cyborg realm, as well, reminding theorists that while the internet is "mediated," so, too, is the experience of the "real" world, mediated through our senses (see e.g., Biocca 1997). It is with such an understanding of mediated experiences where the phenomenological approach to epistemology can be put into an evolutionary context, by looking at the notion of aesthetics as a basic motivating principle for all life. Further studies of this question might help further demystify the notion of "the mind" and reintegrate the mind back in to the body, and back into the physical world, of which it is made, and to which it refers.[18]

Folklorists should reconsider the assumption that folklore is the sole domain of *Homo sapiens sapiens.* I further suggest that folklore studies is well situated to help expand cultural studies into animal studies (and vice versa), generally. What culture is, and how it works, should be rethought, restudied, and reevaluated on a scale much grander and larger than anything we have considered before. Traditions, culture, and aesthetics seem to be much larger than the human condition. Rather, an aesthetic sense seems likely to be part and parcel of the condition of life itself. Acknowledging this, and investigating this, will be a necessary step for the future of folklore studies, and for the future of scholarly understanding of culture, in terms of consciousness, aesthetics, agency, and the evolution of life on Earth.

2

THE APE THAT CAPTURED TIME

Folklore, Narrative, and the Human-Animal Divide

"There have been great societies that did not use the wheel,
but there have been no societies that did not tell stories."
Ursula le Guin, *The Language of the Night: Essays
on Fantasy and Science Fiction*, 1979

While I believe we share so much of our mentality and cultural relations with many other species, including traditions, and folklore in general, what about storytelling? Storytelling, in its various forms, has often been thought of as the folkloric genre par excellence. It may also be the genre par excellence of *Homo sapiens sapiens*, generally. What is it about storytelling that is so special and so effective at building culture?

Considering that many scholars believe that humans are unique among the animals in our ability to tell stories, this schism between human and animal, the story and other folklore, has a great deal to tell us about the outlines and origins of humanity. The question of storytelling may be at the heart of much of the presumed differences between human and nonhuman cultures. This chapter investigates the role of the story in the development of human culture from a variety of disciplinary perspectives.

This chapter is a result of an attempt to answer a simple question: do animals tell stories? Although at one point the idea might have seemed ludicrous, at least from the standpoint of Western science, recent advances in animal studies have shown that we may now speak of animal language (learned, not innate, symbolic communication) and animal culture (again, the socially learned aspects of behavior). Faced with these new developments, the question become a bit less ludicrous. If animals have language, then do they also have stories?

The answer at this time, after a careful review of current data, appears to be no. While I will argue that according to all currently available data, non-hominid animals have not been demonstrated to tell stories, what is remarkable is how very close they come, and this brings to light questions as to when and where storytelling first began, as well as what are the antecedents of storytelling, which one can find in non-hominids.

Such an evolutionary inquiry is not only interesting as a historical exercise, but also holds potential uses towards understanding storytelling, generally. For example, storytelling and narrative comprehension have been noted as key markers of human intellectual development. Usually, children begin experimenting with simple stories around age two or three, and begin to tell competent stories around five or six (Engels 1995). Autism is often closely linked with difficulties in both understanding and telling stories, and a great deal of research into autism and other related developmental conditions has investigated the issue of narrative competence (see, for example, Dautenhahn 1999, 2003; Reilly, Losh, Bellugi, and Wulfeck 2004; Capps, Losh, and Thurber 2000; Losh and Capps 2003; Liles 1993; Loveland, Mcevoy, and Tunali 1990; Flusberg and Sullivan 1995; Flusberg 1995; Klein, Chan, and Loftus 1999). Understanding the evolutionary history of storytelling, and its relation to other forms of animal communication, may therefore have some very real medical and developmental implications for our own species as well.

Animals and People

The history of Western cultures' views on animals is long and complex, but it is safe to say that up until recently science was dismissive of animal intelligence and consciousness. The Cartesion dualistic conception of the mind and body predicated a view of animals as "fleshy robots" acting instinctively, without feelings, thoughts, memories, or awareness. More recently, new findings have produced new theories, and much of the previously assumed human exceptionalism has been revealed to be instead shared with much of the animal kingdom. Scientists had long declared that only humans used tools, but work from chimps to sea otters and even birds revealed tool use to be much more widespread (see e.g., Hall 1963). Tool preparation was the new marker for "humaniqueness," but this too has been documented in other species (see e.g., Ingmanson 1996; Inoue-Nakamura and Matsuzawa 1997), even including birds (e.g., Chappell and Kacelnik 2003). Animal intelligence studies have documented the stunning closeness of our relation to many other mammals, including social and political considerations (de Waal 1982), socially learned symbolic communications (see e.g., Crockford et al. 2004), memories, and even some complex emotions. Chimps outperform humans on some memory tests (Inoue and Matsuzawa 2007). Scientific work in animal studies has documented the symbolic, cultural worlds of many non-hominid animals. Animals remember, think, are often curious about novelty, and even have been documented with instances of complex social learning.

The Banana Canon

In his 1989 article "'Banana Cannon' and Other Folk Traditions Between Human and Nonhuman Animals," Jay Mechling asserted that scholars needed to rethink the implicit assumption that folklore, as shared traditions, only exists between fellow humans, and he provided compelling evidence of traditions shared across the divide of species, particularly in the traditions such as games shared between pets and their owners. He derived his title from one such dyadic game tradition, which was collected by one of his students and labeled "the banana canon game."

> Every morning at breakfast time when John peels his banana, Shana gets excited. She sits on the floor, approximately five feet away from John, and waits for John to play "banana cannon." John: "I take a piece of banana and shoot it like a cannon out of my mouth. She's real good. Gets it from way back." (Lenz 1985)

Although the title example could perhaps be dismissed by some as simply a learned response for food, pet owners would frequently report to Mechling's students on play traditions they shared with their pets. Mechling's analysis of such games revealed shared learned traditions, creating, according to folkloric theory, an interspecial folk group. Recently, Donna Harraway has explored this theme of inter-special influence at length in her 2008 book, *When Species Meet*, which is classified under "posthuman studies."

Nor are such traditions limited to human/nonhuman dyads: inter-special play has also been observed among a variety of animal species, including in adults in the wild (e.g., Fagen 1981). Mechling's article quotes an example by

Bateson of games between two young animals in his care, a gibbon and a puppy, that developed a particular game that both partook in with great delight:

> It is an almost miraculous phenomenon to see the invention of play between members of contrasting mammalian species. I watched it happen between our two pets: a female keeshond puppy and a tame, female pre-adolescent gibbon. The gibbon would come down suddenly out of the rafters of the porch and lightly attack. The dog would react with her normal response to an unexpected tweak of the fur and would give chase; and the gibbon would run away. Not back into the rafters, which would be no fun, but along the floor and corridor into the bedroom. There the whole system was reversed. The bedroom had a ceiling instead of exposed rafters. There were no beams for the gibbon to catch on to, so further retreat was impossible. She would attack the dog and drive her out into the porch again. With that the gibbon got back into the rafters, and then would come down and start another attack, driving the game back into the bedroom. It was a game and they might repeat it six or eight times. Quite evidently both parties enjoyed it. It was the result of an experimental fitting together of the characteristics of one creature with the characteristics of the other; an evolution of a jigsaw puzzle of behavior. Obviously the learning that took place—the fitting together of the two animals' behavior to the evolving rules of the game—was rooted in the relationship between the two animals, not in something happening inside each animal. (Bateson 1982: 7)

I find it hard to argue against Mechling's conclusion that folklore, as shared traditions, must be extended to include other species. Following this, I'd like to propose "banana canon" as an appropriate title for the general proposition that animals participate in folklore. However, it still remains true that until Mechling's work, all folklore scholarship had exclusively concerned humans. Interestingly, folklorists have not only often thought of folklore as being intrinsically a human trait, but have even *defined* humanity in terms of folklore.

From Homo Narrans to Homo Fabulator

Jack Niles, for instance, published a book entitled *Homo Narrans, The Poetics and Anthropology of Oral Literature*, in which he asserted that "storytelling is an abilitiy that defines the human species as such" (1999: 3), echoing what Pierre Janet had stated in his 1928 *l'Evolution de la mémoire et la notion du temps* "narration created humanity" (261). It is interesting to note that in both of these views, it is not folklore as a whole, but rather the narrative genres of folklore, which constitute a specifically human quality.

Logically, if both the banana canon and the "man the storyteller" propositions are true, and it seems likely that they are, then humans are not unique in sharing folklore, but *are* unique in sharing stories. It is this interesting schism between humans and other animals, lying as it does between folklore and the story, that I would like to explore in this chapter.

Precise terminology may be important towards this task. Folklore, it is widely recognized, does not have to involve narrative (and thus, as per Mechling's Banana Canon, may indeed by shared by many animals). Further, narrative language does not necessarily mean a story, even though we may often think of it in that context. An example of narrative language employed in a non-storytelling context would be a radio announcer narrating a horse race over the radio (" . . . and now Lucky Jack is coming up from behind, on the inside, and, Oh! It looks like Georgia is down, Georgia is definitely down, it's Lucky Jack in the lead . . ."). This is narrative language, as the radio announcer narrates the scenario unfolding before him, yet it is not a story, at least as a story is usually defined. A story implies a narrative referring to a time *other than its own* (as the formulaic phrase "once upon a time" makes clear). "Once" may narrate an ongoing scene, but if one were asked to repeat what happened (say at the races), then it becomes a story ("Well, first Lucky Jack didn't look so good, but once Georgia went down, and he got a chance, then he was able to pull ahead and win the race").[1]

This is an important point, because while only humans might tell stories, it is not so clear that other animals do not narrate events. Witness, for example, the role of warning guard animals, the meerkat sentries, with their complex, socially learned, and group-distinct calls for announcing approaching predators, as well as the "all clear" signals once the danger has passed. The translation from any meerkat language would read something like "Lion, distant. Lion coming closer. Run!. . . . Now safe again." Just like our horse-race radio announcer, both animals are narrating ongoing events. Such narration of ongoing events has been frequently noted among chimps who have learned to sign.[2]

Language-trained chimps comment in a wide-ranging manner, inventing neologisms, and engaging in clear playful linguistic behaviors (Savage-Rumbaugh et al. 1993; Greenfield and Savage-Rumbaugh 1990). They frequently comment on ongoing events, including emotional states, and have even been documented signing to themselves regarding their own solitary activities. This is all once more to say, they narrate the present, but they have not been demonstrated to tell even rudimentary stories.

Therefore, it is not true that only humans narrate, although, so far, there has been no evidence that any non-hominids tell stories. This distinction might trouble the phrase "homo narrans," and perhaps suggest a more suitable title as "homo fabulator" (man the storyteller/ the storytelling primate).

Play as Proto-Story

In addition to alarm calls, the category of play is also an interesting site for an investigation of possible "proto-stories." As we have seen in chapter 1, all human cultures recognize play: the category of *homo ludens* was proposed as early as 1938 by Dutch cultural historian Johan Huizinga. Although Huizinga's main point in his book *Homo Ludens* was that play enabled human culture, he was careful to state that play is by no means unique to humans; rather, Huizinga called for understanding play in its evolutionary context. Recent animal science investigations have further confirmed the widespread use of play in the animal kingdom, documenting play behavior in many species, including birds and perhaps even reptiles (see e.g., Beckoff and Byers 1998) Play, then, is an important mode of communication linking human culture with nonhuman cultures

Play behavior is reminiscent of stories in two different ways.

The first is that play, like the story, is "make-believe." "Play," at its most basic, is a set of activities which pretend to be something that they are not. Often, this takes the form of "chasing" or "attacking"—basic skills necessary for nearly every organism in the quest for self defense and food acquisition ("practice makes perfect," as the proverb runs). It is far less dangerous to practice with symbols than with reality. Different species focus on different types of play, often changing types during different points in their developmental process. Hunters tend to play more than prey; social animals more than solitary ones; and "late-learner" animals more than "early learner" animals.[3] But all play shares a common characteristic: play is recognizing that the thing is not the thing. It is meta communication ("this is a play bite, not a real bite"). Also, play necessitates a *recognition* in socially engaging in the "make-believe" game. Not only is the animal "pretend acting," but the animal must recognize that *other* animal also recognizes the play frame. This evidences that there is an acknowledgment of the mental existence of the other, the notion of "someone else in there," including "someones" of different species. This is important in establishing that non-hominids as well may have what is referred to as a "theory of mind," the understanding of the existence of other cognitive beings, other outlooks, and other volitions.

The second story-like aspect of play behavior is that games, like stories, often have a plot, a syntax, and a correct sequence of events. As our earlier examples of meerkat sentries and radio horse-race announcers delineated, narrations can be performed without reference to an outside place and time. While those two examples were both vocal in nature, it is also possible to envision narration in the broader sense of being "enacted." Play behavior, then, is an enacted narrative, although this is still not an enacted story, as it lacks the story's reference to an external situation.

Poireir and Smith's incisive article on "Socializing Functions of Primate Play" points out that "perhaps one of the most useful approaches to understanding the role of play in the socialization process is to consider play as a kind of a "grammatical structure" (1974: 283). As they state, "the rules that a young primate must learn are not without some sort of logical connection of structures. Nonsense grammatical structures are unintelligible, so also are behavioural patterns improperly strung together" (ibid.). Further, they note that "as a primate develops more elaborate and intense play behavior, it orders the rules of the game into the correct sequence for proper functioning in a social unit" (ibid.).

Animals raised in isolation frequently lack appropriate play responses (see e.g., Mason and Green 1962; Mason 1963; Harlow and Harlow 1969). Play is thus not only about learning, but also about sociability. As in humans, learning proper play behaviors is critically important to social learning in many species. Parents play with their offspring as a way of passing on important knowledge. Young adults frequently play with each other as a way of challenging, testing, flirting, and bonding.

Play seems so essential to sociability and social learning that it is perhaps easy to forget about its rather unique attributes. The essential social and pedagogical aspects of play have been noted by animal ethologists as well as human game scholars (e.g., Brian Sutton Smith). It is through play that a great deal of animal symbolic communication occurs, and it is also through play that a great deal of animal symbolic communication is learned. Because play behavior is costly (in terms of energy, danger, etc), it is rewarded by sensations of extreme pleasure. Playing is fun. If it wasn't fun, it wouldn't be play; rather, it would be work. Play, and perhaps some basic games, have been developing on the planet before for millions of years before the arrival of *Homo sapiens*, reflecting a strong component for evolutionary selection. Playing must be very advantageous, to be so selected for over such a wide variety of species, for so long. It may be practice, and this seems to be the main *raison d'etre* of play ("playing" at stalking while a kitten helps prepare the adult feline for adult hunting). Yet malleability and exploring new behaviors is also a hallmark of play.

Another intriguing aspect of play is that, unlike both animal and human "languages," play can be understood, communicated, and engaged in across the special boundaries. The ability to communicate interspecially through play is, I think, a clue to its deeply time-embedded role as symbolic communication in the animal kingdom. What is perhaps more intriguing is that many animals enjoy playing with other species, including our own: I may not enjoy chase quite as much as my dog, but for his sake I participate—and for the pleasure I receive for engaging in play.

Combining what we know of animal *play* with what we know of other examples of animal *language*, we see that much of the hallmarks of the story already can be witnessed in play, yet still without the crucial reference to a specified external time and place. Given all the similarities between play and storytelling, it seems likely that storytelling is built on play behavior, and on the introduction of specific temporal and spatial symbols into play behavior, perhaps through dance, music, or pantomime.

THE STORY OF THE STORY

Having identified the key points of similarities and differences between human and animal symbolic discourses, we may now move on to inquire as to when, how, and why hominids developed storytelling. What sort of narrative abilities and traditions might our hominid relatives and ancestors have had? What were their original, if crude, "stories"? What pushed our ancestors to develop these narrative abilities?

Rather than a sudden, creationist moment when stories emerged, I believe we can instead parse the related social-cognitive abilities in other species, and in doing so gain a more nuanced view of the possible scenarios in the evolutionary development of hominid storytelling.

If we accept the ability and proclivity for much of the animal world to narrate the present moment in symbolic communication (through such activities as our meerkat sentries) then this, as a narrative, accounts for a substantial part of what constitutes a story. There are at least two other requirements: one is the ability to remember episodes, since stories necessitate conceptualizing activities outside of the here and now. The other is the ability to communicate such discrete episodes, a complex task. Due to the complexity, the latter requirement also would seem to require a notion of syntax, in order to be able to create dense layers of meaning from individual linguistic symbols.

Episodic Memory, or "Once upon a Time"

Let us begin with episodic memory. Perhaps, one might justifiably propose, the reason that animals do not tell stories is because they do not conceive of time?

That they live in an "eternal present"? After all, re-enacting episodes presumes a certain type of memory, classified by cognitive scientists as episodic memory. Episodic memory is the memory of events in the past, and seems dependent on the medial temporal lobe, and perhaps particularly on the hippocampus (particularly well-developed in hominids).[4]

Episodic memory is an "advanced" memory. Clayton et al. called episodic memory "mental time travel" and noted that "not all humans are capable of episodic remembering. Indeed, episodic memory develops relatively late, and is not fully developed until about four years of age. It is also the most fragile kind of memory, the first to be lost in Alzheimer's disease and other debilitating neurodegenerative diseases of the mind" (2007: R189). Since originally proposed by Tulving in 1972, the category of episodic memory has been highly utilized by cognitive scientists. Episodic memory can be contrasted to procedural memory, which is defined as the memory of rote procedures. Procedural memory may remember the "how-to," but does not remember "when." In addition to the episodic and procedural, Tulving also proposed the semantic memories, with this accounting for the "what-order" remembering of syntax.[5]

Although episodic memory was once claimed only for humans (as Tulving himself announced in his 1983 work), once again a series of newer studies have lent conclusive weight to the debate, documenting much evidence for episodic memories in a variety of other animals (see e.g., Clayton and Dickinson 1998; Schwartz and Evans 2001; Hampton 2001). Note that some scholars delineate that although other animals may have episodic memory, it is hard to tell, because they do not communicate their memories, preferring instead to characterize non-hominid episodic memory instances as "personal episodic memory." This distinction captures the essential difference: not a difference in memory per se (the memory of an episode happening "in the past"), but rather reflecting that that humans *communicate* their personal memories in their symbolic communications, and it is through this that personal episodic memories become *group* episodic memories, through being communicated as "stories" shared among a wide social network.

Tenses, Time, and Recursive Grammar

As discussed previously, such a complex communicative event referring to an event in another time and place likely requires some sort of syntax or grammar, in order to make sense of the symbolisms and to express ideas of times and places. Syntax and grammar are (of course) more usually considered within the realm of language, and language has been one of the most contentious areas for claiming "humaniqueness." as well as a usual component of storytelling. Human language is far more complex than any other animals' communications. Yet, it is also clear that the faculty of language can be proposed—at least in the broad sense as learned shared symbolic communications—for many other animals as well. Hauser, Fitch, and Chomsky suggest that a helpful distinction can be made between the faculty of language in the broad sense (FLB) and the faculty of language in the narrow sense (FLN) (2002: 1569). While they argue that many animals have language broadly defined and that "the available data suggest a much stronger continuity between animals and humans with respect to speech than previously believed" (2002: 1574), they still find human language unique due to the process of recursion found in human languages. Recursion involves the fleshing out of simple words or phrases by the addition connected, referring phrases ("John says that the monkey is eating the banana that fell from the tree").

Interestingly, it is also the development of storytelling—that is, communicated "packets of time" relative to one another and discrete sequences of events besides those in the "here and now"—that also seems to lie at the heart of Hauser, Fitch, and Chomsky's notion of the unique recursion in human languages. This notion of recursion necessitates not only a notion of grammar (which may be argued to be in much non-hominid FLB), but also a notion of "tensing," of groups of words that refer to "packets" of time, and discrete sequence of events. As Hauser et al. point out, even in the complex communication of alarm calls in studies on meerkats, prairie dogs, and others, the "signals in the repertoire is small, restricted to object and events experienced in the present" (2002: 1576). In my view, there is no recursion in non-hominid languages because there is no tensing (except the default "here and now" present). Again, this is not to say that non-hominids may not think about other times and places, but rather that they have not been able to symbolically communicate such episodic memories to others.

Ultimately, storytelling is communication which includes episodic memory, procedural memory, and syntactical ability; all of which are found, by themselves, in other animals. This important combination likely allowed for the development of tensing, increasingly precise storytelling, and ultimately for the complex recursive grammars of human spoken languages. Storytelling, which requires the expression of discrete episodes in symbolic communication, seems to lie at the very heart of human language grammar.

When?

If the previous section has hoped to answer some questions as to the necessary components of storytelling, we are still left with the question of when storytelling might have begun. Michelle Scalise Sugiyama has been writing on the development of narrative for some time, and has proposed that storytelling was a "product of our hunting-and-gathering past, likely to have emerged between 30,000 and 100,000 years ago" (2001: 234). I think her work concerns many of the key topics of the issue; however, I disagree with several of the points she uses to build her theory, and I think some of her resulting conclusions are subsequently rendered unlikely. Nonetheless, her main points are worth reviewing in detail.

Sugayama states, "Given, then, that modern humans (*Homo sapiens sapiens*) have been in existence for approximately 100,000 years and are the only hominid species or subspecies known for certain to exhibit storytelling behavior, we can safely say that oral narrative is a product of our hunting-and-gathering past, likely to have emerged between 30,000 and 100,000 years ago" (ibid.).

While it is true by definition that *oral* narratives require complex vocalizations, this is not necessarily the same thing as storytelling. The vocal abilities of humans are particularly well-suited to fine nuances in oral sound-making, being able to switch easily between vowel sounds and consonant sounds with our laryngeal modifications and the ability to close our soft palate. The vocal abilities of our nearest relatives, and doubtless of our hominid ancestors, were much less refined. Still, storytelling, especially in its most basic form, would not necessarily require fine vocalizations; those humans with speaking or hearing disabilities are often able to narrate stories, and indeed often participate dynamically in social linguistic life, through sign languages and pantomime. Although humans are vocal communicators, work on primates has revealed that most of our primate cousins rely more on gestural communications, including pantomime, and perhaps even display what may be termed sign proto-languages.[6] Certainly, in ape-language studies, apes have been much more receptive to learning sign language than to learning vocal language.[7(8)]

Hence, there is no reason *a priori* to assume that other related hominids, *Homo neanderthalis*, or even *Homo erectus*, did not relate stories, and therefore no reason to assume an outside date of storytelling with the emergence of *Homo sapiens sapiens*.[9] In seeking the origins of the story, then, it may be more productive to ask, what sort of narrative abilities, might our hominid relatives have had? What were their original, if crude, "stories"?

Recent evolutionary biologists have pointed to the gradual development of fine vocalizations, and have proposed that earlier hominids, such as *Homo erectus*, likely relied on gestural or pantomime, perhaps combined with crude vocalizations, to communicate. Along with Merlin Donald (1991) and others (Hoffmeyer 1996; Arbib 1996, 2008; Corballis 2002; Hewes 1973; Lock 1978; Stokoe 2001), I envision early hominids as likely possessing pantomimetic stories and "mimetic culture," which were important for linking procedural memory and episodic memories

As Arbib et al. point out in their 2006 article "Primate Vocalization, Gesture, and the Evolution of Human Language":

> The performance of language is multimodal, not confined to speech. Review of monkey and ape communication demonstrates greater flexibility in the use of hands and body than for vocalization. Nonetheless, the gestural repertoire of any group of nonhuman primates is small compared with the vocabulary of any human language and thus, presumably, of the transitional form called protolanguage. We argue that it was the coupling of gestural communication with enhanced capacities for imitation that made possible the emergence of protosign to provide essential scaffolding for protospeech in the evolution of protolanguage. Similarly, we argue against a direct evolutionary path from non-human primate vocalization to human speech. (1053)

Even today, gestures continue to play a large role in natural language discourse. Some cultures accentuate this more than others, but all natural language discourse involves body communications (see e.g., Goffman 1967).

Savage-Rumbaugh et al. wrote that we should view the adaptation of modern language as demonstrating the powers of plasticity of the brain, particularly in youth, and that much of human spoken language therefore developed on abilities already extant by a minimum of several million years. These authors link speech acts with bipedalism, "which necessitated reorientation of the laryngeal tract and made closure of the soft palate possible" (Savage-Rumbaugh et al. 1993: vi). They further continue,

> For the first time, such closure permitted mammals to easily produce sounds that could be interpreted by the mammalian auditory system in a categorical manner. When these sounds were paired with the previously extant capacity to produce vowels, it became possible to form "bounded vowels" or sound units that could readily be discriminated as units by the auditory system. (ibid.)

This is to say that the development of fine vocalization necessary for speech may have even been an accidental result of bipedalism generally.[10] It is very possible that vocalizations were adapted for communication *long after* gestural or pantomimetic storytelling were already well developed. Without any evidence, it is difficult to know one way or the other. Yet, assuredly, early hominids would have been much more likely to rely on gestures for their communications, and likely had much more complex gestural codes and sign languages than do gorillas or chimps today. Much of this gestural complexity might have been lost by later hominids, who increasingly relied on vocal communications instead. It could also be that the refinement of storytelling and the refinement of spoken language co-developed, with each supporting each others' advances in a feedback loop model of development. After all, we must imagine a time when the laryngeal modifications were intermediate between ape and modern homo, somewhat capable of vowels and consonants, yet perhaps not enough for full human vocal languages. Perhaps storytelling at that time, such as it was, might have also been a mix of the two forms of language, the gestural and the vocal.

In short, although speech, storytelling, narratives, and language overlap a great deal, and the developments of all of them are woven together in the history of humanity and the hominid line, they are not necessarily the same, and therefore it is quite plausible that earlier hominids might also had some sort of storytelling ability, albeit likely of a gestural and pantomimetic variety.

Why?

Sugayma's view of the evolution of storytelling is one of environmental determinism, and she proposes that stories originated as a way of learning about the group's locale. As she puts it, "the aggregate effect of oral narrative, then, is to provide a broad base of knowledge pertinent to the pursuit of fitness in the local environment" (2001: 245). While it is likely true that being able to tell stories became an enormous advantage in terms of learning about the environment, there is nothing terribly hominid about that—all animals need to know their environment. Also, straightforward determinism is rarely a sufficient explanation of highly complex developments, including cultural ones, which more likely are the result of various underlying causes.[11] Further, it is not at all clear that all stories are all about survival. Mythological narratives, for example, set in a "time before the current world" would seem to have little direct evolutionary advantages, yet clearly play a large role throughout most of the world's storytelling.

Attempting to address this latter problem were Coe et al. in their 2006 article, "'Once Upon a Time': Ancestors and the Evolutionary Significance of Stories." The authors are influenced by Sugayama's work, yet focus on what they describe as "traditional stories." Their definition includes most folk narratives, collapsing the usual distinctions between legends, myths, and tales.

Coe et al. are interested in how stories that promote cooperation or even self-sacrifice can be directly related to the evolution of the species, and they conclude that they are, by the stories' demanding adherence to tradition, as "descendant-leaving strategies," although it is not clear whether they mean actual descendants, or more "philosophical" descendants (those influenced by storytelling). They contrast this demand for adherence to tradition by stating

that "modern" societies instead assert creativity. They see traditional stories'
raison d'etre, therefore, as being "told more to encourage traditional behaviours
rather than motivate the listener to develop new creative strategies" (2006: 22).[12]
Although the role of social cohesion in storytelling—and, indeed, folklore in
general, not just the narrative—has long been recognized (see e.g., Bascom's
classic 1954 "Four Function of Folklore"), it is something a bit different to say
that, evolutionarily speaking, this is why these stories developed.

While it is doubtless true that storytelling has tremendous adaptational
values for the individual and the group, and hence with Darwinian natural
selection, it also is intimately involved with success *within* the group, and hence
with sexual selection as well—and here we are discussing the appreciation
of stories for their own sake, and not necessarily for the sake of adapting to
the local environments, or for enforcing conformity to tradition. The role of
cultural attributes of sexual selection has been explored at length in Geoffrey
Miller's 2000 work, *The Mating Mind*, and critically examined in Blocke and
Dewitte (2006) (see also Ohler and Nieding 2005). To put it in layman's terms:
telling a good joke is a great way to get laid. Multiply that over thousands of
generations, and we can see how the drive towards storytelling can also be
explained at least in part by sexual selections as well as natural (both individual and group) ones. Similarly, the work on the complex political worlds
of chimpanzees (e.g., de Waal 1982) suggests that stories were likely employed
early on in the realm of group politics as well, in such forms as assertions of
power, stories of past events, rumors, and the like.[13]

The reasons behind the development of storytelling seem to me to be
numerous, and overlapping. Undoubtedly, however, the ability to communicate
a great deal of information (including "flows of events") enabled tremendous
advantages for those individuals and groups participating in it. It is one thing
to be able to warn of an approaching lion; it is quite another to be able to
discuss lion attacks that occurred in the past, or that might occur in the future.

Stories on the Savannah

If we seek to understand the reasons behind the evolution of storytelling in
hominids, then perhaps we can begin by agreeing (along with most evolutionary scholars) that one of the most important events in hominid evolution was
the move onto the savannah. Although far from a simple or unmuddied process, much of what we consider hominid developments—including bipedalism,
laryngeal modifications, increased reliance on vocal communications, extensive
tool use, and even pair-bonding—are often tied directly to the movement
from the forest canopies to the open savannah, approximately five million

years ago. The move on to the savannah is likely to be more responsible for the blossoming of humanity (witness the myriad early hominid species) than any other single factor in our evolutionary development, and thus it is likely this step may have put in motion the development of the story.

Understanding how the story resulted from this move may be beyond our reach to ever truly know, and seems likely to have had many converging stimuli.

One important factor may have been an increase in group size, forcing more social communication. Dautenhahn has argued that the evolution of stories was intimately tied to the increasing social size and complexity of social groups (1999), most likely as a result of the early hominid move onto the savannah (for more on this, see Aiello and Dunbar 1993). Dautenhahn proposes that hominids developed a "narrative intelligence," an analogue to the "social intelligence" of primates. This is to say, primates tend to spend a great deal of time physically grooming each other, as a means of negotiating their complex social worlds. When early hominids moved onto the savannah, they likely developed larger and more complex groups, which would have rendered physical grooming ineffectual at maintaining social relations. Storytelling, Dautenhahn proposes, must have been developed to accomplish this task of maintaining the densely complex social relations.

Additionally, the open savannah might have made group coordination all the more important in coordinating hunting or group movements. The wider range of the savannah might have encouraged members of the community to try to communicate on events happening further away than would have occurred in the ancestral forest home.

In addition to the possibilities mentioned above, I would also suggest another additional hypothetical influence from this move to the savannah, which is that it may have resulted in part from the new strategy of scavenging. A number of scholars have argued that scavenging was likely a significant contributor to much of early hominid subsidence and subsequent evolutionary adaptations (see e.g., Blumenschine 1986; Speth 1989; Cavallo and Blumenschine 1989). Although perhaps not terribly heroic, this strategy of chasing large predators away from kills does seem a plausible niche our brainy but puny ancestors could have exploited, not from overpowering but rather, like all good scavengers, by tricking or scaring away larger predators from their kills, perhaps aided by such devices as long spears, slings, noisemakers, or fire. Scavenging by nature pushes animals into a highly inter-special world—not just that of a fight or flight, but rather "trick," that is, understanding the other organism and interacting successfully with it. This, in addition to other influences, may have pushed hominids towards being highly attuned to the "play" frame of "make-believe."[14]

Story Memory, a Play on Words

Once we have "play" communication combined with narrative aspects, we can have narrative play: that is, narrative not of simply the here and now present, but also a narrative about what is *not* going on right here right now, which is to say, a story. Perhaps, in this sense, then, theater and this notion of "a play," provides a likely site of origin for human storytelling. Indeed, it may not be too much to say that theater, as the first story, begat humanity. This is not real, the play frame states, it represents something else. In a theatrical performance, the play frame further states that these actions are occurring not in the here and now, but in the there and then. I am reminded of the classical myth-ritual school, which held that myths are often not simply told, but enacted, they are "played out" (see Harrison 1912). Theater, and the play, seem once more to be at our mythic beginnings.

Communication, perhaps originally mimetic and pantomime, eventually enabled the portrayal of distinct episodes (say, reliving a past hunt with someone playing the part of the prey, while others played the part of the hunters), allowing hominids to experience communication not as timeless representations (such as "hunting") but rather specific episodes ("the last hunt," "the next hunt"). Such a development allows the individual organisms to participate with their own memories in a new, social context. However crude, any discrete tensing would have been a qualitative change beyond anything else in the realm of animal symbolic communication, as far as scientists have thus far been able to document.

To be clear: this is not to say that non-hominids do not have their own internal narratives, or their own internal memories. To the contrary, it would seem likely that many do. It is also not to state that non-hominids do not have culture (defined here as shared symbols and traditions passed down through social learning). Again, it seems highly evident that they do. Hominids and non-hominids alike share in many of the same concerns, emotions, and thoughts, and can easily interact together using syntactical symbolic communication. It is assuredly remarkable that learned traditions can be shared across special boundaries—it is so remarkable, in fact, that it perhaps leaves us with more questions than answers: for example, why would animals develop the ability to communicate, and to play, interspecially? This seems contradictory to Darwinian models of natural and sexual selections of the species, and is practically begging for more theoretical and investigative scholarship. As a starting point, the Banana Canon—that shared cultural traditions exist among non-hominids animals—seems to hold its validity, opening up a new avenue for folklorists to study non-hominid and inter-special traditions, engaging with scholars from diverse disciplines (primatology, animal psychology, etc) working with animal play. Although the thought of "animal folklore studies" might seem bizarre to some at the current moment, we may observe that several other disciplines, such as psychology, also originated in the study of hominids, and only later branched out to study other animals. It is intriguing that folklore as a discipline straddles both: that which is shared with non-hominid animals, and that which seems mostly restricted to hominids alone, the story.

If the story has often been the focus of folklore studies, it is thus no surprise why: it is at the core of hominid communication. Without it, we can still communicate with non-hominids, and even partake in shared traditions with them. To a scientist from Mars, much of our mental processes would seem alike, were it not for that curious twist of humans to begin telling stories, likely linking back to the development of the first crude "play narrative." But the distinction, subtle as it may seem, is of great importance. Humans can pass down stories; animals do not, and, because of this, the capacity for animal cultures to develop complexity over multiple generations is much more limited.

The social function of shared stories gave rise to what we may call the "story memory" of *Homo sapiens*, in which our memories are both recalled and shared as stories, creating the "social memory," and hence identity, of groups. We now recall (through story memory) not only episodes of our own experiences, but also the experiences of others from long ago. This allows for human culture to develop over time in a way unimaginable in the non-hominid kingdom, and allows our stories to function as a vast reservoir of memories, experiences, and aesthetics. We humans now rely on stories, on our discrete categorizations of time, for much of our thoughts about the past. Not only are past events thought of and expressed predominantly in terms of stories, but also the future as well.[15]

We rely so strongly on story memory for our conceptions of the world that at times it even appears able to replace or impinge on episodic memories. The stories of our nations, families, churches, and other groups become *our* story, the memories become shared, all by engaging in stories as memories, and by believing in the reality of the play.

Even our own personal memories are influenced by what scholars such as Rubin have labeled "autobiographical memory"—the memory of the personal past as represented in story form (see e.g., Rubin 1988, 1999) This, too, seems likely to be a "humanique" development, arising out of social storytelling behavior. Dennett has gone so far to say that "our fundamental tactic of self-protection, self-control, and self-definition is not building dams or spinning webs, but telling stories—and more particularly concocting and controlling the story we tell others—and ourselves—about who we are" (Dennett 1991: 418).

This is all to say that the story has not only created us as a unique species, but that it has also created most of what we identify as our own selves, from our concepts of gender, ethnicity, nationalism, regionalism, religion, and even family. All of these identity concerns are developed through stories. Without the story, it is clear we would not be human.

Into the Woods

At the same time, this realization that the story, more than anything else, is what constitutes humanity, might also give us pause to consider the level to which we may tend to be over-impressed by the story as an explanatory device of our surrounding reality, both as scholars and as laymen. For instance, something resulting from a complex mix of actions from many different variables or actors—a "chaotic mess," as it were—might be ill-suited for the straightforward explanatory details of the story. T. C. Chamberlin warned students of science against this in his seminal 1890 paper, "The Methods of Multiple Hypotheses." As he put it,

> It is far easier, and I think in general more interesting, for [young students] to argue a theory or accept a simple interpretation than to recognize and evaluate the several factors which the true elucidation may require. To illustrate: it is more to their taste to be taught that the Great Lake basins were scooped out by glaciers than to be urged to conceive of three or more great agencies working successively or simultaneously, and to estimate how much was accomplished by each of these agencies. (1965 [1890]: 757)

Historians have also noted the public hunger for simple narratives of history, and it is a testament to this awareness that many works on historiography now also include the structuralist narrative theories of the folklorist Vladimir Propp (see Porter 1981; Ricoeur 1984–88). Simple stories are not necessarily more accurate than the fuller, multilayered accounts of various complex variables; rather, they are simply much more appealing and understandable to our story-oriented mind (see e.g., White 1987; Straub 2005).

We humans rely on storytelling for so much of our thoughts about the world that we perhaps at times impose stories on a reality where there was none to be had. If someone wants to know about a chaotic mess, the first thing asked might be "what's the story, here?"—a question that may not be easy to answer, and, further, in answering, we may be imposing our eagerness for a good story on a much more complex and variegated reality.

Concluding Remarks

In my view, the story builds on the elemental notion of *tensing*, a discrete symbolizing of temporal qualities that likely developed out of a combination of narrative and play behaviors early on in our hominid ancestry. The results of this elemental symbolic capture have proved *homo*'s most notable addition to planet Earth, and a most singular attribute of "humaniqueness." The goalpost between human and non-hominid animals does not seem to be speech, or communication, or memories, or even narration, but it does seem perhaps to be the ability to tell a story: absent any forthcoming evidence to the contrary, it would seem that we are the only storytellers on planet Earth. The story is so constitutive to who we are as humans that careful attention to this particular trait may reveal a good deal about our outlooks on time and reality, our developmental stages as a species and as individuals, cognitive abnormalities such as autism and related conditions, and the narrative, cultural, and mental worlds of nonhuman animals as well.

EPILOGUE

Having thrown down this particular gauntlet, I expect, and hope, that it will be challenged. New studies from ethology are an exciting source of data, and, in turn, can correct, or at least moderate, many previous claims. I would not be at all surprised for my claim that only humans have stories to be disproven at some point, or at least attenuated by further data. I would welcome such developments. Since publishing this chapter as an article in 2010, I have kept a close watch on the developments in ethology for any indications of nonhuman storytelling in the animal kingdom. The most compelling study I have observed has been on male orangutans, who seem to announce their future travels to the group—not only that they are planning to travel, but also the general direction they are heading (van Schaik, Damerius, and Isler 2013). This seems close to the idea of storytelling, generally, as I have set it out in this chapter: the idea of communicating actions in a time other than the present. Further replications and refinements of this study may bring additional clarity to the situation, but it is already an intriguing possibility that some of our closest relatives may have something close to what we might call a story—a fact unknown when I was working on this chapter as an article in 2010. Would such a discovery, if definitely established, vacate the insights of this chapter? I would think probably not; even if we can qualify the claims, even if we are not the only storytelling animal, it would still be true that storytelling seems to have a particularly compelling hold on human culture, and a particular level of complex expression.

And in addition to this study, we will surely learn more as more data from ethology studies continues to build. We are just at the bare beginnings, for example, of understanding dolphin, or whale, communications. Might these also contain storytelling episodes? Perhaps, or perhaps not. But one thing is clear: only by learning to listen to them will we ever be able to know what they are saying. And that, I would think, is the most important lesson of all.

3

DO ANIMALS HAVE SOULS?

Mythologies and Worldviews on
the Concept of Personhood

THE CAMBRIDGE DECLARATION ON CONSCIOUSNESS

On this day of July 7, 2012, a prominent international group of cognitive neuroscientists, neuropharmacologists, neurophysiologists, neuroanatomists and computational neuroscientists gathered at The University of Cambridge to reassess the neurobiological substrates of conscious experience and related behaviors in human and non-human animals. While comparative research on this topic is naturally hampered by the inability of non-human animals, and often humans, to clearly and readily communicate about their internal states, the following observations can be stated unequivocally:

> . . . . *the weight of evidence indicates that humans are not unique in possessing the neurological substrates that generate consciousness. Nonhuman animals, including all mammals and birds, and many other creatures, including octopuses, also possess these neurological substrates.*

Rather than asking what animals *are*, the next two chapters focus on the fundamental ways that people frame the question. What do we *think* animals are, and why? Such answers are deeply embedded in cultural systems, including our own. For most of the history of Western discourse, humans were people, and animals were (are) not. This paradigm (of "fleshy robots" versus soulful people) has been constructed over a great arc of time in Western thought, drawing not only from scholars, but also other pre- and non-academic thinkers, who often fused their philosophies with religious ideas on personhood, most clearly in the idea of souls.

Such distinctions (what has spirit, and what does not) are elemental ontological cultural categories, closely linked with our foundational mythologies, the sacred origin stories of how things came to be.

Chapter 3 takes a look at the concept of souls and its role to personhood in two distinct mythological traditions writ large—the Abrahamic and the Native American—for the sake of comparisons. While posthuman views of the animal kingdom may seem like revolutionary news to much of Western thought, Native American cultures reveal a widespread and profound acceptance of the idea of animals as people, and their close relationship to our own species. The question "do animals have souls?" offers a way to trace the constructions of various cultural views of animals in a way that ties together the role of formative sacred stories—mythologies—and the ongoing cultural categories that influence daily discourse, both scientific and lay.

THE CONSCIOUS WORLD

The beginning of the new millennium witnessed a dramatic growth in scientific knowledge of nonhuman mental worlds and abilities. Dolphins have individual names for themselves, expressed in whistles (King and Janek 2013). Hyraxes speak different socially learned languages (Kershenbaum et al. 2012) Octopi are playful, intelligent creatures who learn quickly from one another (Kuba et al. 2006). Fish use tools (Brown 2012). Such scientific discoveries not only overturn years of scientific thought, but also are in direct contradiction to much of the religious and lay discourse in the Western world regarding "humans versus other life" as well.

Not only must we recognize that animals are "a lot like us," sharing fundamental characteristics heretofore unrecognized, but we must also begin to question the very nature of "us." Such powerful questions tug at accepted definitions of essential words— "person," "human," and "animal"—while troubling widely accepted ideologies, traditions, language, and beliefs. In animal studies, specialists are now having to confront the study of animal culture, animal communications, and animal mentalities, all of which lead towards the discussion of personhood beyond the human.

In her comprehensive overview of the "animal turn" in recent scholarly discourse, Pauliina Rautio (2012) praises the utility of concept of interspecies articulation, where the focus becomes the connections between the human and nonhuman, rather than focusing on merely our own species, or on a divide.

From the human-oriented disciplines, the animal turn has been a tectonic shift: "humanities" takes the human as a starting and ending point—if there is anything other than our "animal nature," it is merely cast as a shadow, perhaps as a fault to be overcome. As Tonutti wrote, "we can say that humanism turned its back no nature; it assumed *humanitas* as a subject of speculation and totally dismissed humanity's natural dimension" (Tonutti 2011: 187). The binary divide between humanities and the natural sciences helps reinforce the seemingly intrinsic boundaries between human and animal, yet as these boundaries have proven more fictions than real, the implications have destabilized the underlying organizing principals of "nature versus nurture" or "wild versus cultured."

Anthropology is in a similar bind. Culture has long been presumed to be an entirely human affair. Anthropologist Ruth Benedict wrote that "culture is the sociological term for learned behavior. . . . The degree to which human achievements are dependent on this kind of learned behavior is man's great claim to superiority over all the rest of creation; he has been properly called 'the culture-bearing animal'" (1942: 138). Yet now we know most certainly that culture is not the sole province of humans.

Rethinking these basic definitions and their implications forms the backbone of posthumanism: the general intellectual movement to re-examine what it is to be "human." Ironically, perhaps, much "posthuman" work done in this arena has focused on how humans have thought about nonhumans—which is to say, still taking the human as the appropriate venue of inquiry, albeit destabilizing the assumptions of essential separation between humans and animals.

One exception to this is Scott's 2006 "Spirit and Practical Knowledge in the person of the Bear among Wemindji Cree Hunters," which takes animism as centered on an essential ontology which allows for nonhuman agency and personhood—an epistemic decentering of the agency away from the human, and towards nonhuman personhood: in a word, animism. Here, taking his cue from his Cree informants, he notes that such a proposition of animal souls allows for nonhuman agency, even within animism itself. Or, one might say, non-hominids contribute to animism, too. Thus, in his view, animism can be seen as more than a spiritual or religious outlook: instead it is also an ontological (and, following this, epistemological) system of understanding the world.

A concurring recent anthropological study is Eduardo Kohn's 2013 *How Forests Think: Toward an Anthropology beyond the Human*. Here, too, the author becomes interested in ontologies, and here, too, interested in native (South American) ideas of the thinking forests, plants, and animals. According to him, for the Runa, with whom he studies, animism is "grounded in an ontological fact: there exist other kinds of thinking selves beyond the human" (94).

Ontology has deep links with mythology, which is a branch of folklore, yet the discipline of folklore has likewise remained focused on the human, even while it is increasingly obvious that many of its core subjects (tradition, games, music) are widely shared throughout the animal kingdom. Combining these insights with those afforded by animal studies, and by Scott's view of animism as ontology, we are now in a better position to examine core difference in Native American mythology (enmeshed in animist ontologies), with those of non-native, Western mythologies, based instead on an anthropocentric ontology.

There are some inherent difficulties in large-scale comparative mythological studies and associated worldviews. Perhaps the most pronounced is the reluctance of many scholars to admit that there *are* widespread mythologies and associated worldviews. This may be due to two distinct trends: the universalists and the particularists. Universalists, such as Carl Jung and Joseph Campbell, argued for universal mythologies, held together by the "collective unconscious." These approaches have been now largely discredited from scholarship, as contemporary scholarship has instead documented the wide cultural differences in different mythologies (see e.g., Dundes 2005).

On the other side of the spectrum, anthropologists and ethnologists often tend towards site-specific research and conclusions. The complexity of mythology and its close relationships to culture, language, and society, make comparative research difficult. Specialists often dedicate their careers to a particular mythological path. The emphasis on in-depth understanding of mythologies, including learning the source language, and extensive participant observation of the group, have provided for rich, specialized works.

Still, mythologists have long been aware that related mythologies do span immense territories, revealing large-scale similarities and differences in different groups. Frazer, for example, famously cited the widespread story of the "Failed Animal Messenger" (the macrotype for the Garden of Eden story) found widely across Africa and the Middle East. Working with Native American mythologies, Rooth (1984) proposed a grand total of eight macrotypes.

Further, there can be much to gain from comparative investigations. Both similarities and differences in core cultural categories are often revealed by the corresponding mythological traditions. For our case study, we can compare and contrast the widespread myth associated with Abrahamic traditions (that of the

Garden of Eden with its inherently anthropocentric cosmos) with the variety of myths found in native North America, which tend to feature nonhuman actors in creating the world, and a mythic time when all the animals talked and acted like humans.

This key conceptual difference in the creation of the world, and of humankind, grounds resulting philosophical differences in the role of human versus nonhuman animals in Native American societies and traditions, contrasted with Abrahamic-inspired ones. Such elemental mythic constructions echo down millennia of discussions.

This, chapter, then, juxtaposes Old World and New World systems of thought, as they relate to nonhuman animals. In doing so, I do not mean to stress a uniformity in either Abrahamic or New World mythologies or philosophies, nor deny the ongoing influences on each other, but rather try to display what I see as a fundamental (as in the structure of the world) disjuncture between the two. Such a view takes a postcolonial as well as posthumanist look at mythologies and worldviews. Such an investigation is not merely an academic exercise, but, hopefully, one that leads to a better understanding of current scientific and lay discourse, and to a better understanding of the contours of the wider topic at hand: that of how to envision our relationship with other species.

IMPLICATIONS

Theoretical studies on such topics can have real-world implications. Scholars from a wide variety of disciplines are questioning human-animal connections and the roles of sentience in terms of personhood, the mind, and other related concepts. These scholarly studies both reflect and shape industrial and legal practices, even everyday practices, as people continue to navigate their ongoing relations to nonhuman living things. These newer studies challenge much of what has been claimed as uniquely human, and, as such, have been used in support of new laws and regulations for nonhuman animals. In the EU, cosmetic companies can no longer perform tests on live animals (Kanter 2013). In India, dolphins have been declared "nonhuman persons," with rights to live freely and not in captivity. In general, a discourse towards a stricter enforcement of "animal abuse" statutes seems to herald new concerns toward humans' relations to other forms of life.

Yet if there is a general agreement on the idea (if not the specifics) of "universal human rights," what can be said regarding our proper relationship to other living things? Here there is no such agreement, and instead a wide, often conflicting variety of ideas on the proper relation of humans to other animals, and even to the rest of life on Earth.

All the while, the topic is growing, and is of growing importance. Today, the largest enemy to humans around the world may not be—for the first time in a long time—each other, but rather from the wholesale collapse of ecosystems: the shuddering collapse of much of life on Earth. Our greatest danger as an entire species may lie with our own lack of sensitivity to other living things, and our greatest hope for survival may be our ability to become more attuned to our place in the ecosystem—our kinship, if you will.

THE ENVIRONMENT, THE ENVIRONMENTAL MOVEMENT, AND MYTHOLOGY

In the US, the environmental movement owes much of its intellectual traditions to Native Americans. As George Cornell put it:

> Native Americans have made enormous contributions to the growth of modern conservation. These contributions are not romantic or political rhetoric, but rather, represent the popularization of Indian practices and perceptions by figures such as George Bird Grinnell, acknowledged as one of the "fathers" of modern conservation, and Ernest Thompson Seton, the renowned naturalist and one of the founders of the Boy Scouts of America. (1985: 105)

Both these figures were enormously influential in forming early twentieth-century nostalgic yet practical ideas on the importance of wilderness, and in installing an appreciation of wilderness on the American public. Both authors attempted to translate various Native American traditions to American youth and young adults, stressing the Native American precepts of respect for nature, alongside their wilderness skills. In addition to these figures examined by Cornell, we may add another: the charismatic founder of the Sierra Movement, John Muir.

Muir, the famous conservationist, traveled to Alaska early on in his career, growing familiar with the Tlingit Natives. In particular, a Tlingit named Kadachan impressed and influenced him with his ecological views. Kardachan told him of a theological discussion he'd once had with a missionary, who was preaching on the importance of the human soul. He asked the missionary if he believed that wolves had souls. The missionary responded in the negative. Ah, Kadachan said, they believed that wolves have souls (Muir 1915).

Such intimate encounters with animist viewpoints, which regard all life as connected, helped Muir form the background of much of the environmental movement through his tireless advocacy.

In these and many other ways, Native American views have continued to impact non-native views in spite of their political disempowerment. Yet this continuing influence also reveals the stark difference between the two worldviews, that of the "New World" of the various Native American cultures and societies, and the "Old World" from whence came the invaders, regarding the fundamental properties of life. Due to this, a comparative view of the Native American mythology, and that of Euro American society, may provide valuable insights into the benefits of postcolonial theory, being able to learn anew from previously discounted cultural discourses of knowledge. By nature, such a large comparison will paint the picture in broad strokes, at times doing a disservice to the variety of different traditions in both worlds. Yet I hope that it may still also be able to illuminate critical differences that bear directly and indirectly on the subject of human relations with the natural world.

The global environmental movement has become one of the largest social and political movements of the late twentieth and early twenty-first centuries. Not surprisingly, concern for nonhuman life (both lay and academic) is linked with the wider environmental movement. Environmentalism as a general movement links wide varieties of disparate groups, individuals, and communities: from local organizations, vegetarian and vegan movements, anti-GMO and/or anti-chemical movements, anti-pollution, indigenous tribes, sustainability advocates, and many more. Environmental movements urge awareness of environmental impacts of human activities, and curbs to development where appropriate in order to safeguard natural environments (determining "appropriate" being the contentious part). Environmental groups and movements play key roles in policy-making, research, and in helping to form everyday sensibilities and practices.

SACRED NARRATIVES FOR EVERYDAY LIVING

In studying Native American traditional culture, one is inevitably struck by the strong sense of connections to other living things—animals, plants, even stones and forces of nature. This has spectacular local variations, yet the central theme can be found throughout a wide geographic area, part of the larger animism-shamanism area of the circumpolar and the Americas. Animals play active roles in nearly all genres of Native American folklore, from myths and legends to dances and names. If I were asked to propose the single most striking difference between Native American cultures and those of Western societies, my answer would have to be in this regard. Although people might feel uncomfortable with widespread comparisons, there is no escaping the wide gulf between how Western and Native American societies portray their kinship with animals.

This elemental split in the categorization of the numinous can be traced to the cosmogonic myths, the sacred stories of how the world (and other things) came to be. Myths explain not only the cosmos, but they also explain one's relation *to* the cosmos. Myths answer the big questions: What is life? What is thought? What is my place here in the universe? Myths are a sacred charter for our most everyday, mundane actions, as well as for our ritualized ones.

In the myths of the Abrahamic and related faiths, the most common and well-known mythic story is the creation of Man and Woman, as Adam and Eve. It is noticeable that the divine entity appears to resemble human beings, as the Bible states "He created Man in His image." The implication, and the later iconography, being a male human-looking divinity, who creates the cosmos, the Earth, and mankind, as well as rules the cosmos, and the spiritual realm.

THE ELDER BROTHERS

Contrast this to Native American myths. In nearly all of them, the world, and humans, are instead created by divinities that are explicitly non-hominid. Coyote, for instance, often creates the world, or humankind. Or he educates people, teaches them how to use tools, fire, and language.

But Coyote is no Jehovah—instead of a perfect, omniscient creator, Coyote is instead a trickster, falling prey to his own base instincts of greed, or lust, often in humorous encounters in the mythic narrative. One is left with the distinct impression that this world, instead of being some clock-like heavenly plan, might instead be a bit of a mistake, something of a joke. Sometimes the world, or people, are instead created, or educated, by Raven, a figure somewhat similar to Coyote in the Northwest of America. In one widespread myth, the "Earth-Diver myth," the world was water, until the ducks, or muskrat, dive into the waters, to pull up Earth, and make their trademark floating nests. Sometimes it was a council of animals who created the Earth, or at least helped in this construction.

In many Native American myths, there is a great deal of slippage between the worlds of men and animals. Animals often act and hold councils, even using canoes or tipis, and frequently turn into people. People, likewise, are often revealed to be animals. In the Dena'ina folklore, the animals are people, too: they call humans "the Campfire People," just as the beavers might be called the "Chewing People," and so on. Thus, even the word for "person" reflects this distinction: does personhood only refer to *Homo sapiens*? Western discourse tends to say yes. Linguistically, the Dena'ina myths claim the opposite categorical definition—animals are people, too. There are many, many Native American narratives of people marrying animals, and even having offspring with them, again oftentimes reflecting the blurry line in identity, shifting back and forth in the stories.

Stemming from such widespread and important myths, non-hominid animals are often acknowledged, as "Elder Brothers" or some similar title acknowledging their mythic importance, and their existence prior to humans. Such an outlook reflects an interesting spiritual tradition, with ramifications for prevailing notions about the role of animals and other living forms, and our relations to them.

GOD THE FATHER AND THE THREE LITTLE PIGS

Compare this, then, with Western traditions, and the myths shared by the Abrahamic traditions. This is salient especially because the Abrahamic faiths of Judaism, Islam, and Christianity are the dominant faiths in over half the human population, and they are the dominant faiths in most of the nations of the world, barring only parts of Asia.

One of the most widely known creation stories in the world is that found in Genesis. In this anthro- (and andro-)centric tale, a man god rules the universe and creates mortal man in his image. The only active role of animals in the tale is that of the snake (commonly identified with the Devil/Satan, although the Old Testament does not state this). The snake tricks the pair into eating fruit from the forbidden tree of knowledge, causing their expulsion from Eden by Jehovah. The animal here, is clearly the bad guy.[1]

Further, when God banishes them, he states that the land, the plants, and the non-hominid animals are under their control, saying, "Be fruitful, and multiply, and replenish the earth, and subdue it: and have dominion over the fish of the sea, and over the fowl of the air, and over every living thing that moveth upon the earth" Genesis 1:28 (KJV).

The overall narratives of Genesis seem to reflect an agriculture, patrilineal, and patriarchal cultural outlook. This outlook accorded well to much of the culture in the Near East, North Africa, and Europe (minority religious traditions notwithstanding). It also helped propagate an explanation of the cosmos in very anthropocentric terms: the spiritual realm, heaven, is all about *Homo sapiens*. The rest of this life stuff is ours to do with as we please, without any spiritual significance in the grander scheme of things. People are numinous, other life is mundane. In the Abrahamic mythic traditions, the universe is created and controlled by a human-looking male figure ("God made man in his image") for the purpose of mankind. The categorical split is obvious: humankind versus everything else.

This is not to say that individuals, and folk traditions, may not disagree with this view, but however compelling their personal appeal might be, the official view from the Abrahamic faiths is that only humans are spiritual beings. Wolves, affirmed the missionary, do not have souls.

The story of the Garden of Eden translated well into Christian Europe, where the common iconography was of the fig-leafed couple biting into the fruit of knowledge and being transformed into a delicious red apple, and the snake representing the *Summum Malum* was the sum of all evil. This scene is one of the most widespread of the Abrahamic faiths, encapsulating the powerful messages transmitted through such mythic tales.

As Roland Barthes, Alan Dundes, Lévi-Strauss, and other scholars of myth have shown, myths do more than offer fantastic stories; they also organize our basic principles about how we organize our cultural lives, from all the other genres of our expressive culture through basic conceptions of what it is to be human, what is a good life or deed, and what it is to have a soul. The story of Genesis has been taken as a template for many a marriage, and many personal names in the world are derived from the story of Genesis as well. For many people, the story of Genesis further explains the nature of our relation to other life forms: the relationship has been decreed to be one of dominion.

Since the use of agriculture became widespread, agriculture has remained the dominant way of life for most people on the planet, until very recently. The Garden of Eden seems to reflect this agricultural lifestyle, which may have been one reason for its widespread acceptance. Unlike in the New World, the Old World civilizations domesticated many species. People increasingly saw themselves as lords and masters of nature—herding cattle, irrigating fields, changing the very landscape itself. Domestic animals were good, and under the command of humans; wild animals tended to be bad, threatening human society. If it was all very hard work, one could take comfort in the thought that this was in line with the cosmos: the sacred myth decreed that toiling the fields was God's command.

Throughout the Middle Ages, this myth provided all the answers needed regarding the beginning of the world: enshrined as one of the most important stories of Christianity, the textual version was held to be literally and factually true, a merging of history and the divine. Stemming from this category of "humans as divine," the relationship between Jesus Christ and humans reflected this model: Christ was seen as a "shepherd," or a "fisherman," of people. Animals were to people what people were to God. A feudal hierarchy of being was observed, of men as lords and masters of their fields and flocks, while "good servants" of the Lord.[2]

THE "ENLIGHTENED" VIEW OF ANIMALS

Following the Reformation and the decline of feudal Europe came the Enlightenment, and the rise of science-based learning. In challenging faith-based knowledge, the new philosophies sought to extol the role of the individual and rationality. Although this presented a challenge to the church on many fronts, one aspect that proved ironically harmonious was a continuing anthropocentrism.

The single most influential scholar regarding this issue was doubtless René Descartes, whose ideas shaped the modern view of man, now with a critical distinction between the mind and the body. Only humans had a mind, in Descartes's view, and this proved humanity's essentialism. Other living things, therefore, had only a body, and no real sense of thought or even feelings of pain. For Descartes, and for most of science for the next four centuries, animals in this view were viewed as completely separated from hominids, not even sharing basic fundamental qualities like thought processes, emotions, memories, etc. They were instead viewed more or less as "fleshy robots," simply displaying responses to stimuli. This widespread notion continues to influence much of Western culture, as is evidenced from the categorical use of "animals" as meaning "non-hominid animals." Much of Western culture still displays widespread rejection of animal thought, language, and culture, although the scientific evidence establishing each of this has been made apparent.

TALKING ANIMALS ARE FOR BABIES

In other European genres, we can notice talking animals, such as in the *märchen*, or fairy tales—those traditional narratives told not to discuss true things, but rather for fun and entertainment, and perhaps a bit of pedagogy, and often directed at children. *Märchen* are not true stories but merely stories told just for fun. In European traditions, this genre is thickly populated with talking animals, from the Three Little Pigs to Chicken Little. In this genre, predicated on non-belief, domestic animals are often portrayed as good, while wild animals, those outside of human dominion and control, are portrayed as bad, as in the Big Bad Wolf. There is a split between "good" domestic animals, and the "bad" wild animals, especially those that may threaten the agricultural livestock, like the "big, bad wolf."

Western society holds anthropomorphicized, talking animals as appropriate for children, as any quick review of children's toys, literature, and fashion apparel makes abundantly clear. We may see how the idea of talking animals are held to be fantastic, categorically un-true, and appropriate only for the "innocent" age of childhood.

By comparison, then, we can note how easily Westerners have associated animism with a "childhood stage of religious development." Talking animals, Western societies says, are for children, and societies who have traditions of them, then, such as the Native Americans, are likewise viewed as childlike. This move employs a long-held metaphor for Native Americans to be "like children" or in a childlike state of cultural evolution. It was yet one more way for the conquering people to denigrate the culture of the conquered, one more example of colonialism. In a clash between two mythic traditions, the militarily successful society trivializes the others' mythic, sacred traditions.

From the Garden of Eden, through Descartes, and into the trivialization of Native American spiritual traditions, the question of the relation between *Homo sapiens* and the other animals has been consistently dismissive, defensively so, of close links.

We may note that the science of evolution was noticeably slow to develop in face of an abundance of evidence. It wasn't until Darwin's *On the Origin of the Species* (1859) that a compelling argument was made to establish a model of the past not dependent on the Garden of Eden myth. In the United States, approximately one third of the population continues to disbelieve the scientific story on this topic, and prefer instead the mythic explanation. This rate, unparalleled in the developed world, reflects the high rate of religious belief and practice in the United States. I believe that this extreme obduracy to this one issue can be explained at least in part in terms of the power of sacred stories. Many people do not feel comfortable with the idea that we could be "related" to "animals"; hence, for them, evolution must be false. Even the words themselves contain this idea; even though we know that we are animals, we *never* use the term in this regard (except as an insult).

We are animals, but we will not say it. We were created out of animals, but we do not feel comfortable believing it. This is the continuing power of myth.

THE VIEW FROM TURTLE ISLAND

By contrast, throughout much of Native American myths, animals play resplendent roles. Indeed, Native American traditions are wholly consonant with the idea of evolution in the general idea that animals were here before us, and that they created us, or our world, long before we arrived on the scene. Further, we may remember that this was true long before Western science believed this to be true. Early on, Western science felt secure proclaiming its superiority over native viewpoints, all the while being wrong on this important point, until the *On the Origin of the Species* and the resulting scientific discussion. Throughout remained, and still remain, many traditions of people learning from animals in Native American discourse, and indeed of animals learning from other animals. There is an intense engagement in the natural world, especially the living world. Animals play central roles in many genres in Native American culture, in stories, dances, clothing, songs, names, and, of course, the religious observances regarding maintaining the proper relations with the spirit realm, with its many animal denizens. It is difficult to overemphasize the role that animals, in particular, play in Native American cultural traditions.

At the heart of it all is animism: the generalized outlook that spiritual forces flow through all life, as well as some other occurrences that would not be usually classified as living by Western thought, such as earthquakes, wind, or stone. Rather than have a centralized church hierarchy to reflect a canonical text, spiritual authority in animism is more commonly located in the natural world, and the individual's abilities to interact with it, including but not limited to the role of the specialists, the shamans.[3]

In animism, animal spirits are often the creators and teachers of mankind. Such animal spirits are rooted in the role of real animals (the eagle, the mouse, the coyote) but also in the heightened spiritual role of teachers and guides to mankind. Even those native societies long adapted to agriculture retained many of the myths of animals as founders of the world. Nor should contemporary scholars dismiss such beliefs as all extinct or archaic—many Native Americans continue animist spiritual beliefs and practices.

In animism, human society is seen as dependent on this spiritual relationship with the natural world. Hence, inter-special communication is not only viewed as a distinct possibility, and reality, but even as a necessity. This is why the animals figure so highly in so many genres, including dances and costumes—there is a phenomenological element to ritual: in imitating the actions and behavior of animals, one can begin to understand perhaps a bit better into that animal's worldview, and glean how to better interact with them.

From ritual to tales to even personal and clan names, the importance of inter-special communication resounds loudly throughout Native American culture.

For example, hunting, in animism, is thus viewed as an inherently spiritual activity, an interaction between two spiritual, soulful beings, and an exchange of flesh, skin, and sustenance. Following this, when spiritual relations with the animals, and the rest of the natural world are good, then so are the material rewards, in the form of animals giving themselves up to humans. By the same token, when hunting is bad, this means that spiritual relations are bad as well, and very often the animal spirits may be angry at being disrespected, for example when hunters do not offer them appropriate prayers, thanks, and funerary rites. The imposition of the "disrespectful behavior" of non-native culture is held to have significant environmental consequences. John Iniuq, a Caribou Inuit, stated, "Now-days, look around. Animals are insulted. They might go away forever. This can happen. It is not like when I was a child. People don't understand animals any more. People who have to go among animals, out on the land, they still understand" (quoted in Normal 1990: 144–45).

At times these traditions could be mundane, such as accounts of old people near my home area who learned to communicate with ravens. The ravens would help them hunt: the ravens, after all, being cunning scavengers known to guide hunters to their prey. Other times, the accounts of inter-special communications are more spiritual, and visionary, although there may be no clear line between the two. As Samson Autao a Cree put it, "In the old times, people and animals talked with each other, just like I talk with my family every day" (Norman 1990: 143).

Folklorist Alice Legat's 2012 *Walking the Land, Feeding the Fire: Knowledge and Stewardship among the Tlicho Dene* explains how among the Tlicho Dene, the concept of dè signifies not only the environment itself, but also of being aware of one's place in that environment, an elemental form of knowledge for them. Such knowledge is both physical and spiritual, and therefore implying respect, and a recognition of the spirit power of the nonhuman.

Anthropologist Rodney Frey writes how the Coeur d'Alene would describe their relations with the nonhuman world: "Within this web of kinship relationship, the members share in an *equality* with one another, in what the Coeur d'Alene term *unshat-qn*" (1995: 41). Such equality is expressed especially by respectful speech and behaviors, for example in asking "permission" to harvest plant life, and in using all parts of the animals hunted.

And, as Howard Harrod put it, in *The Animals Came Dancing: Native American Sacred Ecology and Animal Kinship*, "Oral memories were rich with examples of how animals gave their bodies to the people, often agreeing to become food because they had established kinship relations with humans"

(2000: xii). In this way, Harrod states, this reciprocal arrangement contrasts with the non-native, Euro American utilitarian views of animals.

A general notion of reciprocity is shared by many ecocritics and posthumanists, and echoes Tonutti's call for "articulation." If we know we share an ontology, in what manner do we rethink our relationship to that ontology? In other words, now that we know animals are much more like us than we ever thought, how do we change other, related beliefs, outlooks, and even terminology regarding other living things? Also, now that we increasingly perceive our precarious balance of life on planet Earth, how does that, as well, change our moral and ethical outlooks to other life? In what ways might we re-imagine or re-categorize our ontological relationship with the nonhuman world?

SIDE BY SIDE

There is an explanatory value to myth: in this sense, it is not unlike a folk science (for an excellent analysis of the overlap, see Schrempp 2012). At times myths can be productively consonant to scientific explanations, and at times they may seem in direct contradiction. In the Native American traditions, their mythic stories of animals creating the world of the humans harmonizes well with what is scientifically known to be largely correct, and in direct contrast to the competing anthropocentric myths of the Abrahamic faiths. We also have seen that Western science was wrong on this for a long time while the Native Americans were right, all the while denigrating their traditional explanations. This is not to state that Native Americans were Darwinists, or employed his notions of biological evolution, but rather that their ontologies tended to concur with Darwin that we are all, indeed, kin.

We may now speak (as good scientists) of animal cultures—that is, socially learned, not innate, patterns of behavior. Animals have words, in languages. Animals have been demonstrated displaying episodic memories, the distinct memory of time and events, and even planning ahead for future events. Not only are we closely related to animals through our bodies, sharing many of the same genes with wolves and even fish, but even through our very humanity—ideas of family, or jealousy, of politics, and fairness are shared with our Elder Brothers. This is a concept that, although well documented, still sits uncomfortably for many people in Western culture.

Certainly, there are many things that stand out about humans: we are indeed a most remarkable species. Yet, at the same time, we may also notice how much of who we are we find in other species, and how remarkably intelligent many other species are as well.

Alongside these scientific advances in our understanding of the mental worlds of animals has been a general reassessment of the proper moral relations between humanity and other animals. It is unclear what form this will take. There is certainly a radical fringe, some of whom have engaged in violent or other highly controversial actions, in the name of animal rights. Yet there is also a growing middle ground, as can be witnessed in the increase of animal rights legislation. Animal protections of some variety are now standard in many legal systems.

As Donna Haraway wrote, "Movements for animal rights are not irrational denials of human uniqueness; they are clear-sighted recognition of connection across the discredited breach of nature and culture" (2001: 2271). Such "clear-sighted recognition" often finds itself in direct contradiction to prevalent current discourses.

STRAINS ON THE SYSTEM

Several concepts now current in popular understandings of the natural world also reflect this new discourse. Global warming has cast into stark light the limits, and dangers, of enforcing man's will on the natural world. The increasing environmental stress on the world system is looking particularly ominous, and we may yet have to pay a horrific price for our anthropocentric ways.

That, in itself, should lead us into inquiring into other cultural systems and worldviews, particularly of those sensitively attuned to the natural environment now so severely threatened. Even following the concept of anthropocentric utilitarianism, one could argue that it's in our (human) best interest now to pay attention to the planet, an attitude reflected in the growing "Dominion Theology" of Abrahamic-based environmental approaches. Yet it may also be worth remembering that it is precisely such a philosophical approach that got us into this environmental mess in the first place.

We now talk in terms of ecosystems, and ecological balances, yet these are relatively new terms to our scientific discourse. These concepts do largely agree with Native American mythic traditions, and we can note once more that Native American traditions were very consonant with these terms . . . including, of course, in earlier times when such ideas were *not* yet formulated in scientific discourse. Further, it seems highly likely that Native American traditions were formative of such shifts in scientific and popular thought.

This explicit comparison between these two worldviews is not meant to equate folk knowledge with scientific discourse, or to say that folk discourse is "just as good" as scientific discourses. They are, of course, different discourses. However, mythic themes can influence a society, including that society's scientific discourses. Abrahamic myths of an anthropocentric universe have in the past created hurdles in understanding the natural world, particularly in terms of its overlap with our own. Myths work at creating ontologies, which are then carried forth in other discourses, including that of science.

I believe science may learn a great deal from examining traditional Native American mythic traditions, not only about the rest of Native American culture, but also of larger questions of our relation to the rest of the natural world. Investigations into mythology allow us not only to see the categorical ontologies that had influenced Western discourse, but also, more tantalizingly, they allow us to witness other ontologies, in this case the animist ontologies revealed in Native American mythology and worldview. It is in this context that we may appreciate Graham Harvey's 2006 article "Animals, Animists, and Academics," in which he argues for a re-evaluation of the utility of the concept of animism within academic discourse, as well as Scott's (2006) assertion that the animist outlooks of his Cree informants helped provide them with objectively better wildlife data than was available via Western science.

DECOLONIZING SCIENTIFIC DISCOURSES:
POSTCOLONIALISM AND POSTHUMANISM

And, if we admit that the Native American traditions were right on such major issues regarding our relations with other animals, vis-à-vis Western science, on evolution, animal consciousness, animal languages, and other issues, for many decades, then it is at least worth asking, rhetorically, on what other issues might they also be correct? And what of similar views of other minority groups in various locations around the world? Postcolonial science opens itself up to the inclusion of considerations of other schools of thought, other epistemologies, and offers possible avenues of thought out of the dead-end of anthropocentrism.

Postcolonial outlooks can also lead us back to potential of posthumanism: towards realizing the knowledge that can be gained at listening to the overlooked, the under-heard, and those with agency and personhood denied. Such moves allow for a less culture-specific lens through which to view the relations between humans and other living things, and to allow for dialogue, for articulation, between different cultures and different ways of viewing the world: in this case, both the Native American, and that of the non-hominid world as well. Postcolonial philosophy, and posthumanism, may in the end be the best of allies, as Western discourses to learn from other, previously overlooked systems of knowledge. Improving our understanding of our interconnections with life on Earth may, ultimately, assist us in learning how to use such knowledge to help build a healthier, more sustainable world.

4

YOU SEXY BEAST

Animals and Sexuality in Western Discourse

Another way to approach ontology is through relations: what we are can be deduced, at least in part, by looking at what we are related to. The question of our relatedness to nonhuman animals has been at the heart of a great deal of philosophizing, with large roles played both by religious and mythological outlooks (Abrahamic religions marking our absolute separation from nonhuman animals) and scientific discourses, which increasingly note our close connections to the animal kingdom. One major way that relations are established, and performed, biologically and culturally is through the lens of sexuality. An examination of some of the ways we discuss sexuality in Western culture reveals a strong role played by nonhuman animals to discuss and mark our own sexual nature. People frequently discuss human sexuality in terms of nonhuman animals. Sexuality is linked with our "animal nature," revealing specific constructions of how we think about sexuality, humanity, and animals. Our own sexuality is "beastly," that problematic part of us that remains uncivilized. By extension, this implies a cultural belief that animals have unrestrained, "wild" sex lives—in contrast to civilized, cultured, and sexually repressed humans. Discourses on sexuality reveal an interesting nexus on this human-animal binary in Western discourse, revealing ideas of mind versus body, spirit versus flesh, and wild versus domestic. Such notions contain deeply rooted cultural ideas about humans, animals, and the nature of civilization.

The thesis explored in this chapter is that such beliefs and vernacular expressions express and reinforce the cognitive binary of human/animal embedded in our language, culture, laws, religion, and society. Edmund Leach's 1964 "Animal Categories and Verbal Abuse" sought to understand the ritual and symbolic roles of different categories of animals on an essentially social continuum. For Leach, people referred to animals as a tabooistic discourse of referring to their own social situation, as well as their relationships with others. The use of animals as cultural symbols has been explored in further works, perhaps most noticeably *American Wildlife in Symbol and Story* by Angus Gillespie and Jay Mechling (1987). Yet while it is most assuredly true that people do comment on their own social relations by metaphorical use of animals, I would also hold that in doing so, people are also commenting on the animals themselves, and their relations to people. That is, calling a woman "foxy" is a comment on the perceived behavior of both the woman and foxes as well, establishing an interesting link between the behaviors of human and nonhuman animals. Working towards approaching the subject in this more posthuman light, this chapter traces this cultural binary and its effects further back, ultimately to its mythological origins, in order to illuminate how representations of the "sexy beast" connects to the "human-animal divide." The question of why we discuss our own sexuality in terms of other species provides an interesting viewpoint of this cognitive binary, especially in light of the ongoing intellectual movements brought on by the "animal turn" and posthumanism, generally. Such an investigation attempts to correlate recent moves of investigating how we "think with animals" with a particular focus on how we utilize animals to think about and express our own sexuality.

DOMESTIC AND WILD

Along with the general binary of humans and animals is a further, somewhat complicated divide of animals into the categories of domestic versus wild. Like humans, domestic animals often find their sexuality ("breeding") to be tightly controlled. The phrase "animal husbandry" reveals long cultural interpolations between androcentric gender roles, sexuality, and livestock with central ideas of the domesticated us, the civilized. Domestic animals are liminal figures, both us and not us, neither civilized nor wild. Their own placement sits uneasily in this balance, at times seeming to replicate our own categorical divisions: the idea of "taming the wild beast" represents both the domestication process, and the process of civilizing ourselves.

Domesticated animals offer a way to discuss human sexuality in ways particularly close to home, yet still distinct from the human world. Closest to the family home, we can observe that the word "pet" is loaded with sexual implications—"my pet" is a term of affection, while "heavy petting" means some sort of (forgive me) "monkey business." There are two main pet species for humans: cats and dogs. Both reveal particularly gendered constructions, which shape particular ways in which the species are used in the tabooistic discourse of sexuality.

Cats in general are identified with the feminine. The male cat is often called a "tomcat," implying that the base category of "cat" is, essentially, a female one. The "crazy cat lady" is a common figure of American folklore but with no corresponding "crazy cat man" figure (see McNeill 2007). "Cattiness" as a trait is associated mostly with women and/or feminine behaviors, and the female witch's cat is well-known staple in folk concepts and popular culture. A "cat-fight" can refer to a fight involving only women. Cats are often directly identified with aspects of female sexuality. The word "pussy" is perhaps the most elemental example, with two very distinct meanings: cat, and female genitalia (in the eroticized sense). The popular American use of the word "cougar" refers to middle-age women "on the prowl" for younger men.

This gendering is reversed in the case of the other main companion species, the dog. While "doggy style" is the common name of one of the most common sexual positions, the overall gendering of dogs leans heavily towards the masculine.

The dog is often labeled "man's best friend." The word "dog" has the male noun as the base term, while the proper term for the female dog ("bitch") is now primarily encountered as an obscenity, occurring mainly as an insult towards women. The female dog is problematic: ugly women are "dogs," angry women are "bitches." Meanwhile, women may complain that "men are all dogs" (by which they mean overly sexual).

Moving further afield among the domesticates, we continue to find sexualized, often strikingly gendered representations. "Horny old goat" refers exclusively to men. Goats in general tilt towards the masculine: note the hyper-masculine great god Pan, and the aspects of him later assigned to cultural representations of Satan. Cows and sheep seem tilted towards the feminine. Of course, some species already have gendered terms, such as bull, stallion, stag, or hen, each of which can be integrated into the discourse as well. Of these, the male chicken is perhaps the most elemental of the sexual representations in English: the word "cock" is about as clear a masculine symbol as you can get.[1] Other gendered terms are frequently employed as well: bachelor parties in England are commonly called "stag parties," while bachelorette parties often are referred to as "hen's parties."

The Wild

But while domesticated animals seem to reflect an emphasis on human gender divisions and their proper regulation, the category of "wild animals" seems far more important in the elemental "human-animal" divide, and more central to the construction of this as a central ontological category.

Domesticates live in the human world, but wild animals are (supposedly) free from it. We "husband" domesticated animals, but we hunt, on the prowl, for wild ones.[2] This construction reveals the binary of "civilized/non-civilized," evident in the idea of "wild animals" as lacking society and social constraints, and, conversely, humans as largely constructed from both, and the suppression of our "animal" natures. This dichotomy has played a role in stories since at least the *Epic of Gilgamesh*, the oldest known recorded myth, wherein Gilgamesh is repeatedly contrasted with his brother Enkidu, raised by wild animals, in a mythic representation of civilization versus its antithesis.

Wild animals are often used to portray unconstrained human sexuality, with the word "wild" often connecting the two. Sexuality as "wild" is a pervading metaphor throughout Western discourse, and one could (should?) be "wild in the sack." People can find themselves "wild with lust," a theme of associating sociability itself with the repression of sexuality, and with "the wild" as an idealized state of unrestrained sexuality and sexual fulfillment. We can see how, in this move, Western society projects its fantasies of *unbridled* sexuality onto other species, as in letting our "animal natures" to "run free and wild." Nor is this imagination restricted to folk speech alone: animal-print fabrics are used to denote a sense of sexuality, in clothes, accessories, and bedding.

Such representation does not come from nowhere; to the contrary, the expressive folk taxonomies express underlying cultural categories[3] and therefore offer one avenue towards uncovering these frequently unconscious basic cultural and linguistic categories. In this case, we examine a basic cultural binary of human versus animal, expressed particularly in the relative constrainment of aggressive and (most particularly) sexual impulses, enforcing the binary of "tame" versus "the wild."

Us versus(?) Them

This taxonomy is a part of a wider discourse about humanity and what it is to be human. Although we are animals, we are not animals. Such an oxymoronic statement requires cultural elucidation—after all, the long-held religious and cultural assumptions of qualitative distinctions between humans and animals are, simply, wrong. Once again, *Homo sapiens are* animals. A stark recognition of this popular fallacy allows us to question anew the underlying cultural role of the cultural binary, and to understand the resulting cultural expressions. Not only are *Homo sapiens* animals, but animals are us: that is to say, the category of animals shows a profound overlap with what previously was assumed to be human, a key point of posthumanism, and the "animal turn," generally. The understanding of non-hominid cultures, and non-hominid social dynamics, calls into question the idea that human culture is based on repression of individual instinctive desires (particularly aggression and sexuality). As in commonly the case, notions of the "natural" tend to reflect cultural ideas, and underlying myths, more than they do "nature." Western ideas of animal sexuality are just that—ideas, which seem to be based on a sense of "othering" more than on nature itself, and emanating and reflecting our culture much more than reflecting the actual lives of animals.

For example, far from wild animals having unrestrained sex lives, sexual repression is not only for *Homo sapiens.* Many non-hominid animals also live out their lives in tightly knit social groups that demand input and attention, and the suppression of individual desires for the overall good of the group. Among many animals—including many primates—sexuality (along with aggression) is tightly regulated by the social hierarchy. This is all to say, sexual repression is not unique to human societies; there are many sexually repressed non-hominid individuals out there who manage their sexualities individually and socially as best they can, often in ways strikingly similar to how humans do.[4]

Given all this, how and why would not our society instead recognize that our sexuality—like many other of our aspects of our being—is shared in multitudinous and interesting ways with our close relatives, rather than representing an essential binary of free versus constrained?

ANTHROPOCENTRISM AND ITS SHADOW

Anthropocentrism has been increasingly singled out for a number of errors on the history of Western discourse (both lay and scholarly) in the widespread deconstructive critique now generally glossed as the "animal turn." In recognizing anthropocentrism as a cultural viewpoint, new philosophical moves incorporate emergent scientific findings regarding sentient life. These critiques are found often in the emergent movement of posthumanism, which, among other goals, seeks to re-examine our notion of what it is to be human and what it is to be.

Alongside this, historical studies of Western science have become more aware of its anthropocentric past tendencies, and its unfortunate obfuscation in scientific understanding: for many years, science steadfastly denied the existence of animal language, intelligence, complex emotions, culture, and society . . . in contrast to the available evidence, and also in contrast to some other non-Western discourses.[5]

Mythologies and Scientific Paradigms: An Archaeology of Origin Stories

To understand the growth of anthropocentrism, and the human-animal binary, I trace backwards in time the foundational ideas of what it is to be human, back to our mythic origins. After tracing these formational ideas back to the Garden of Eden itself, I then move forward along similar lines, back towards the present moment, regarding the proper role of sexuality. This back-and-forth investigation displays two overlapping threads: one regarding the basic ontology of humanity, and the other, the ways that this ontology is reflected in ideas of sexuality. Both these aspects, I believe, are components of the tabooistic discourse of using animals to discuss our own natures.

For many people, what it is to be human is largely the remit of psychology, the science of how people think. Often, psychology is held to not only *the* study of human personalities and mentalities, but also a stand-in for our very ontology, the answer to the question, *Who am I?*

One starting point for our Janus-faced investigation could begin with Sigmund Freud, the author of one of the most major origin stories of our contemporary ideas of human ontology. In his thoughtful and influential work *Civilization and Its Discontents* (1930), Freud proposed that the repression of individual desires (aggression and, even more so, sexuality) is what gave rise to civilization. As society demanded repression of "animalistic" urges (most elementally a repression of incest and creation of the incest taboo), a feedback loop was created, and humans spent their increasingly repressed sexual and aggressive energies in culture-building tasks, like creating beautiful art—the very definition, for Freud, of sublimation.

In Freud's origin story, humanity is the sole bearer of civilization, which it achieved by its qualitative differentiation from all other animals in the suppression of "natural" urges of aggression and sexuality, our "beastly" nature. Like all origin stories, such accounts are powerful in framing categories for thinking about the world.[6] In Western discourse, such stories have long supported the pronounced anthropocentric trend of Western culture.

Freud's insistence on the importance of the repression of sexuality was doubtless connected to the zeitgeist in which he worked. The zeitgeist was an unsettled one: colonial-era Europe was conflicted about the topic of sexuality and social relations, in part because of a heightened sense of sexual repression, and in part due to the colonial experience itself. Travel accounts proliferated, revealing (and imagining) radically different approaches to sexuality, titillating audiences with the supposed free sexuality of various peoples all over the world—perhaps best exemplified by the South Sea Pacific Islanders, made famous in paintings by Paul Gauguin (1848–1903). In anthropological accounts, Bronislaw Malinowski's 1929 *Sexual Life of Savages* states that sexuality "dominates in fact almost every aspect of culture" (xxii), and this pronouncement helped to shape the belief that Western society was sexually extremely repressive in comparison. These sentiments were later echoed in Margaret Mead's 1928 *Coming of Age in Samoa*. The popularity of locating sexual freedom in others reveals a great deal about Western culture, as well as its conflicted relationship with both self and other.[7] In Freudian terms, this is all repression and transference. One could both condemn and remain fascinated with the sexuality of others as both an effect and assertion of Western society's own sexual repression. Freudian theories not only applied to individuals, but also societies as a whole, and the complex relationship between the two.

For Freud, this was caused by the general "rise of civilization," and it continued to contribute to man's conflicted nature—the wild beast constrained by culture. Even the Freudian notion of the conscious/unconscious mind draws from this, wherein the civilized mind represses the "animal" urges, refusing to acknowledge them and relegating them to an unconscious existence. The essential Freudian assumptions for the rise of civilization depended on the individual's own suppression of bodily (animalistic) urges. This tension can be seen as an elaboration of the mind-body split already firmly embedded in basic ideas of Cartesian Dualism. According to Descartes, only humans had "minds," whereas animals merely had bodies. Cartesian dualism viewed animals as mere "fleshy robots," while rights, political representation, feelings, rational thought, and other aspects were the provenance of humans alone.

Continuing to work backwards, we may also observe how Descartes's vision was, in turn, a modification of the previous canon, that of canonical Christianity's insistence that it was the "spirit" and "soul" that was unique to humans. While Descartes used the terms "soul" and "mind" nearly interchangeably in his work, he is remembered for establishing the modern theory of the "mind." In this way, Cartesian dualism reworked Abrahamic ideas of the "soul" or spirit into the Enlightenment view of the "mind." In both, only humans had the benefit of mind/soul, and animals were constrained to the body alone. In this way, the Enlightenment further cemented, rather than challenged, the mythic binary split between humans and other animals in Western discourse.[8]

All of this archaeology of ideas has led us back towards religious origin stories—which is to say, once more back to mythology. At the end of this particular trail, we arrive at the gates of the Garden of Eden, where the categorical split between humans and animals was first established by God. The story tells us that a man-like divinity creates man (and later woman). Although at first they live in a state of nature, when they eat the fruit of knowledge, the god banishes them to mortality, making them suffer, yet giving them dominion over the animals. Abrahamic religions are notable for this very anthropocentric (and androcentric) mythic orientation. The cosmos is all about man (I use the gendered term here purposefully). God is represented as a man, and Abraham himself is a man: both are father figures. The world was created by a man-like divinity ("God created Man in his own image"), for the purpose of mankind. In Abrahamic traditions, only humans are numinous, only people have souls; all else on Earth is mundane. There is an obvious emphasis in this story on the importance of the categorical distinction between humans and other animals.[9] The scholar and priest Anne Benvenutti states the biblical passages are "the key sources of the widely held Western notion that by divine design humans are distinctive, superior, and even godlike compared to all other animals" (2014: 12).

We have in this way excavated the ontology of the human along mythic, canonical lines; first Freud, then Descartes, then the Christian church, and back to Abrahamic mythology itself. We can see how the foundational mythology of Abrahamic traditions continued to be re-cast in the Enlightenment, in modernity, and in science in canonical discourses on the essence of what it is to be human, and further that this category is established in opposition to the category of "animal." Finally, we can observe how this discourse of human vs. animal provides such a rich cultural resource for thinking about what it is to be human—perhaps nowhere as intensively as regarding sexuality.

Feel Shame, but Go Forth and Multiply

Alongside the mythic categorical distinction that only humans are numinous, only humans have souls, and only humans are in God's image, is the charter for the proper role of human sexuality. Human sexuality is revealed both in Adam and Eve discovering shame (having eaten the forbidden fruit), and receiving the command from God to "go forth and multiply." In this mythic view, human sexuality is at once shameful, against the will of God, yet still valuable when harnessed for the purposes of lawful reproduction. This lawful reproduction can be seen as replicating the divine human male image of God in the correspondingly patrilineal, patriarchal earthly societies: God's presence and likeness on Earth. Yet, even within this divinely granted exception, sexuality still contains negative overtones: the disciple Paul, for example, urged his followers not to marry, so as not to be spiritually marred by sexuality. This outlook can be seen as well in the prohibitions against sexual activities for priests and nuns within the Catholic Church. Similarly, both the "divine man" of Jesus Christ and his mother Mary are theologically held to have been born free of the taint of sexual intercourse. Sexuality, for Abrahamic religions, is largely antithetical to spiritual purity.

In contrast, animal sexuality, unlike human sexuality, is completely mundane, unashamed, unregulated, and lacking of any sense of sin. This can be witnessed even today in its generally deregulated status. Displays of human sexuality are strictly regulated, but displays of animal sexuality are not. Moving images of non-hominids copulating are freely and unproblematically shown on all-ages public television shows. Animal sexuality is mundane in its general categorization, and not a topic of any importance in Abrahamic mythology, Cartesian dualism, or psychology (there is no "Oedipal complex" for nonhumans, but instead mere appeals to "natural behavior").

Although the inherent sinfulness of human sexuality is a large component of Abrahamic beliefs, it is not a component for many other mythic viewpoints.[10] For example, although sex remains powerful and potentially dangerous in Native American outlooks, there is no conceptual framing of sexuality as "sinful" (which would necessitate a ruler deity whose law one was breaking). Rather, sexuality tends to be looked at as an important animating force of life on Earth, more celebrated than denigrated.

The exception of sinful human sex in Abrahamic outlooks is sexuality employed in the service of the deity's command to "go forth and multiply," ideally within the church-sanctioned marital relationship.[11] In Western discourse in general—both scientific and lay—there has long been an emphasis on reproductive sexuality as "natural," and non-reproductive sexuality as "unnatural." The category of non-reproductive sex as "unnatural" has also been used to describe, and denigrate, homosexuality, masturbation, and various other manifestations of sexuality.

This terminology and underlying belief is, however, clearly *cultural* and not *natural*. Non-reproductive sex is instead quite common in nature. Scientists have increasingly come to understand how sexuality is often used for more than reproductive purposes. Perhaps the bonobos (*pan paniscus*), one of our closest relatives, make the most compelling example: the bonobos, like their namesake deity Pan, use sexuality in a remarkably varied manner, engaging in many non-reproductive sexual activities (homosexual, solo, pre-reproductive, and so on).[12]

Rather than such taboos against non-reproductive sexuality reflecting actual comments on what is "natural," the power of myth in making culture appear natural is revealed once again. This is one of the primary ways in which creation stories create a charter for everyday life; as Bruce Lincoln put it, myth can be "ideology in narrative form" (1999: 146).

Animal Lovers

Among the tabooed practices of "un-natural" (non-reproductive) sexuality, bestiality (inter-special sexuality involving *Homo sapiens*) is, for Abrahamic religions, one of the most problematic. Thomas Aquinas wrote that of all the "unnatural" (e.g., un-reproductive) sexual activities, bestiality was the worst (Part II, *Summa Theologica*). Such concerns with what is "natural" continue to reveal cultural conceptions lodged in a particular cultural worldview, rather than revealing much about nature, or sexuality, itself. Here again, animal studies have instead documented that inter-special sexuality is a common feature among wild animals.[13]

In Western discourse, the idea of non-reproductive sex as inherently sinful, combined with the idea of humans as inherently separated from other animals, has combined to make bestiality a particularly unpalatable subject. Few taboos are more strongly upheld in Western discourse than the general prohibition on sharing sexuality with nonhumans. In this way, the functioning and enforcing of this taboo reveals and maintains the categorical opposition between humans and other animals, allowing us to locate our sexuality outside of our humanity, and among the non-hominids.

Taboo topics—why study them? The answer is simple: we study them because taboos are one of the most informative aspects of cultural variations. What is taboo in one culture, and not in another, often reveals culturally important schema for organizing conceptions of the world, and peoples place within that world. Very frequently, taboos relate to the heart of cultural concerns—what to do with dead bodies, for example. One solution, cannibalism, is extremely taboo in Western culture, but has been a culturally accepted practice in many cultures. In Western culture, we eat animal flesh (Jehovah gave man dominion over the animals), but not human flesh. Perhaps because of this taboo, cannibalism is symbolically important in Western religious traditions—most particularly with the miracle of the Eucharist, where bread and wine become the body and blood of Christ, ritually eaten by his worshipers.

Sexuality is, arguably, even more central to how various societies and cultures structure and regulate themselves. What is taboo in one society might not be in another, or might not be in a different time period, and this is perhaps nowhere more evident than in sexuality. Sharing sexuality with nonhuman animals is one of the greatest taboos of Western culture, perhaps on a par with the incest taboo itself. Yet herein lies an important distinction: although anthropologists have long declared that the incest taboo is a universal attribute of all human societies (and, as such, one of the few true human cultural universals and hence a topic of great discussion: see e.g., Fox 1980), the same cannot be said of bestiality. Prohibition against incest may well be a universal building block of human societies (requiring families to exchange ties and gather alliances), but the same is not true of bestiality. The cultural attitudes towards this topic are much more varied, with great ranges in how societies viewed the practice, with various cultures glorifying, encouraging, accepting, discouraging, banning, or demonizing the practice.[14] With such a great range in cultural reactions, the Western culture's attitudes begin to stand out in detail.

The category of interspecial sexuality strikes at the heart of how humans relate to animals. The English word "bestiality" is loaded with negative connotative meaning, lodged in other uses of the world "bestial"—not merely "animal," but as animal at worst, containing connotations of dangerous aggression as well as sexuality.

Nonetheless, the fact that it *is* a taboo topic in Western discourse probably explains the dearth of scientific inquiries into the topic. Scientists, after all, are also members of the societies, and therefore are frequently also influenced by their culture's taboos. This makes studying taboo topics difficult, but all the more important. Only a critical examination of the taboos of Western culture will allow us to increase our knowledge of the ways in which taboos operate in determining various cultural aspects, many of which may be unconscious.

Taboos and Comparative Mytho-Cultural Categories

The idea of a strong taboo against interspecial sexuality has a long history in Western discourse, dating back to the myths themselves. While there may not be a direct connection between what deities do and actual human practices, there does seem to be an indirect connection, wherein the categories narratively proposed by mythologies are enacted in people's everyday lives.

A glance at classical Greek mythology reveals numerous examples of interspecial sexuality: Zeus raping Leda in the form of a swan is one of the best-known episodes, while his raping of Europa in the form of a bull founded the nomenclature of "Europe." The fearsome Minotaur, in another example, was said to be the offspring of the Queen of Minos and a bull, perhaps hearkening back to the Minoan rites of bull worship. Pan, the Great God of the countryside, and particularly of the shepherds, was figured as a mix of goat and man, and known for inspiring wild, unbridled sexuality. All of these images were cultural institutions that lasted for millennia, being re-enacted as entertainments at various times, for example, in the Roman coliseums. In Rome, one of the most celebrated works of literature, *The Golden Ass*, revolved its entire plot around the idea of sex with donkeys and its strong popularity among Roman women. Meanwhile, Roman entertainment frequently enacted scenes of bestiality from Greco-Roman mythology (Masters 1962). This practice seems common across much of the ancient world: in the Byzantine Empire, the beautiful prostitute who would later become the Empress Theodora, one of the most powerful women in the history of the world, gained early renown as a spectacular enactor of the sexual encounters of Zeus as a swan and Leda.

Ancient Egyptian gods were frequently mixes of animals and people, from Bast to Anubis, and both Egyptian religious and secular practices often included humans having sex with other animals. Early writers commented on ancient Egyptian peoples' general proclivities for engaging in sex with various species, including cows, dogs, monkeys, goats, and even crocodiles (Miletstki 2000). Cleopatra was said to have a box filled with bees to use for stimulation, somewhat akin to a modern vibrator (Miletski 2002: 3), which brings up the interesting point: this would be illegal in much of contemporary Western society, while sexual activity with an inanimate machine—the modern vibrator—is most decidedly not.

In North America, as we have seen in chapter 3, Native American mythologies usually narrate that humans were created by animals, and animal deities and spirit forces play active roles in nearly all genres—legends, dance, music, costumes, and more. The importance of human kinship with animals in Native American traditions is difficult to overstate. Native American cosmologies and worldviews tended (and tend) to emphasize the similarities and connections between humans and other animals, congruent with the common overall view of animism.

Coyote, perhaps, plays one of the largest roles in Native American mythology. Coyote, often labeled a "trickster god," is often responsible for the world, or for sunlight, or for bringing the knowledge of fire to mankind, or other important aspects of the cosmos. Not only is a non-hominid one of the most important creator deities in Native American mythology, but Coyote is a decidedly lascivious deity as well, frequently having sex with women, as well as other animals, in countless stories. Nor is Coyote the only animal figure to have sex with people in Native American lore. Instead, interspecial sexuality is a very common theme in Native American folklore, often explored in graphic detail. Again, this is not to assert a straightforward link between mythology and cultural practices; this is often decidedly *not* the case with mythology, but it is worth noting that such representations of the divine admit and explore connections between humans and animals, holding animals to have souls, intelligences, emotions, and sexuality, much like humans, and also admitting the possibility of humans interacting with other animals on these terms. Unsurprisingly, there are many early ethnographic accounts documenting a much more accepting view of interspecial sexuality among Native Americans than among the colonial powers from Western Europe (see e.g., Voget 1961; Talayesva, Simmons, and William 1942).

There are multitudes of ethnographic examples from around the world, but suffice it say, viewed in a global context, followers of the Genesis myth tend to take some of the most hostile views on having sex with nonhuman animals. This view has been increasingly globalized, with most nations in the world now dominated by one or more Abrahamic religions. To understand this taboo, then, is to understand some of the roots and developments of Abrahamic religions, and, in turn, to understand the continued anthropocentrism of Western thought.

Given that many neighboring religions openly celebrated animal gods, one marker of early Judaism seems to have been its clear exclusion of non-hominid animals from the cosmological world (reflected in biblical stories, such as the early Old Testament heresies of errant Jews worshiping the golden calf). This exclusion from the cosmological world is also tied to its exclusion from the sexual world: while Leviticus made any bestiality a crime on penalty of death, neighboring religions celebrated both beasts and bestiality. The Egyptians offer the most obvious, and perhaps most important, contrast.

Bestiality became an even more particular concern of the Christian church later on in Europe, with witches particularly singled out for engaging in this practice. One of the primary activities of witches' sabbaths, according to the church inquisitors, was having orgiastic sex parties, and in particular in engaging in sex with animals. The devil was often said to appear as a goat, with which women engaged in sexual relations. It was during this period that bestiality took on its darkest tone in Western discourse—rather than being simply bad, or misguided, or a poor substitute for human-human sex, it now became demonic, literally evil.[15]

It may have been deemed demonic, but it is clear that the practice of bestiality continued, verified by the frequent court cases brought forth on this subject—and not just against women, but also frequently against men for engaging in sexual relations with livestock. The early colonial courts of America witnessed many such cases being prosecuted (Miletski 2002: 30). In these and later American courts, bestiality was often considered along with homosexuality to be "sodomy" (ibid.).[16]

Similarly, the horror and revulsion that often greets bestiality in contemporary culture seem to be an indirect result of this same Genesis myth. God made man in his image, and Jehovah is never to be represented in any form other than a man-like one. To be mixing the species, then, works against this cosmological construction, the very morality of the universe. Perhaps this may explain the reason why Satan and other monsters are so often represented as part-human, part-animal—the very embodiment of evil. Evolution likewise mixes the species, in admitting our relationships with other animals. Ideas of non-hominid animals having advanced cognitive abilities similar to our own—so long denied in the academy and only recently being somewhat grudgingly acknowledged—also troubles these cosmological binary constructs. Sharing sexuality between humans and other species seems to similarly engage this same taboo of troubling the human-animal binary division.[17]

RULES: MADE TO BE BROKEN?

In spite of the taboo, bestiality has continued to be a part of the cultural landscape.

Alfred Kinsey's landmark studies on American sexuality in the late 1940s found that between 2 and 5 percent of Americans admitted to sexual contacts with animals. A later study in the 1970s suggested a slightly lower number, between 1 and 3 percent overall, perhaps in part due to the widespread shift in population from farms to urban areas.[18] There have been no major studies on this since the 1970s, and so one is left a bit in the dark as to the developments in the last forty years, including, obviously, the introduction of the internet. A 2013 survey of undergraduates at Yale reported 3 percent admitting to bestiality contact, yet this survey was limited in scope and reliant on self-reported activities (Hua 2013).

From the generally illegal and taboo status of interspecial sexuality arises a plethora of jokes, insults, and epithets directed at the practice, often directed at distinct groups of people—the lonely shepherds with their sheep, sexually frustrated fishermen spending months at sea with seals, and so on. As a known but tabooed practice, this discursive area provides a productive font for denigrating others.

Cyborg Beasts

Although most of this has a tremendously long historical trajectory, the recent development of the internet has profoundly influenced the discourse on the topic.

With the rise of the internet, cultural constructions and taboos are put into sharp contrast as they clash and merge on the information superhighway. While bestiality is illegal in California, it is legal in Hungary, where there is a thriving pornography industry specializing in this theme. As discourse globalizes, bestiality's questionable status becomes an interesting touchstone of cultural concerns.

Internet porn is a powerful, and perhaps vastly underestimated, cultural force. Pornography has been globalized in a way unimaginable only a few short years ago.[19] This is true not only in cosmopolitan urban areas, but in every country with unfiltered internet access around the world, in every conservative village, in every religious household.

While the larger topic of what this intense sublimation of sexual energy into two-dimensional audio-visual stimuli means for human society is beyond the scope of this chapter, it is worth noting that internet porn has created a panoply of socio-sexual relations and interest groups. Like cyber groups generally, cyborg sexuality allows for multiple overlapping identities to form around specific user interests. As various scholars have explored, these new interest groups can be powerfully organizing forces, perhaps particularly for interest groups normally outside the mainstream of society. While one effect of the internet may be a homogenizing force, stemming especially from Western culture, another effect seems to be formation of various distributed identities—"digital enclaves," as Robert Glenn Howard (2011) put it.

The topic of sexuality between humans and non-hominid animals has seen a fluorescence of social activity, forming numerous discussion groups around these topics. As of this writing, beastforum.com boasts over 1.3 million members, with membership drawn from all over the world. Although only one of many such online communities, its mere presence documents the clashes between the vernacular and the institutional in the cyber realm. The taboo aspect of the topic is what gives such large social groups their *raison d'être*, as the individuals would often be marginalized in their "real" world groups.

Another important lesson from such work is that cyber sexualities are not merely passive consumptions, but often very social affairs, creating and maintaining group identities, and often acting as advocates for particular points of view.

Animals R Us

In addition to those interested in actual zoophilia are other groups perhaps even more firmly enmeshed in the overlap of human-animal sexualities. One notable example is the "furries." The furries lie within the larger realm of cosplaying identity groups. Nonetheless, the approach is significantly different, in that furries commonly dress *as* animals, act out animal-human actions, and interact with other humans similarly dressed as and acting as nonhuman animals. The furry community, therefore, does tend to be legal in its approach, since the participants are all humans. Nonetheless, the taboo nature of this group (as evidenced in a recent chlorine gas attack at a recent furry convention)[20] reveals that the group similarly troubles the human-binary divide. Like the zoophiles, the furry community has grown alongside the development of the internet,[21] as the internet both allows for and fosters such alternative views within the larger "mainstream" societies.

Even within mainstream culture, there is a changing relation between humans and nonhuman (especially domestic) animals. Pets are often given human names. Animal advocates urge that the term "pet owner" be replaced with "companion," a word which invites the overlap of sexual and non-sexual connotations. Many people sleep with their animals. "Animal lovers" as a term reveals this strange overlap, between lovers in the platonic sense, and lovers in the sexualized sense of the term (both zoophiles and non may identify by this term). In many ways, the lines between human and animal have become troubled.[22]

The Exotic Other

Rather than "unnatural," we may now view the taboo against interspecial sexuality as reflecting culturally specific and strongly held categorical notions of binary separation between "humans" and "animals." Following Lévi-Strauss, we may view such distinctions as both constitutive of definitions ("definition in opposition"), and as reflected both in cultural practice and in mythologies. As with any "othering," the other can become a repository for the fantasy fulfillment of repressed desires, perhaps most particularly of sexuality. Here, then, the rest of the animal kingdom plays a role not unlike the exotic "Orient" played to Europe, as detailed by Said (1978). Just as the Orient was imagined to be a place of wild, free sexuality—attractive and repulsive at the same time to the "Occidentals"—so too do non-hominid animals play a similar role in contemporary Western culture.

To understand the category of the "unbridled animal sexuality," then, it is necessary to understand the role of "othering," generally: the imaginings of unrestrained sexuality as a way of coping with the social repression of one's own individual desires. [23] And in Western society, "wild" animals are our greatest Other, representing our dreams of freedom from social constraints.

CONCLUSION

The inquiry into the role of animals in Western discourse on sexuality reveals the effects of a profound cultural cognitive binary between us and them, people versus animals, with instantiations ranging from the ancient myths to modern jokes, and implications for our use of language, and our philosophical and scientific inquiries. In Western culture, this binary construction plays a major cultural role—so much so that its omnipresence in Western discourse may have hindered previous scholarship and understanding of our relations with other animals. Taboos, such as those regarding sexual practices, can reveal a great deal about a society: in this case, I suggest this powerful taboo against actual inter-special sexuality in Western society can be seen as part of this overall binary of humans versus animals, and, importantly, with our sexuality as inherently "animal" as well as sinful, often in opposition to our muzzled "humanity." Yet, at the same time, by imagining animals as enjoying lives free of sexual restrictions, and by associating our own sexuality with our "animal" nature, we locate our own sexuality among the animals: our repression and sublimation of our own sexuality in turn helps sustain and fuel this concept of animals as inherently sexy, yet sexually repulsive. Such a complex construction provides rich resources for a variety of cultural expressions, and a source of endless jokes, insults, and eroticisms, ranging from *Playboy* bunnies to tiger-print bedsheets.

This investigation of vernacular expressions reveals elemental cultural constructions, with ties to science, popular beliefs, religion, and mythology. Such investigations have the potential to inform us about ourselves, including the ways in which Western cultural constructions influence scientific understanding of our actual kinship with other animals (and vice versa). The "animal turn" has forced the anthropocentric western discourse to see its own animal face in the mirror, and face the gaze of countless cousins. In this particular instance, we have investigated the way that western discourse utilizes notions of "our animal self" to continue to refer to a life free from social restraints, perhaps nowhere more so than in the realm of sexuality. Yet, the sexual lives of other animals reveals that this is a projected utopia, not a reality: rather, social suppression of sexuality is a common occurrence in many animal societies. In the end, we are left with our own distorted gaze upon ourselves. As long as Western discourse insists on qualitative distinctions between the human and the animal, and the notion of human sexuality as inherently "animalistic" and sinful, then the tabooistic discourse using animals to present our human sexualities will likely continue. Like the parable of Derrida's cat, in front of whom Derrida was curiously ashamed of being naked,[24] it is not so much about the actual beast involved, as it is a profoundly powerful—if at times misleading—discourse we tell each other about ourselves.

PART 2

BECOMING CYBORG

The other main branch of posthumanism looks at the impact of the digital realm on human ontology. The digital realm can be seen as influential even in its very architecture, the way that the constructions enable social behaviors and tradition building online. We can trace posthumanism's ascendancy in large part with the development of the internet. Other interesting theoretical moves are also implicated in these historic shifts, perhaps most noticeably postnationalism (defined loosely as the lessening importance of the nation-state as a locus for identity)[1] and postcolonialism (the lessening importance of colonial powers, as well as the state of being for the many nation-states created via colonialism).

We are witnessing a truly epochal transformation with the introduction of digital discourse, creating a new way for people to think about themselves.

The following three chapters look at some of the ways that the digital era has brought the idea of cyborg identity to the fore. Cyborg identity, the linking with biological identity and virtual identities, tie together human cultures in a unique way. One of the most noticeable attributes is in the de-spatialization. In old-time folklore, you had to be in the room to hear the story. In cyber folklore, you, and the storyteller, could be anywhere. Such new formations of social groups and culture destabilize the geographic bases for culture, and trouble notions of the "imagined communities" (as per Anderson 1984) of the nation-state. Like it or not, we are becoming a global village, and a cyborg one, at that.

The chapters in part two examine some of the changes in human aesthetics in such things as music and visual images—the performative contours of how people are performing their global, cyborg selves.

These chapters trace the expressions of joys and frustration of becoming cyborg: cyborg aesthetics, political beliefs, legalities, and cultural expressions are all vernacular expressions of profound ontological tensions brought on by our current conditions. If we can think of the "cyborg" as part-human, and part-not, then in what way do we perform that identity? What are the dangers, frustrations, as well as joys and exultations, of becoming cyborg?

5

BEATBOXING, MASHUPS, AND CYBORG IDENTITY

Folk Music for the Twenty-First Century

This chapter discusses two new artistic musical traditions, beatboxing and mashups, in terms of their communal, changeable forms as displaying hallmarks often associated with folk music. Investigating the relationship between aesthetic choices and identity concerns highlights the central theme of the man and the machine, the cyborg, and the interconnected cognitive functioning of man and machine—all increasingly a part of reality at the beginning of the twenty-first century.

INTRODUCTION

I begin this chapter with a look at beatboxing. Beatboxing is a very popular musical form, and I have witnessed it being performed in nearly every part of the world. It nonetheless remains, for the most part, out of the realm of the recording industry, record charts, and copyright offices (with some important exceptions). Beatboxing, I will attempt to show, has moved into the global realm, with global signification, in large part due to the internet. As such, beatboxing makes an interesting starting point from which to examine the processes, functions, and aesthetics of computer-mediated musics. It further provides useful context towards understanding the new artistic forms which are both computer-generated and -transmitted, and the other genre with which it often blends, the mashup. Mashups are an enormously popular musical form, with hundreds of pieces being created and uploaded every day. Like beatboxing, mashups too fall outside of our usual definitions. Neither copyrighted nor reproduced by the media industry, mashups have become a sign of our times, speaking volumes to the internet's potential at allowing the common man to produce new artistic forms, and new aesthetic choices, to promulgate new identities, at once both global and deeply connected with the basis for the globalism: the computer.

I. BEATBOXING

At first glance, beatboxing might seem like an odd choice to observe the cyborg, as it is so often encountered as a live performance. If one travels to any major cities in the world, one may well encounter the sounds and performances of the tradition performed in the street, the train, or indeed just about anywhere: the sound effects coming straight out of the performer's mouths, the *thump-ka-thup* beat, the occasional inclusion of sounds which resemble electronic sampling, the mimicking of the "scratching" of a phonograph needle grating against a vinyl LP, and so on. Sometimes, someone else might be in the performance, perhaps rapping over the top of the one-man rhythm section, or perhaps an accomplice passing the hat around the audience gathered in the street, but most often it will be one person alone, *a capella*, creating all this sound, one person with, at most, a microphone.

I was led to the topic of beatboxing by my undergraduate students during a lecture on folk music. I was showing various examples of folk music from around the world on YouTube, while explaining and discussing the different aspects of folk music. I explained that for music to be considered folk music, the music must display all the hallmarks of folklore, as per Dundes's famous definition of folklore as evidencing "multiplicity and variation" (Dundes 1999, vii), Ben-Amos's performance-aware "artistic communication in small groups" (1972), and I further added that folk music should be, for the most part, un-authored and un-copyrighted, existing outside the realm of the culture industry.

One of my students asked, "What about beatboxing?" I typed it into the search engine, and, lo and behold, there came a return on YouTube of over 35,000 entries, many of which had been viewed tens of thousands of times (some into the hundreds of thousands of times or even millions of times).

Once I heard the familiar strains, I immediately realized that I'd heard this genre before—in the streets of Los Angeles, San Francisco, New York, Marseilles, Dublin, and, indeed, nearly every cosmopolitan area I'd ever visited for any length of time. Also, as my initial foray in the class had quickly revealed, many of the performances (and even more of the viewings) of beatboxing take place in cyberspace, mostly on YouTube, or similar sites featuring user-generated content. YouTube is not only a method of distribution, but also another site of performance, where the music can be watched and commented upon, absorbed and recreated.

Although YouTube displays recordings, it is not the same as a television or movie—the internet is a "pull" technology, meaning that people have to seek out the videos. Furthermore, the decidedly vernacular emphasis of the videos reveal YouTube as a place where ordinary people can engage in critique by leaving comments and responses, becoming an "active audience." A "hit" video is always noticeable due to the large number of "hits" as well as the ratings and comments. Cyberspace, like any space, provides opportunity for performances by people.[1] People perform and create art, and people observe the art and give feedback. In terms of beatboxing, there are good performers and not-so-good performers, popular pieces and not-so-popular pieces. Yet the tradition is highly stylized, highly traditional in its aesthetics. Most of the same elements can easily be witnessed in the various versions, even though the versions are literally from all over the world. How did this come to be?

Pasts and Presence

The first "historical" moments of beatboxing are dated to 1980, when performer Doug E. Fresh (Doug E. Davis) claimed to have invented the genre. During the early 1980s, Darren Robinson of the Fat Boys (originally the Disco Three) brought beatboxing to the national stage. Others, however, state that beatboxing arose in the multitudes of anonymous artists, as authors TyTe and Defenicial stated on their website article "The Real History of Beatboxing: Part 1" that "the history of Beatboxing is blurry. It appears, like graffiti, to have begun it's life as an urban art form."[2]

Since the term "beatbox" originally referred to an early drum machine, the modern genre of beatboxing clearly owes a great deal to hip-hop culture, and to the development of a specific genre of "rhythm-speech" with stylistic and aesthetic concerns linked closely with hip-hop culture. It was through the commercialization of this hip-hop genre that beatboxing reached its largest, most mass audiences, and hip-hop still flavors, to varying degrees, the production of beatboxing around the world.

All the same, beatboxing has been received, and subsequently produced, differently in different parts of the world, at times blending with other cultural forms of rhythm speech, and other forms of folk music. Musicologists have documented a worldwide distribution of mouth rhythms, or "rhythm-speech" as Atherton (2007) dubs it. African American hip-hop performers themselves drew upon a long-standing cultural legacy of mouth music, found in bar-bershop, jazz (scat) singing, and much more, including where vocalizations were used to mimic percussive instruments. Early blues performers such as Lead Belly (Huddie Ledbetter) can be heard inserting vocalized percussion sounds in some of their live performances. Similarly, around the world are many example of "rhythm-speech," perhaps most famously in India, with its *bol* form, and in "Celtic" regions, with the *port beil*, or "mouth music," much of which was specifically percussive in nature. Atherton (2007) cites other example genres in Ghana and Australia.

Regardless of any possible links with these traditions, beatboxing may still be difficult for people to conceive of as a folk music. For one thing, it is an urban development, and as Bohlman, in his 1988 *The Study of Folk Music in the Modern World*, stated, "Urbanization topples one of the most sacred tenets of folk music theory: the distinction between the rural and the urban" (126–27). The rural, was of course, the home of the *volk*, linked by writers such as Herder to specific places, and whose removal from modernity helped create the fictional unities of the early nation states (see Wilson 1973; Anntonen 2005).

A search for "folk music" on YouTube brings in a total of 85,000 entries, most of which seem to be recordings of traditional folk music, from Nepalese to Azerbaijanian. While not labeled as such, and not showing up on the "folk music "search, beatboxing is all the more interesting because it fits all the definitions of folk music without being widely recognized as such. Why this is so has a great deal to do with the past of the discipline, particularly in Europe, where the notion of folklore was contrasted to the urban, literate realm. It also frequently carried (and carries) notions of ethnic and national identity.

Ethnic and national identity was thought to be "natural" descending from Herder's formative ideas. Many times, romantic ideas of folk music are explic-itly held to geographical "roots," and folk music is occasionally referred to as "roots music." To be "rootless" is therefore, by this logic, an inherently bad or inauthentic aspect.[3] In the case of much of the research on "folk" or "world" music, to be rootless is equated to being inauthentic. To be divorced from the geography of the tradition's genesis was to be "schizomogenic," as Steven Feld (1994) put it. Anthony McCann, in an article addressing the cultural codes of transmission in Irish folk music (which he holds are based on the "idea of gift"), asserts that "the further that music moves from its register of origin, the more likely, it seems, it is to be commodified" (95).

The negative views of rootless music have been summarized, and challenged, by Steve Jones, who, in his article on computer music, stated that "much writing in popular music, academic and journalistic, fixes on the notion that geographic location of a particular group or sound is a good thing, for, at the very least, achieving a kind of specificity, an anchor, within which to understand a particular socio-historical moment. When movement is invoked, it is largely used to denote a dispersion and diffusion of values, a loss of aura and authenticity" (2002: 213).

I am in agreement with Jones not only that this is the overarching paradigm for many conceptions of "roots" music, but that this formation is ill-equipped to deal with the new realities of global communication and emergent vernacular musical forms. As Stokes noted, "music does not then simply provide a marker in a prestructured social space, but the means by which this space can be transformed" (1994: 4). In this case, this space is the new frontier of cyberspace.

Computers, Music, People

There are many emergent artistic forms on the internet, and a great deal of overlap with computer-generated music. But one of the things that interested me about beatboxing is that it is not, in the main, computer-generated. For the most part, it is a form that is performed live, with no equipment at all; or, more usually, nothing more than a microphone and an amplifier.

Beatboxing occupies an interesting position in terms of people, computers, and music, as the genre is generally geared towards live performances, including street performances, creating a semi-professional avenue for aspiring musicians. It mimics the sound of computer-generated music; it parodies the computer in live performances relying on the human voice alone. Yet it also blends seamlessly with computer distribution and computer-generated music, and the cut-and-paste pastiche of many of the new digital-based user-generated art forms. In my research on the web, sometimes the music was performed explicitly for the production of web-distributed videos, at other times, the music was performed in some other public venue and filmed by an audience member, who later placed the video on the web.[4]

There has been a good deal written on "global music" or "world music" (e.g., Feld 1994; Erlmann 1998), which I've touched on in some previous research (Thompson 2003), yet my main interests in this chapter lie slightly apart from much of the previous literature. What interests me most about "world music" in this context is in what so many scholars assume as natural—usually, again, that a traditional form of music, firmly rooted to place, has been disrupted and cheapened by global distribution.

What can one learn, then, by examining global music that also reflects a distinctly postmodern (the imitation of samplers) and urban aesthetic? This question implies different answers, and different questions, than can be explored by a historic-geographic outline of oicotypical variations of folk music; different, even more so, than can be explored by noting long-held notions of folk music as reflecting long-seated ethnic and/or national identity.[5]

Still, some questions that scholars of folk music have been asking carry over well, and these, I propose, are the ones dealing with aesthetics and its relation to identity negotiation. Earlier, in my paper on emergent musical forms in Alaska (2003), I proposed that aesthetics is a mediating step between expressive culture and identity concerns. Although identity concerns could easily be discerned by the researcher, for the most part they were not cited as influences by the performers. Rather, the performers engaged in the forms they saw as "fun" or "cool" or otherwise aesthetically pleasing. Let me restate this thesis: aesthetics is a mediating step between expressive culture and identity concerns, and it is this mediating step that is most widely and consciously recognized by the performers and audiences of the tradition.[6] By and large, people sing songs because they like them, not because they feel compelled to proclaim their identity.

Following this, then, I will ask in this chapter, what are the aesthetics of beatboxing, mashups, and more? And how do these point towards concerns with identity? As many have argued (e.g., Dundes 1993; Oring 1994), folklore and identity are inextricably linked: scratch the one, and you find the other.

I hope that a brief review of some of the forms observable on YouTube will prove instructive, although it should be noted that this is only a partial sampling, since beatboxing exists outside of YouTube as well, in the streets, subways, school basements, parking lots, churches, and concert halls of the world. Nonetheless, YouTube has proved a valuable resource in terms of user-generated documentation of performances, and an important means (although certainly not the only one) of diffusion of the tradition.

First, we might examine the "traditional" beatboxing in the street.[7] Someone "sings" the part of the drum machine plus sound effects, and someone has made a recording (with or without the knowledge of the performer) and placed it on YouTube. Such examples come from literally all corners of the world: Korea, Algeria, France, Australia, Iran, Ethiopia, Samoa, Greenland, etc.

One thing we can note right from the start of our investigation is that beatboxing now is a widespread, if not fully global, form of vernacular music with a strong sense of traditionality alongside its variations. No matter what the continent, what the country, the examples are all clearly recognizable as belonging to the same genre, with the same "thump-ka-thump, ka-thump *kish*," imitating the drum machine, plus the imitations of sample sounds and effects. Very often these examples blend these generic markers with their own cultural forms of mouth music and "rhythm speech."

Also highly noticeable is a strong aesthetic of combined human and computer: in this case, the human is attempting to sound like computer-produced music. A "beatbox" originally referred to a "drum machine," a machine that created drum patterns from sampled sounds, which was often critiqued as being "soulless"—the "drummer in a can." Yet, these performers are using that same aesthetic and broadening it with some crucial human performance elements.

Although modern beatboxing may have started alongside rap as a street performance, with shared beginnings of sampling, it has been embraced by a wide variety of performers in a wide variety of contexts, and has been a natural for YouTube videos. We can also easily notice the other performative qualities—the hand movements, bodily movements with the rhythm, and so on, all of which help guide the viewing experience.[8] The performer often appears to manipulate invisible machines (including "scratching" vinyl LPs), and the audience plays along with this noisy miming. In beatboxing, machines are an omnipresent absence.[9]

The idea is a simple one that many people can attempt to perform. Beatboxing is global, and therefore it makes sense that it speaks to global rather than local concerns: in this case, the concern is man and machines.[10] There are no language barriers, and few barriers as to different tonal or rhythmic systems. The equipment required is minimal, and thus there are few economic barriers. Yet this is not to say it does not have a traditional form; indeed, one of the most striking things about beatboxing is the coherence and cohesiveness of the genre. The same sounds, in the same manner, are being performed in all the corners of the world.

Further, it has achieved a high level of performance qualities, and has been taken in by a staggering demographic of people as an enjoyable musical form: for example, one YouTube beatboxing video had listed over 20 million views.[11] Has this entered the market? Of course it has—as have most folk musics. It has also been accepted by other musicians, and brought on stage in hybrid formats all over the world.[12] In 2008, Vodafone France released a television ad featuring French beatboxing star Joseph "Poulpo." In fact, beatboxing is such a global phenomenon, that you can watch and appreciate, and yet not be entirely sure where the music, or the performer is "located." It quickly becomes apparent that this is the wrong focus: the music is somewhere, it is many wheres—it is on the web, and on the streets, of the world. If before one could tell one's nationality, perhaps ethnicity, perhaps even language, by hearing one's folk music, with beatboxing, emergent vernacular forms no longer carry conspicuous signs of geography, and, hence, ethnicity.

Recordings and Performance

Although in the first section I discussed beatboxing as a live performance, perhaps in part to fulfill some imagined criteria for "folk" music, I'd like to expand this discussion beyond mere recordings of live events.

Indeed, much of what passes for "recordings" can hardly live up to the term. Ever since Les Paul pioneered multi-tracking, and the Beatles' *Sergeant Pepper's Lonely Hearts Club Band* expanded this idea to new musical heights, most musical releases from artists are not recordings of live performances, even if many of them continue to mimic the aesthetics of live performances.

Like geographical place, "live performances" have often been viewed as a criterion for authenticating folk music. This hearkens back to the idea of simple, unmechanical folk, who ideally crafted their own crude instruments and shunned the degenerative influence of modern technology, preserving for the rest of us some romantic, hazy agricultural Eden. I have to say, I'm not a big proponent of this idea: yes, folk musicians did often fashion their own crude instruments, but this was usually due to poverty, not because they were luddites. Folk music in Ireland, for example, readily and eagerly incorporated new instruments and new technologies.[13] Similarly, while beatboxing may have emerged from a desire to imitate expensive drum machines cheaply and easily, the aesthetic concerns were nonetheless completely modern.

While beatboxing involves an aesthetic concerning machines and computer produced sounds, at other times beatboxing and other new musical genres incorporate computer-produced sounds, rather than simply imitating them, often in a cut-and-paste montage.[14] Is this acceptable? Although one may not see it performed in the street, I believe that this shows the other side of emergent musical global genres. While man and machine is a central aesthetic, I don't think it is man *versus* the machine, but rather man *as* the machine. That is to say, the new identity is a global, human one, but I think it is not only that. I think it is also one of negotiating a new sort of man-and-machine identity, a synthesis between human and computer.

Beatboxing has much in common with the aesthetics and generic styles of hip-hop sampling.[15] However, it is somewhat separated from these other forms due to its human-produced sounds which imitate sampled sounds (which imitate live performance). A circularity, from live performance to computers and back again, completes this feedback loop, spilling out onto the web and onto the streets of the world, among those who are interested.

This is a far cry from the Herderian notions of folklore and folk music, and this is precisely my point. While at one time songs were performed in physical space, and people didn't travel all that much, folk music could reasonably be correlated with geography. But this has changed, and changed dramatically. The new technology, the user-generated content, has created new opportunities for artistic expressions, dealing with global identity concerns. The "place" of this music is the world wide web; the "roots" are virtual roots. We are now in the realm of "Folklore 2.0."

II. MASH IT UP

Mashups are a combination of two or more digital songs, videos, or images that are mixed together in new ways.[16] One might have Johnny Cash vocals over, say, the music of the Ramones. One could then use that soundtrack and put in some other videos over the top: perhaps samples of a commercial movie, or a "home" movie downloaded from the internet. Digitization has allowed each tiny little piece to become disassembled and reassembled into an endless variety of new productions. This is one of the most popular new art forms, with hundreds of mashups being released, usually for free, every day. This is not to say that they are all masterpieces, of course, but it is to say that there is a widespread interest and participation in mashups, most of which have no commercial aspect.

Mashups cover a wide variety of styles and examples. Some are audio-only, while others focus on audio-visual material. For those audio-visual (movie) examples, there are many different styles and approaches.

Sometimes video material is simply dubbed with new audio. Very often, these examples overlap with the mashups composed of various pastiches. There are numerous examples playing off the contrast between "children's" characters such as Ernie and Bert, Barny, the Teletubbies, and so on, with more adult themes.[17] For example, the children-oriented *Sesame Street's* Ernie and Bert characters are often provided with dialogue portraying them as a gay couple. There are many videos and stills off of the "Bert is Evil" theme, portraying Bert with Hitler, Osama bin Laden, and the like.

Sometimes, the use of two similar videos can be very artful, both amplifying the other in unique ways (Divide & Kreate's "Sharp Dressed Party" mashup of Pink's "Get This Party Started" and ZZ Top's "Sharp Dressed Man").[18]

Mashups are commonly used for political commentary, humor, and critique. At times, politicians' recorded words or videos are mashed up with other components. Examples include a popular mashup of Sarah Palin and the movie *Fargo*, playing on Palin's disastrous first interview with Katie Couric along with her similar accent,[19] Senator Ted Stevens's famous declaration of the internet as a "series of tubes,"[20] or the mashup-produced theme of George W. Bush "beatboxing."[21]

Interestingly, not all examples of popular culture are selected for mashups, but some are. Notable examples include: *Star Wars*, *The Lord of the Rings*, Teletubbies, *Sponge Bob*, and *Sesame Street*. These, and some others, seem to be being embraced as iconic characters, plots, and themes, in the new art culture.

Alongside commercially produced material, user-generated videos or sound may also become very popular ("going viral") and become the basis of numerous other compositions. These can be combined with or follow a certain theme, providing intense networks of authorship and collective creativity.

A further development was introduced by Ophir Kutiel, better known as Kutiman, at his site thru-you.com. Kutiman developed a series of artful music videos in which the music and film are drawn from a pastiche of user-generated music videos on YouTube, from all ages, nationalities, and musical backgrounds. The result is a stark question to prevailing notions of originality in art and authorship, and his videos have drawn a large amount of attention.

Who's in Charge, Here?

Mashups challenge our current ideas of authorship (and, by extension, copyright): who is the author of such hybrid products? Johnny Cash, the Ramones, or the person who put them together in his basement? Interestingly, how well some songs fit together with other songs makes one question the whole notion of "original songs" altogether. Mashups operate in the grey areas of the law (and very frequently will be removed form sites like YouTube due to possible copyright violation after a complaint by one party). In a sense, they are, like beatboxing, also an extension of some of the issues which arose with early sampling techniques (see Demers 2006), although with mashups it is not just using one sample, or video, but often creating new works entirely out of the works of art of others.

It is refreshing to see vernacular forms arising from people's artistic impulses, rather than being slavishly dominated by the "culture industry," as the Frankfurt School had at one time feared. Indeed, these new musical forms often find themselves in direct conflict with the culture industry, particularly regarding the issue of copyrights. This has caused great headaches for the recording industry and the copyright regime as a whole; both of these closely followed the model built to deal with the effects of the printing press (that same technological innovation that was supposed to spell the end of folklore). Before the recording industry, there was no distinction between popular music and folk music; they were one and the same. With the recording industry, the radios, and all of the rest, this changed. Folk music was supposed to exist outside of these realms, however much this "outsider" cachet was marketed and commercialized by the industry.[22] But the industry is having a harder time now controlling these new emergent forms. Now (and once again) cutting-edge popular music and emergent folk music are hard to distinguish.

Increasingly, the idea of *a* copyrighted work, not to be altered, is becoming obsolete. People enjoy taking what they know and reconfiguring it in new ways, giving it that lively "multiplicity and variation" that folklorists all know and love.

Meanwhile, corporations have increasingly turned toward lawsuits to put a stop to such creative remixing. In one example, EMI, the Beatles' publisher, threatened an early mashup artist with a multi-million dollar lawsuit, demanding that the artist turn over the hundreds of thousand of people who downloaded his work.[23]

Several of the top scholars on these new art forms have seized upon examples such as this to decry what they see as the overly litigious and restrictive use of copyright. Lawrence Lessig, in his book *Free Culture* (is "free" here an adjective or verb for Lessig, or both?), makes the distinction between "read-only" culture and what he calls "read-write" culture. As he put it, "Read-only. Passive recipients of culture produced elsewhere. Couch potatoes. Consumers. This is the world of media from the twentieth century. . . . The twenty-first could be different. This is the crucial point: It could be both read and write" (Lessig 2005: 37).

As Lessig points out, some of the most exciting new art forms are just this: "mashups" embracing "read-write" culture. New art is developed using pieces and bits of other pieces of art. Works are often collaboratively formed, collaboratively improved, sometimes with attribution, sometimes without. Lessig is one of the leading legal scholars on these notions, yet I believe that his formulations still could be improved by turning his lawyerly gaze towards folkloristics, and to the "read-write" culture, outside of copyright, that has long defined folklore and folk music.

Taking folklore (including folk music) into such account is easy enough. Before the printing press, there was little concern with copyright. Copying was enormously difficult, and expensive, undertakings when manuscripts were copied by hand. It was only with the development of printing technologies—the "Age of the Book"—that copyright issues were defined and delineated.[24] As time went on, this included music, whether on player-piano rolls, gramophones, LPs, or other forms. The production and distribution of art was consolidated into large corporations. Fewer people then produced art; it was mass-copied, and many people consumed.[25] Many people—including academics—associated these developments with the end of folklore. Who needed folk music when you had Elvis and the radio? Although this notion was gradually and painstakingly revised by showing the persistence of folklore in modern times, it nonetheless helped place folklore in the minds of most as a premodern, or at least marginal, form of entertainment.[26] Now, there would not be multiple versions and variations, but rather one mass-produced version, controlled from the top by ever-more-powerful media corporations.

Still, limits remain: for example, Disney cannot presume a copyright on Sleeping Beauty, or Cinderella, because folklore has long been considered un-copyrightable. Lessig reveals the Disney corporation's remarkable successes in copyrighting, perhaps nowhere as apparent as in the case of Mickey Mouse, who began his career in "Steamboat Willie" (even though, as Lessig points out, "Steamboat Willie" was a direct knock-off of Buster Keaton's "Steamboat Bill").[27] One cannot publish a "new" version of Mickey Mouse without risking direct legal conflict with Disney. But one *can* write all the stories one wants about Cinderella, Sleeping Beauty, Hansel and Gretel, and the like. Even Disney could not write the Grimms out of the history books, and the Grimms make it clear that they were not the authors of the tales, simply their collectors and editors. Nor were their informants the authors: rather, their informants were copying, creatively, the stories they had heard from other storytellers, mashing them up a bit, and retelling them anew.

In terms of music, authorship and copyright have followed the pattern set by the printing press and the culture industry. Classical composers long relied on folk music for inspiration and melodies, and the trend continued into popular music released in the new media formats (radios, and from player piano to phonograph and beyond). Stephen Foster, the "father of American music," relied heavily on folk music—particularly African American folk music—to create his wildly popular songs. It is unclear to what degree Foster "created" his songs, or merely adapted them, and this is true for a great deal of the use of folklore in authored mediums. Nonetheless, work produced in the folk medium is often thought of as un-copyrightable, while the "authored" work produced from folklore is now more heavily protected than ever, a position that has led to a great deal of legal wrangling throughout the world.[28]

III. PERFORMING THE CYBORG

In "The Aesthetics of Interactive Computer Music," Guy Garnett stated that "it is now possible to use the machine, the computer or any and all electronic and physical devices, without the dichotomy, to join the mechanical power of the machine to the nuanced and 'subjectivizing' control of the human performer. This, ultimately, is itself an aesthetic value for our new age" (Garnett 2001).

The "subjectivizing" control mentioned by Garnett is of crucial importance towards understanding performance. Theoretical understandings of folklore have frequently turned to studies of performance in order to attempt to understand the relationship between the personal and the social, the embodied and the mental, and the creation of the subject through repeated, and internalized, performances.[29]

The creation of the subject overlaps a great deal with the creation of identity, although there are differences. Identity has an institutional feel about it, as identity can frequently be imposed from outside, and one is not always free to take on new identities. Further, having an identity does not, by itself, imply any agency—one can have an identity as a purely passive (even brain-dead!) being. But being a subject implies something different: it implies having a subjective relation to the world, becoming aware of one's own subjective stance vis-à-vis that of others. Human subjectivity is a reflective stance as well, as we are all aware that we are surrounded by other subjects, other rational, thoughtful humans. As Elizabeth Fine wrote, "Performances link us to 'the Other' through aesthetic experience not, simply cognition" (1992: 7). Subjectivity is not free from institutional constraints by any means, yet implied in the word is a self-actualization of identity concerns. Subjectivity, or the awareness of being a subject, is perhaps a preferable term here to "identity," since identity so frequently is used in terms of official status, or objectively imposed descriptions, whereas subjectivity includes at once the idea of having identity and also of engaging in the world in an aesthetic, individualized reaction, in the phenomenology of corporal existence, and an epistemology of selfhood, groups identity, and their interactions.[30]

Much work has been done on understanding the performance of identities and subjectivities, from performing ethnic identities, gender identities, national identities and more. For example, Fine also wrote that "performance . . . makes or constitutes cultural identity, as well as imitates it" (1992: 9). Performances allow for the display of at once both group and individual identities, displaying both agency and restraints. Through performances of all types, the subject self-actualizes his/her identity concerns. As de Certeau has pointed out, one may be enmeshed in a system from which there is no real escape, yet one still has agency as well. In de Certeau's terms, these are the "tactics," employed by the relatively disempowered, to attempt to maximize their rewards from the confines of the larger system (Certeau 1988). Performances can be seen as yet another such tactic, and a very symbolically powerful one at that. Performances can both proclaim and disclaim identity, establish subject positions in the greater milieu of other subjects and institutions, and appeal for public recognition, legitimation, and other rewards for the performer and/or for the symbolic implications of the performance.

Performance Online

Due in large part to folklore's intense interest in performance, folklorists were quick to take note of the internet as yet another site for performance. As Kirshenblatt-Gimblett put it as early as 1995, "The new media challenge disciplinary assumptions of face-to-face communication, oral transmission, performance, community and identity" (73). Although in the mid 1990s, the technology and the lore were somewhat limited, since that time the technology and lore have been expanding at a dizzying pace. Now the folklore spread on the internet is not just text-based alone, in the form of jokes, urban legends, and the like, but has become something else, something more. More and more people are performing on the web, in an increasing number of genres.

Donna Haraway (1991) has envisioned "cyborg identity" as a new, and newly important, facet of identity. In particular, Harraway was interested in the ideas of the cyborg as destabilizing gender identities, and causing us to rethink our "natural" assumptions of gender identity. She further stated that "a cyborg is a cybernetic organism, a hybrid of machine and organism, a creature of social reality as well as a creature of fiction. Social reality is lived social relations, our most important political construction, a world-changing fiction" (1991: 149).

This has been borne out in the development of the internet, where identity has become much more fleeting, fragmented, and constructed. One can have an "avatar" (an formerly archaic word now rejuvenated for the new cyborg realities) of any gender . . . or no gender at all. One may not be sure, in communicating with a person, what gender they are. Also, gender is not the only identity to be subverted by the subjectivizing performances on the web. Even more important, perhaps, is that the cyborg subject can leave *all* previous identities behind, or, indeed, invent new ones. Not only is one not sure of an online subject's gender, but also of the subject's nationality, age, wealth, and many of the other previously iron-clad subject positions. To perform the cyborg is to perform humanity, yet it is a different type of humanity, with different possible identities and subject position, that is being performed. And it must be performed through the computer; once one steps away, one is back to being gendered, aged, nationalized, and all the rest. Of course, one *can* bring these subject positions online as well (as has been explored in Nakamura 2002), but this is no longer a requirement. Instead, performing the cyborg is performing a new way of being human, and perhaps the best demonstrations of this are in the new artistic forms performed via the computer. Beatboxing relies on the computer to establish a new style of folk music to be performed on the streets as well as the information superhighways; mashups and such exist solely in the new communicative realm. Yet both of these new forms point towards novel aspects of performance, of subjectivity, and of new ways of being human.

IV. THE POSTMODERN LOOKS A LOT LIKE THE PREMODERN

In the realm of expressive culture, the postmodern seems to have many similarities to the premodern. In many ways, the re-involvement in cultural production by the masses is very reminiscent of the folk culture that predominated life before the printing press and the mass, industrial production of cultural forms.

This is not to say they are the same, as other scholars have recognized. Media scholar Henry Jenkins dubbed this new phase as "convergence culture," a coming together of all sorts of participants (commercial, vernacular, institutional, etc) in common themes and stories, together with what he labels "participatory culture."

He argues that "that convergence encourages participation and collective intelligence" (255), pointing out that in the postmodern age "people are learning how to participate in such knowledge cultures outside of any formal educational setting" (259). This certainly has its analogues to the folk cultures of premodernity as well.

RG Howard has outlined how web discourses are somewhat vernacular, and somewhat institutional, a hybrid sort of production. Howard states that

> while mass-mediated communication technologies have empowered the institutional, participatory media offer powerful new channels through which the vernacular can express its alterity. However, alternate voices do not emerge from these technologies untouched by their means of production. (2008, 192)

Further, he also points out that

> insofar as we engage with participatory media, either by consuming or producing them, we too are the agents of their creation. Just as we are vernacular, so too are we the institutions. More than ever before, it is the responsibility of researchers and critics to avoid romanticizing the vernacular as some object held wholly separate from any taint of institutional power. Instead, the vernacular is now, more clearly than ever, hybrid. (ibid., 212)

There is a great deal of variety in cyber culture, with some websites or software programs not enabling participatory culture at all and others being completely based on participatory culture, from the planning stages through the distribution. While there has been an explosion of user-generated art on the internet, bypassing much of the previous institutional limits on cultural production, the institutional is still always a presence in cyber culture, with regulation and enforcement of appropriate conduct.

Folklore is mostly ephemeral, existing in the performances, and in the minds of people. Web culture may be somewhat ephemeral, as well: very often, for example, mashups will be removed from YouTube or similar sites because someone (or some corporation) complained about possible copyright violations. One never knows, from one day to the next, what will be still available, and what will be mysteriously missing. Yet, there is an archival quality of the new media as well: unlike the more traditional folklore scenario of telling jokes at the office water cooler, telling a joke online always has the possibility of being archived, copied, distributed to outsiders, and held open for examination.

The newly emerging forms on the internet, often branded as illegal and as "outlaw art," are new forms of folklore for the twenty-first century. Like all types of folklore, these forms spread from person to person (or, one could say, "peer to peer"). The main differences between this ("folklore 2.0") and classic ("analog") folklore is that digital communication is mediated through the computers: this allows for a variety of participants, serves to archive performances, and perhaps more importantly, severs the long-assumed tie between (cultural) place, and (geographic) space: with audio-video connectivity on the rise, even "face-to-face" takes on a placeless potential. Cultures and cultural groups can exist in a hybrid of place and cyberspace, involving both the institutional and vernacular. Thus, to track culture now involves more than geography of cultural forms, more than even the tracking of diasporas and transnational groups; it now also necessitates understanding information flow via the digital realm, the production and consumption of culture in the twenty-first century.

Production and consumption of culture in the age of modernity ("Art in the Age of Mechanical Reproduction," to use Benjamin's terminology) crafted the important, legal distinction between popular and folk music (and other art forms). Copies become a commodity, and culture is expressed through these forms. Today, we are undergoing yet another technological revolution, one likely to be even larger than that brought on by the printing press and mechanical reproduction. We are now looking at art in the age of digital reproduction, which is a new beast altogether. Mashups turn the tide on the printing press regime, ushering in a new era of performance that has much in common with the old. Whereas before the author/composer could freely use folk music to create an "original" piece, now artists are using previously published materials to create new folk art.

V. CONCLUSIONS: FOLKLORE 2.0

With the onset of digitization technologies, copying, including creative copying, became once again in the hands of the masses. This has shaped up as an epic battle between "the copyrighters and the copylefters." Although much excellent scholarly work has been done on this matter,[31] I am more concerned in this chpater with the impulse of people to create art, using the materials that form their lives, rather than the legal issues surrounding such actions.[32] Increasingly, our lives include sights, sounds, and scenes that the media industry has generated. Also increasingly, people are realizing that the power to (re)produce and distribute art, to manipulate these generated realities into new forms, is once again in their hands. Not only this, but this is occurring on a global, de-territorialized scale. If folk music is closely enmeshed with identity, then what sort of identity does this global, computer-mediated folk music herald?

Of course, not all humankind is linked in together in the cybernetic world wide web, and certainly not evenly so, but the various online communities numbers are impressive: how many YouTube users? Second lifers? *World of Warcraft* players? Online newspaper readers? Online professional or hobby organizations? The trendsetters of the world *are* highly interconnected via the computer, and the trend shows no sign of slowing. Cell phones are wildly popular in much of the third world due to their affordability. These are not telephones in the old sense of the term, but instead miniature computers in their own right, connecting even impoverished people to the world wide web, and to the discussions and movements occurring therein.

If it is true that identity is constructed and reconstituted by actors in performance rather than passively expressed through them (as per Bauman 1972), then I believe that identity concerns can be discerned by looking at the aesthetic concerns with the artistic performance. In this case, the aesthetics in both beatboxing and mashups point to an identity concern with computers. In a nutshell, they perform this idea that we *are* the cyborg. We still have a sense of self, yet this now includes an interconnected cognitive function with the machine, and it is this new identity concern that is being negotiated by new forms of folklore, the realm of "folklore 2.0."

In a sense, this should not be surprising. Other scholars in diverse fields have also pointed to the cyborg quality of modern life, and the resulting questions for notions of identity.[33] Just as the printing press ultimately proved decisive for the development of national identity (as outlined by Anderson 1991, among others), so too will this new media provide for new identities and new subjectivities.

We have given birth to a new kind of cognitive functioning, a new sense of self. One of the best ways to witness the formation of subjectivity in action is through observing new vernacular musics like beatboxing and mashups: the aesthetic choices of people throughout the world point to new subject concerns, new negotiations about who one is. Only this time, it is not just humans in the mix. Welcome to the folk music, and folk groups, of the twenty-first century!

6

NETIZENS, REVOLUTIONARIES, AND THE INALIENABLE RIGHT TO THE INTERNET

What are the implications of these new genres such as mashups? For one, they are part of the formation of new aesthetic communities online, which intersect in increasingly complex ways with previously assumed identities, such as the national. Formations of new identities are frequently contested by the older forms, as vested interests weigh in on shaping the newly emergent cultures. The cyber realm has created new categories of belonging, and has questioned in particular the long-dominant nation-state identities. This brings our views to *postnationalism*, the outlook that examines the relative decline of the nation-state in terms of cultural identities, belongings, and performances. If who we *were* for the last couple of hundred years had been often expressed in national terms, postnationalism holds that the cyber realm, with its de-spatialized communications, has changed these discourses.

These changes bring pragmatic challenges: vested interests rarely fade peacefully away. For analogy, the ideology of the nation-state brought on by the revolutions of the printing press did not automatically dissolve the old aristocratic order; rather, the epochal changes were enacted with a great deal of struggle and bloodshed, and in some cases have never fully disappeared (as in the persistence of the United Kingdom's House of Lords). Similarly, the postnational changes in identity are not a claim that the nation-state will suddenly dissolve and disappear. Instead, they indicate profound struggles for controlling the future of identity and communications. This chapter investigates these processes, the intersections of culture and politics (writ large) in examining some of the tensions between large vested interests, and the emerging global realm of the netizen.

REVOLUTION 2.0

On January 25, 2011, citizens, protestors took to the streets of Egypt, demanding democracy and a change in regimes. An election held in November 2010 was largely denounced as a sham. The eighty-two-year-old leader and thirty-year autocrat, Hosni Mubarak, quickly moved to shut down the internet in an effort to counter such user-generated social networking sites such as Twitter and Facebook (see Ali 2011). Egyptians exploded in anger—who was he to control who they, the people, could speak with? There were appeals to the internet as a human right, and debates on those appeals.[1] After a week of the massive protests, the internet was restored in the hope of mollifying the community; some saw the move as a doomed ploy by the government to regain some semblance of authority. But the Egyptian people harbored no illusions about their national government; they were well aware of the wider world, and of issues such as freedom of the press, freedom of organization, freedom of religion, and true (rather than nominal) democracies. They were well-informed of global discourse. And more importantly, they were *participants* in this global discourse.

The events in Egypt were not an isolated national story, but rather part of a wider movement, quickly dubbed "Arab Spring." Occurring first in Tunisia in December 2010, but spreading quickly to other countries throughout the Arab world, populations erupted in the first world political uprising in which social media figured as a prominent constitutive factor in the revolution,[2] as well as in the public recognition of the discourse involved, before, during, and after the Tahir Square, Egypt (among other protests in various countries and/or locations). The world witnessed a global first: Revolution 2.0. While there have been previous organizations which made good use of global media in revolutions and social uprisings, such as the Zapatistas (see, for example, the account in Lindholm and Zuquete 2010), the events unfolding of a citizens' uprising against despotic national regimes nonetheless mark the first direct, successful political impact of Web 2.0 social networks. The implications of this are momentous: participatory culture and participatory social networks include global networks, the birth of a truly global discourse, and the birth of the postnational citizen.

In Egypt, before digital media, and especially the internet, communications were much more controlled. Under Mubarak's reign, Egypt had been under "Emergency Rules," suspending due process of law for over thirty years. Most "troublemakers" to the Mubarak system could be easily silenced by a brutal secret police force. Newspaper editors, television programmers, and the rest of the citizenry participated in this common game of hegemonic discourse, one that ultimately confined the knowledge of citizens by confining the media stories available to them, and very often with explicit and implicit exhortations to nationalism.

But now their citizens were using the internet to communicate, and the regimes lost control of the story. When the unlikely protests started, in reaction to those in nearby Tunisia, the Egyptian government identified the immediate threat of the internet: the ability for protestors to organize mass protests online. Unquestionably, it was this concern that motivated the Egyptian government to close all access to the internet at the first signs of civil unrest. Such a view makes sense from the standpoint of the despotic government, but the larger story may lay elsewhere: that being, their citizens became participants in a global discourse, no longer beholden to the nationally produced narratives. The move of the national government to deny them access to the global realm was no longer an acceptable possibility. Egyptians from all walks of life used the internet and engaged in discourse on a global scale. Who was Mubarak, or any national government, to deny them this? The emerging ideas in the global realm were more important (and more impressive) than the petty regional claims of the national dictators. The reign of national media, national stories, and national control of social discourse was annihilated—swept aside—in a simple shift of public discourse, and a refusal to submit from an overbearing version of the national.

A ham radio operator in the Egyptian desert was able to bypass the internet clampdown and get word out to other hobbyists via Morse code: "Internet not working. Police cars burning." Another sent out the message: "Today marks a great day for Egypt." The messages were relayed to the internet, and global internet-based groups such as Telecomix, Anonymous, and all sorts of others helped ensure that these dispatches remained circulating in the global discourse, bypassing the Egyptian national authorities (see, for an in-depth account, Ryan 2011[3]). When the protestors' demands were met, and Mubarak stepped down from power, the influence of such discourses were acknowledged and celebrated. Gamal Ibrahim, a jubilant young Egyptian father, named his child "Facebook Jamal Ibrahim," honoring the power of global social networks to provide a new life, and a new political way of living, for his daughter (Olivarez-Giles 2011).

A new global right—the right of free speech in a global discourse of the internet—may be a new ethical, civic, and political demand of our time. These ideas of global rights created by the internet highlight the important role of new identity relations between individuals and global discourse, mediated through the internet. It also suggests that new means of identity may be superseding national identities; with this comes profound implications for nation-states as *loci* for continuing political power in the world today. This is particularly relevant because many of the ways in which collective identity is being forged online are highly derived from individual interests (including occupational, hobbyist, political, ethno-national, local, religious, etc.).

THE MECHANICAL NATIONAL MEETS THE DIGITAL GLOBAL

Censorship used to be so easy. A nation only had so many printing presses churning out national books, newspapers, and magazines, so it was easy to know who had printed what. Shipments coming in from other countries could be stopped at the border by ominous-looking border guards who could inspect deliveries and prevent "dangerous foreign" texts from entering the country.

Increasingly, "keeping a lid on things" became difficult. Printing became cheaper, and more widespread. International trade, tourism, international agreements, satellite television, and various other developments all allowed people to gain more knowledge, and have more connections, to people in other nations. As mechanical technology improved, travel—of goods, people, and information—became much easier and more common. Along with these new international connections came increased global discourse, including on such issues as universal rights, democracy, freedom of press and religions. Diasporas became more common. Refugees, immigrants, and visitors traversed the world, creating complex overlaps of place and culture: San Francisco's Chinatown; Indian communities in Kenya. The pace of communication technology, linking far-flung parts of the world together, continued its astonishing developments: the telegraph transformed the world of its time, as did the radio and then television. The ideal of the nation-state was already creaking at the seams by the time of the arrival of the internet, which pushed globalizing, democratizing communications into hyper-speed.

To be sure, globalization and postmodernity are also economic transfor-mations, bringing people from widely separate geographies into business and economic relationships. Industrial production is increasingly global in production and consumption. Supra-national organizations of all kinds are also common. Tourism, currently the largest industry of the world,[4] continues to swirl together people and places, and thoughts thereof, at an increasing rate. Yet even with all these forces, it is the internet, and digitally based communication in general, which represent the most pronounced site of global participatory culture. This is precisely what makes the idea of the online culture inherently postnational, and, as such, a threat to despotic national governments. National governments used to be able to control much of the discourse of their citizens, and, therefore, what their citizens thought about the national governments. A recursive system was set between political control and control of discourse *about* politics; in a word, hegemony.

Through the promulgation of national languages, textbooks, national holidays and celebrations, official religions, national museums, and controls over print, radio, and television networks, national governments have long enjoyed a near-totalizing formation of geographically based discourses and "imagined communities" (in the famous phrase of Benedict Anderson 1991). This has been outmoded by the development of digital communications and the internet, which allows anyone in the world to share in the same discourse.

Subsequently, many nation-states have attempted to tighten controls on the internet, perhaps nowhere more famously so than China, where the "great firewall of China" is an enormous effort to exert state control over their citizen's digital discourses. It is easy to understand the motivations: the Chinese government is not democratically elected by the will of the people, and thus allowing citizens rights to free speech and free exchange of information is a threat to their continued existence. But to erect and sustain such a monumental project of monitoring and controlling the people's discourse requires an enormous amount of, for lack of a better word, spies (that is, people who are paid to monitor and control information). The great firewall of China is designed explicitly with the goal of national control of discourse, yet such a construction runs the danger of becoming a house of cards: a system built to protect itself, run by people who may no longer believe in it. In China, the great firewall has already been challenged by a brand-new creature, the grass mud horse.

THE GRASS MUD HORSE

Perhaps the most famous reaction against censorship in China (although far from the only one), the grass mud horse (*cao ni ma*) gained popularity via the internet in a series of videos. On the surface, it is a story that proposes new ancient mythic beasts, the "grass mud horses," who are peaceful grass eaters living in an idyllic territory invaded by the evil River Crabs.

The pointed joke is that the word used for "grass mud horse" is a close match for a rude obscenity (the only difference being between tonal variations) meaning, essentially, "fuck your mother," while the "river crabs" refer to censors. The message, coming from a nation chafing under despotic national control, is clear: the netizens, however "profane" they may be, are the heroes, while the censors, the vile River Crabs, are the villains.

The idea of the grass mud horse became enormously popular among China's netizens, with videos of an accompanying "folk songs" sung by children, alongside music videos and "documentaries." Rap songs portray the same song. Videos and other references proliferate. Toys of the "grass mud horse" (based on the alpaca) are hot sellers. The Chinese government now attempts to censor any mention of the grass mud horse (making itself look somewhat ridiculous, petty, and fearful, in the process), a move denounced by China's netizens as "another invasion of river crabs," but oblique references are now common and widely understood. This may have been another instance of locking the gate after the horses have bolted: henceforth. China's censors, active as they are, are represented in popular discourse as evil river crabs, destroying the idyllic life of the peaceful grass mud horse. And the story, too, predicts an ending: the crabs will be destroyed, with the grass mud horses emerging victorious.

GADDAFI SINGS ZENGA ZENGA

Another compelling internet sensation resulted from the 2011 uprising in Libya (also following the mass protests in Tunisia and Egypt). Head-of-state Muammar Gaddafi delivered a series of fiery threats to the protestors on state television, vowing to hunt them down "inch by inch, house by house, home by home, alleyway by alleyway." An Israeli DJ, Noy Alloshe, created a mashup of this excerpt of his speech with the music of "Hey Baby," by rapper Pitbull (and featuring T-Pain).[5] The song was adopted by the Libyan opposition, and requests flooded into Noy Alloshe from around the Arab world and abroad. Early on, some fans of the mashup asked him to create a second version, minus the scantily clad dancing girls of the first video (in order to be more acceptable to elderly, more conservative people), and he did so. Multiple versions have since appeared on YouTube, many from the Arabic world. The mashup was an enormous worldwide hit, with pointed political commentary. Gadaffi could not control the internet, and could not stop the parodies. The video was easy to copy and easy to spread around. Neither he nor his national government could control the story. Political control had to devolve to an almost medieval level of overt, brutal display of physical power through military force to try to maintain control.

"Zenga Zenga" was an enormous hit, enjoyed by an astonishing worldwide community of people, nearly three million in its first week alone. The aesthetic characteristics present the idea of control of representations moving away from despotic national regimes and national media, and instead, via the digital global realm of the internet, transmitted person to person, occasionally changed in the process. It is not so much what the video says against Gaddafi—after all, it uses his own words, even if they are indicative of his well-known and often-mocked violent ramblings—but rather that it wrests control away from him, and caricatures him in a way of the artist's choosing. The postnational aesthetic can also be seen in the worldwide spread of the video—although particularly popular in Libya, and other parts of the Arabic world, the viewership has been truly international.[6] Like the grass mud horse, the grassroots artistic efforts reveal a celebration of postnational identity, overlapping local and global, the "glocal"—something new in human history.[7]

Other autocratic nation-states have seen the writing on the wall, starting to preemptively assert control over online communications. For example, the Russian government has taken increasingly aggressive steps to control internet communication. In August 1, 2014, President Putin signed into law the requirement that "popular" bloggers must register with state authorities and comply with strict controls in terms of acceptable statements.

Within a year, it became clear that this law would apply to memes as well. On April 7, 2015, Roskomnadzor (Russia's state internet regulator) posted a reminder about the law on their home page on the popular Russian social network Vkontakte, stating that the law prohibited "using a photo of a public figure to embody a popular internet meme which has nothing to do with the celebrity's personality."[8] This reminder seemed to respond directly to the recent proliferation of memes featuring public figures, including, of course, Vladimir Putin. Although many of these memes were laudatory, the form of expression also allowed for easy expression of dissent in critical or sardonic memes. The popularity and ease of production and distribution of these images allowed for a much freer range of discourse than available from state-approved media outlets. Alongside restricting the memes themselves, such moves restrict everyday artistic communication in general.

A similar situation occurred in Turkey, where insulting the president is against the law. Dr. Bilgin Çiftçi, a physician, was arrested and put on trial for a meme that placed photos of the country's president, Recep Tayyip Erdogan, next to photos of Gollum, the creature from the *Lord of the Rings* movie series. Simply placing the photos next to each other was taken to be a crime, since it seemed to insultingly suggest a remarkable physical similarity between the two.[9]

In general, the more authoritarian nation-states are attempting to reinforce their control over their citizens' communication, particularly their international communications.

OTHER OWNERS

Nor are autocratic governments the only claimants to control the new everyday culture. Especially in capitalist societies, other large claimants towards ownership of online discourse are large media corporations.

Consider, for example, the case of the "socially awkward penguin." This meme is just one of the numerous everyday visual arts that people share, modify, and pass on. The image consists of a photo of a penguin, a marked blue triangular background, and various texts inserted over the top. There are hundreds if not thousands of varieties of "socially awkward penguin," most with a bipartite textual comment humorously regarding incidences of feeling socially awkward, e.g.:

> "Can't pronounce menu item / Doesn't order it."
> "Tries to jump in conversation / Gets completely ignored."
> "Looks away to avoid eye contact / Ends up making eye contact with someone else."

In 2015, Getty Images began a series of aggressive letters to various bloggers demanding money for the meme[10]. It turns out that the penguin in the image was taken from an image owned by Getty Images. Yet that image has been reused and recontextualized over and over again, thousands upon thousands of times, by all sorts of everyday users, using the meme to discuss life. Getty Images appears to employ automatic searches to try to find and target users of their images, and it appears to be, for them, a lucrative endeavor.[11]

While this is, perhaps, a silly example, it is meant as an illustration how even those using the most nonconfrontational examples of everyday art are still threatened by claims of illegality. The idea that trivial, jovial artistic communications between people should be subject to criminal prosecutions should be frightening to anyone.[12]

OWNING CULTURE

As the examples in the sections above seek to demonstrate, there are powerful claimants towards ownership of culture, most notably governments and corporations. These two groups are often in bitter disputes with the general populace of global internet users over the ownership of cultural expressions.

The assertions of proprietary claims are interwoven in overall cultural discourses regarding originality and authorship. Most of the arguments claiming corporate ownership of culture stem from modernity's long involvement with mechanical reproduction of culture, and the (linked) development of the nation-state. To a great degree, the crisis surrounding ownership of culture stems from the differences between these two epochs: the digital versus the mechanical, the global versus the national, and the postmodern versus the modern.

The legal claims of the ownership of culture are expanding dramatically, at the same time when more and more culture is being shared freely. This is the battle for the future of human culture—whose culture is it? Who gets to say? The question has already toppled dictatorships, and has met fierce reaction from insecure autocracies around the world. Corporate control of expressive culture—both of media corporations and governments—is profound, and simultaneously, is being profoundly challenged. Technology outpaces limits placed on it, and the people of the world want to communicate freely.

MODERNITY IN HINDSIGHT: CYBERFOLK AND
THE GUTENBERG PARENTHESIS

In the folkloric model, culture is created via interpersonal sharing: a story is heard and then repeated later. This allows folklore to constantly be adapted to new times, new situations, and new groups. My own definition of folklore is that folklore is "the stuff we learn from other people," which is to say, not from books or from formal institutions. Folklore is replicated through performances, and that this process ensures that folklore continues to change, adapt, and mutate. This slipperiness and changeability of folklore is precisely its greatest strength. Unlike literature, folklore is always contemporary, always current.[13]

When ordinary people began using the internet for their daily lives, folklorists quickly noted the amount of folklore that people were sharing (see e.g., Kirshenblatt-Gimblett 1995). Urban legends spread like wildfire. This early trend followed pace with the explosion of digital communications around the turn of the millennium. Many younger folklorists focused their research efforts more and more on online folklore, noting the ways in which scholars can view much of the online communication as inherently folkloric in nature. This allowed folklorists to be able to use many of their usual disciplinary tools, theoretical outlooks, and approaches.

Other scholars have also taken note of vast changes in the modes of communication in the digital age: University of Southern Denmark professor Lars Ole Sauerberg offered the phrase the "Gutenberg parenthesis" to describe that brief 500-year period when culture was influenced by mechanical reproduction. This phrase has given prominence in the work of his colleague, literary and cultural historian Thomas Pettitt, and has now become used by numerous scholars as a way of thinking of digital communication (see Pettitt 2010)[14]. The phrase captures a view of modernity in hindsight: the impact of the Gutenberg era, and its replacement by digital communications. Converging on the same conclusion as folklorists, Pettitt proposed viewing the emerging online culture as a "secondary orality" (as per Ong 1982). "Orality" may be a bit misleading, since not all folklore is oral, and since so much of internet culture is also visual. In 2012, folklorist Anthony Buccitelli investigated how digital performances may be a better fit for the category of "folk objects" than for orality, due to the temporal "stickiness" of both folk objects and internet communications. Another key difference between cyber lore and traditional folklore is that in cyberlore, performer and the audience may be (and often are) at opposite sides of the world. Space is often re-imagined online (for a theoretical perspective, see Buccitelli 2013).

Still, this postmodern, digital, form of culture is noticeably folkloric in its "multiplicity and variation," loose sense of authorship, acknowledgment of collective creativity, and general ways in which the culture is shared in a largely non-hierarchical sense. Memes and mashups both display a form of "folk visual art" in their communicative processes[15]. The debates that surround the ideas of free expression, or the lack thereof, result from the tension between models of folkloric communication and those based on models of authorship, descending from modernity and the Gutenberg era.

COPYRIGHTS AND WRONGS

At the present moment, images of all of Renoir's paintings are—and always have been—free to use, but the socially awkward penguin, taken from an obscure photograph, is not.

The history of this legal difference stems from the introduction of the copyright regime during late modernity. Copyright emerged in England as part of the "royal charter" system of allowing business monopolies. Early on, copyright was mostly limited to books, providing limited monopolies for limited time to a small amount of commercial printing ventures. Over time, more and more parts of culture were granted copyright. Copyright has become a tremendously big business, potentially covering most of what can reasonably be described as human culture.

The copyright regime was enacted to limit publishers in terms of what they could reproduce. "But with the birth of the Internet, this natural limit to the reach of the law has disappeared. The law controls not just the creativity of commercial creators but effectively that of anyone" (Lessig 2004: 19). Prompted by the money to be made via copyright claims and the growth of the culture industries, copyright claims themselves grew, and grew, and grew. Now implied in copyright is ownership not just of the item, but also of the art, the image, and ultimately the very idea, itself. At this point in time, in the US, any creative thing one crafts is automatically assumed to be copyrighted, even a doodle on scrap piece of paper or graffiti scrawled on a bathroom wall.[16]

Such formulations have at their root a belief in originality, which is to say a belief that the origins of creative expressions are singular, and to be located within a singular individual. Yet, as Valdimar Hafstein proposes, we can instead view each performance in terms of both tradition and novelty, a sliding scale of originality that acknowledges the act of "creative copying" as well as "social creativity" (2004). Opposing "traditional" and "original" then (the cornerstone of "literature versus folkore") is revealed to be a false dichotomy, infused with cultural value statements (originality good; traditionality bad). Because of the differing philosophical assumptions, this more complex view of the process of artistry as being expressed on a continuum of creativity does not fit well within the copyright regime as a whole. One either has copyright or one does not: copyright is always expressed in absolute, binary terms of cultural production.

The emerging mashup culture, therefore, is inherently a difficult match for the expanding legal regime of copyright derived from the printing press. As Lessig put it, "There has never been a time in our history when more of our 'culture' was as 'owned' as it is now" (2004: 12).

STATE PROPERTY: "PROTECTING HERITAGE"

In addition to outright censorship and enforcement of prevailing copyright regimes for the purpose of the culture industries, the nation-states have one more arrow in the quiver for proprietary claims for owning culture: heritage. Heritage is an assertion of a particular inherited proprietary relation to culture, often through the prism of ethno-nationalist strains of governance.

"Heritage" is an up-and-coming word which has generated an enormous amount of literature, legislation, and funding in recent years and has been investigated by numerous legal, political, social, and cultural scholars.[17] While the concept of "world heritage" does allow for global claims for culture, the heritage regime instead more often embraces the ideology that the "heritage of" means a specific—usually corporate—group. Heritage invokes the idea of inheritance, and being an heir, and this connects legalistic claims to culture. This takes particular rhetorical form in the case of tangible heritage—items claimed to "belong" intrinsically to one nation-state—and takes an even more extreme rhetoric when applied to the category of "intangible heritage," claims for the intrinsic ownership of cultural practices. In this rhetorical and governmental move, past cultural practices are turned into ownable objects. The major assertions are brought forth by governmental groups—primarily nation-states—and followed up in their international discourses, such as the United Nations, which has strongly supported these ideas. Corporate industries, most notably WIPO (World Intellectual Property Organization), have been deeply involved with furthering these legalistic developments.

Thus, nation-states are increasingly claiming ownership of "their" culture. Yet what "their" culture is remains highly contestable and contested[18]. Consider the case of Nigeria, one of the most ardent followers of the UN recommendations (as are several other African countries). According to Nigerian law, one must obtain permission from the federal government in order to "publish," "distribute," or "reproduce" folklore (for an extended discussion on this, see Kuruk 1999). Given that folklore includes genres ranging from epics to proverbs to dirty jokes, the sweeping claims of government ownership are breathtaking. Even attempting to shoehorn such institutional claims into the problematic discourse of romantic nationalism proves to be difficult. Nigeria, for example, is the home of over 500 ethnic groups, 500 linguistic groups, and a variety of religious groups, many of which also traditionally exist in bordering nation-states as well. Who owns Hausa folklore, therefore, is necessarily a battleground for contention: Nigeria? Niger? Or any of the many countries in West Africa with a sizable Hausa population?

Or one could look at the illustration of a similar case of Azerbaijan, which has laws very similar to that of Nigeria. Azerbaijan has been locked in disputes with neighboring Armenia regarding ownership of cultural forms, trading official accusations of "heritage theft" over such issues as publications of cookbooks,[19] folk music, fairy tales, and so forth.[20] In 2010, the Azerbaijan copyright agency posted an article on its own website, "Stealing of Azerbaijan culture and morality samples by Armenians." In 2014, the country sent a list of "offending examples" of "heritage theft" to several international organizations.[21] By the spring of 2015, the conflict between the states (particularly the disputed Nagorno-Karabakh region) boiled over into bloodshed. The overlap between this vociferous discourse over heritage, and the military conflicts resulting in blood spilled and lives lost, cannot be ignored.

Viewed in these practical terms, the "heritage regime" is yet another owner-ship claim: the idea that a particular corporate body (usually a state) owns the right to use and reproduce the culture. And, unlike even the most restrictive forms of copyright, there is no proposed end date for heritage claims—no mat-ter how widespread the culture may become, the logic of heritage, or owning folklore, extends in perpetuity. The ownership of culture is moved from an individual, or group, and into the nation-state system of governance. Nation-states are expanding these ownership claims even as the relative coherency of the nation-state as a locus of political representation is in decline.

If, as per Benedict Anderson's famous claim (1991), "print-nationalism" cre-ated the modern nation-state model (through standardized national languages, print controls, the production of national news, censorship, and the like), the internet has enabled global communication and the rise of sharing communi-cation with far-flung individuals. Hence, the rise of the importance in "national heritage" can be seen in opposition to the ongoing globalizing tendencies of human culture. Likewise, the increased claims of "national heritage" can be seen as a rearguard action against the epochal changes in human culture, and a structural decrease in the importance of the nation-state, generally.[22]

FUTURE POSSIBILITIES FOR EARTHLING CULTURE

A 2016 BBC survey indicates that most people in the world now identify as "global citizens" rather than national ones.[23] This is a trend to watch, but it makes complete sense: politics follows communication. Communications establish communities, and communities constitute political bodies. The rise of global discourse foretells the rise of global identities, including global politi-cal identities.

Directly following the remarkable successes of the Arab Spring movement in toppling long-standing autocratic regimes, many scholars began to theorize internet access as a new, fundamental human right. A UN commission specifi-cally made the recommendation that access to the internet should be declared and considered a "fundamental human right."[24] Yet what is "access" without "engagement"? Accessing only official information would move directly against the heart of the issue, which is the right of people to communicate freely via the internet, globally.

The shadow side to proprietary claims to culture, is, of course, the creation of the category of illegal art. What are the implications of art being controlled by elite, moneyed forces, and forbidden to the people in their everyday communications? How can people try to imagine a future world if their art is deemed illegal, their artists as criminals, and their everyday expressive communications increasingly owned by large corporate groups?

Artistic communication and performance are the building blocks of group identity. While the culture industries still exist in the new, mediated world, they are no longer the predominant form of cultural distribution. The majority of culture consumed in the world has quickly shifted from a hierarchical model of the culture industries and nation-state governments towards the folkloric model of vernacular participatory culture, mirroring the epochal shift from mechanical to digital modes of communication. The battle over these two modes is a battle over the very nature of culture, and for the future for humanity. Will our culture's everyday artistic communication be increasingly free, or increasingly owned? And, if owned, by whom?

REPRESENTATION AND THE FUTURE OF AUTHORITY

Who controls the story? *Qui parle?*, as the French say? If we admit the tremendous power of narratives in shaping social reality, then we must investigate how the larger, unifying stories are formed and influenced in order to fully understand how societies work. In ancient Egypt, rulers would periodically enforce a retroactive censorship, removing all evidence of a particular ruler, or even of whole historical periods. Historical records inscribed in hieroglyphs in the temple areas were chiseled away, literally stricken from the record. During the periods of literature, periodic purges of past material have been common, as different ancients came in and out of favor—and where there were few copies, destruction was often more complete. Many times, as folklorists are well aware, such repressed lore would live on in oral traditions, even (and perhaps especially) when forbidden or purged from the literary realm, only to sometimes re-enter that realm later on.

During the Medieval era, prefiguring the modern, literacy was a tool of the political establishment and, even more so, of the Church. Yet the reality of Europe's Medieval, and largely nonliterate, society, was that it was a constant struggle of the church and the political leaders to control the grand narratives of society *vis à vis* the robust role that oral lore played among the populace. The explosion of literacy after the development of the printing press propelled the role of literature in transforming society and organizing large-scale national identities in previously unimaginable ways. National governments were quick to become major factors in setting the "grand narratives" (as per Lyotard 1982) as whole citizenry identities were established through national education systems, national museums, national press, standardized national languages, and the like.

ENTER THE NETIZEN

"Netizen," I would argue, is a particularly apt term for describing the move into global discourse mediated by digital technology. The term itself is a global one, particularly popular in Argentina, and in several Asian countries, such as South Korea, Singapore, and China—reflecting the far-flung Pacific nations. Increasingly, however, the word is being used by people around the world, rapidly appearing with ever more frequency in newspapers and other media.[25]

"Netizen" is a conscious reworking of the term "citizen," and as such contains claims of political and social identity. If the "citizen" descended from ideas of civic social realities (participations, obligations, and the like), then what has been shifted is not so much these fundamental ideas and ideals, but rather their scope and locale. This is not entirely new, either: long before current ideas of citizenship, the ancient Greeks held that the idea of citizens applied only to city-states and the community-led governments by elite aristocratic men, representing the noble lineages. The Romans made great use of the Greek ideas of community and civilization, and the notion of "the citizen" grew along with the Roman empire, creating differing levels of belonging at different times over its history. In the Medieval period, people in many towns and cities often regarded themselves as *citizens*—with rights and privileges, as well as obligations—to the local town or city. This is the direct predecessor of the idea that the "national citizen," and the concept was expanded alongside the idea of the "national community." Efforts to formulate an idea of *international* citizenry still rely on the nation-state as the primary locus of political belonging (see Archibugi 2008).

Contrary to this formation, a netizen sees social and political discourse as via the internet rather than via national media, and the place of social interaction as global rather than national or even international. As historian Mark Poster asserts, "nation-states are losing their cultural coherence by dint of planetary communications systems" (2002: 98). Poster also sees that "the political formation of the netizen is already well under way, bringing forth [. . .] a humanity adhering not to nature but to machines, not to geographically local identity, but to the digitized packets of its own electronic communication" (103).

Netizens are in touch with each other, however physically separated they may or may not be. In this way, these online forums manage to help folk groups form new identities, ideologies, and political sensibilities.

The idea of citizenship as participation in public life has moved from the local, to the national, and now to the global. But how is this new participatory culture constructed? If the division is not territorially based, what constitutes the various levels of membership and participation? This is where a folkloristic approach may be useful, especially in examining the relationship between groups of participants and group identity, or analyzing a social group in terms of its performances.[26] Folklore is enjoying a tremendous renaissance online. Without question, online folk groups have become important in establishing new forms and thoughts of identity. This presents folklorists with a vital task: the opportunity to document the tremendous growth of new social and cultural networks. But what are the contents and contours of such expressive culture? Who takes part, and to what degree, and in what groups? All of these, and more, are useful questions to search for insight into the ways that the new netizen identity is being constituted.

CHANGES AND IMPLICATIONS

Increasingly, the notion of place as a solid foundation for culture and political representation has become contested. The same technological advances that brought the printing press and modern nation-states also enabled large-scale population movements, both by choice and not, a trend that has only intensified over time. As anthropologists Akil Gupta and James Ferguson (1992) explain:

> Both the ethnological and national naturalisms present associations of people and place as solid, commonsensical, and agreed-upon, when they are in fact contested, uncertain, and in flux. (12)

One of the main ways in which the concept of the netizen is challenging the formerly supreme nation-state is by altering the fundamental ways in which people interact with place, and the long-standing tendency to equate culture, and hence identity, with geography. If modernity was based on the individual and the national, then postmodernity has given new questions to these formerly accepted bases of personal, civic, and political identity. There is still, to be sure, the local: the actual space that one inhabits and in which one participates. You can always talk to a neighbor about the weather, no matter where you are in the world. The local remains powerful, yet it co-exists at the same time with a new discourse of the internet. The local and the global overlap, and easily so, giving us the increasingly useful neologism of the *glocal*. The glocal describes the ways that local groups link to international societies, often leapfrogging over national concerns. But the local is no longer the only realm of folklore groups; both place and other earlier forms of identity instead exist as various *imaginaires* online, within which one can evoke identity discourses, or not.

It is true that one can still speak of a "digital divide" between the haves and the have-nots inhabiting this online agora, yet the massive expansion of the digital communications have been a major democratizing influence on global discourse, swiftly empowering many previously excluded peoples and groups to voice their concerns and opinions. Digital communications have spread into many places that never witnessed electricity, and are surely one of the most dramatic makeovers the planet has witnessed in terms of human communication, and hence, human society. Places that were never before modern can now be postmodern, and tribal groups and others who have remained outside modernity and nationalism are often now eager participants in this new global discourse. Elders can now be videoed telling oral stories in languages never written; the stories then can be shared with the world at large. In many uneducated slums, street youths teach one another to be literate through their self-learned media proficiency.[27] And throughout much of the third world, cell phones have become ubiquitous,[28] linking the user to the larger global media networks of the internet. World affairs now can easily become everyone's affairs.

We may be witnessing for the first time the development of a truly new sense of citizenry, pointing the way for future global (or glocal) governance. Yet this would suggest a vastly different structure than the United Nations, a group that is built on the predominance of the nation-state in world affairs. Grass mud horses and rapping dictators may reveal a sense of frustration at the vast world netizenry against what is perhaps perceived as the dangerous, often violent quarrels of nationalism.

CONCLUSIONS

The *vox populi* is now being heard loud and clear, as never before.

The emergence of folk groups online, sharing folklore and participatory culture, brings with it a renewed importance of folklore studies, generally. After all, for over 200 years, folklore studies has cultivated an expertise in the study of communally created shared culture, as well as the relationship between such participatory culture and identity. Identities are forged, confirmed, and celebrated in large part through shared expressive culture, and the social contexts of such performances are important. The digital realm allows an individual to have a corporal, local experience as well as a digital, virtual social life. It is important to note that the corporeal still implies face-to-face interactions and the importance of locale, while the digital does neither. And the two may often overlap: the local frequently plays a vigorous role in the online world. Importantly, what is eclipsed in this emergent discourse is a need for the nation-state as a locus of representation, and by extension, citizenry. National territory, the "imagined community," fades in relevance in this newly emerging discourse.

With postmodernity in full bloom, postnational aesthetics are on the rise, signaling, in my interpretation, an emergent sense of global identities and global citizenry, with consequences for understanding an ongoing revolution in the philosophy of global civics, political identity and representation. This is not to say that the nation-state is likely to disappear overnight. The nation-states still control resources, and armies, print money, and the like. Yet, as discourse globalizes, the nation-states seem to be moving together as well, joined through various organizations ranging from the United Nations and international law to nongovernmental organizations such as Doctors without Borders. The European Union promulgates law for its "sovereign" nation-state members, and various such supra-national groups connect nations in an overlapping web of regions and interests.

Further, the nation-state will most certainly continue to be a strongly held source of identity, even in its *imaginaire* state online: already one can witness online "nations" of dispossessed peoples. In the transnational world of vast diasporas and worldwide flow of peoples, the idea of the nation-state may still remain an important "imagined community" for many people, blending with the ideas of "homelands" and the other geographical *imaginaires.*

Yet, alongside the development of the global agora, there are many more sources of identity besides the national available, and people will likely increasingly identify themselves in strikingly postnational terms. The tensions between the national interests, and the emergent folk groups online, is already one of the most dramatic of the emergent postmodern world. The questions concern nothing less than the future of identity: who will our children/grandchildren consider themselves to be? We might like to assume that identities are fixed, but history shows us this is an error. In times of great societal flux, in particular in great shifts of communicative technologies, identity itself has become open for questioning and for change.

In order to improve our understanding of this emerging situation for human culture, we must examine this new folklore and its emerging aesthetics—who is sharing, who is performing, what do they perform, and what does it mean to them? It is the same old field of folklore studies, albeit in new contexts, and with critically heightened importance. In this way, the study of online folklore—"folklore 2.0"—may help us to understand these new identities, which in turn may be the grounds for new political representations and philosophies.

Communication builds groups. Forms of communication create forms of political groups. The age of the nation-state relied on print technology and mechanical culture to push the nation-state as the dominant locus of political power and representation in the world (as the current supreme global organization, the United Nations, makes explicit).

Now, we have entered a new age of humanity, one relying on digital communications. Digital communications are notable for fostering global discourses, and hence global political thinking. Along with all the tremendous social and political change brought by these new technologies (including the toppling of several dictatorships), the world recently witnessed the introduction of a brand new global human right: the right of internet access (as the UN report committee has already recognized). Every person's voice, it seems, should be able to be heard in the forum. The rights of the netizen, the first truly global citizenry, are being formulated and proclaimed. Multitudes of new groups, new social formations, and new identities are being formed. The postnational glocal models of citizenship and politics will have to grapple with the reorganizing of our societies and philosophies, in building a new future for humanity.

Any investigation of cyborg identity must recognize the global (or glocal) components, which sharply reduce the ontological impacts of the nation-state, national identity, and the ethnic and/or "tribal" identities out of which the nation-state grew. Belonging and citizenship—the "political body"—are being reshaped globally. Posthumans, it seems, are also postnationals.

PART 3

US AND THEM: RE-IMAGINING ONTOLOGY IN THE CYBORG AGE

Part three examines the emerging posthuman identities in such figures as trolls, ghosts, aliens, androids, and AI. These figures are our *others*: those that are *not* us. "Others" can reveal much about the human condition. Ghosts, for example, clearly reflect core ontological philosophies: what is that nonmaterial part that makes us *us*?

From a folkloric perspective, supernatural others are always a revealing category of beliefs for a society: what we fear, or hope for, provides insight into the hearts and minds of diverse cultural perspectives. We imagine who we are by imagining who we are *not*: in doing so, our supernatural others cast shadows revealing our vernacular ontologies. The next three chapters examine a variety of "others" in hopes of illuminating the unconscious discourses of vernacular posthumanism.

7

GH**O**ST ST**O**RIES FR**O**M THE UN**C**ANNY VALLEY

Androids, Souls, and the Future of Being Haunted

The introduction of artificial intelligence (AI) problematizes our discrete categorizations of folklore and folk groups. As humans interact with AI more and more, folklorists must ask to what degree is AI a part of our social and cultural worlds? To what degree will we become cyborgs, fusions of human and technology, and to what degree will we allow for nonhuman actors to be a part of our social networks?

This process will doubtless take many forms. This chapter considers AI as embodied in robots, commonly called androids,[1] and proposes that as androids and artificial intelligences become increasingly prevalent, our understanding of personhood will be necessarily expanded. So, too, will our understanding of personhood after death: we will soon find ourselves haunted by their ghosts. Ghost stories have been studied heavily throughout the history of the discipline of folklore (perhaps most notably during the time of Andrew Lang in the British Folklore Society), but it now appears we are quickly approaching a new era in ghosts. This chapter offers a view of posthuman personhood by examining the more specific possibility of android ghosts. Importantly, this is a genre of folklore which has not yet materialized; this chapter offers a decidedly futurist outlook, examining ghosts that have yet to materialize but which may be reasonably anticipated. Further, this chapter argues that such future ghosts can be useful guides in crafting new philosophies of "android ethics," to avoid being haunted by our ethical failures. Utilizing folkloristic knowledge about ghosts, liminality, and personhood, we can prepare for the vast cultural changes heralded by current technological developments, and the subsequent challenges to our ethical systems, by viewing the possibility that expanded views of personhood will give rise to new spirits that haunt us.

FOLKLORE AS FUTURISM

Currently, the role of folklorist does not commonly overlap with that of "futurist." Folklore is, rather, often associated with the past and past traditions, and it has only recently (and partially) moved towards a study of contemporary cultural phenomena. It is therefore unfamiliar for folklorists to move away from certainties to consider possibilities and trajectories. At the same time, other disciplines such as economics or climatology are often explicitly futurist in their orientation.[2] This chapter takes up this kind of futurist approach, investigating trajectories and likely futures in folklore, rather than establishing and examining folk culture as a *fait accompli*.

Futurism is most commonly associated with science fiction, the realm of authored literature, rather than folklore. Yet, while folklorists have not often played the role of futurist, there are many traditional takes on futuristic thought, and much of the sci-fi realm has been reworked by vernacular means. Think, for example, of mythic narratives of the end of the world, including not only the biblical apocalypse but many other mythological "end times" as well (Wojcik 1997). Prophecies and fortune-telling have also long been a staple of folkloristic discourse (Simpson 1978; Silverman 1988; Mould 2003, 2005; O'Brien forthcoming). From this vantage point, we might plausibly assert that folklore has been involved with the future since its beginnings.

Given that we have long studied the ways that cultures perceive and predict future events, folklorists should not shy away from taking on the new role of futurists, bringing our insights to predict, plan for, and shape the swiftly oncoming future. Folklorists-as-futurists can have important roles in collaborating with the developers of technology, to help them become aware of the social and cultural implications of the introduction of these technologies on our communities, families, and lives.

THE UNCANNY VALLEY: GHOSTS, ANDROIDS, AND US

The "uncanny valley" is a term that appears frequently in android literature. The term refers to the perception of things that are human-like in appearance, but not human. These can include various entities, including monkeys, dolls, corpses, animals, animations, reflections, robots, and, increasingly, androids. The use of the term "uncanny valley" was introduced into the android literature by Masahiro Mori as *Bukimi no Tani Genshō* in 1970. According to the author, the "uncanny valley" presents a hurdle for android developers to overcome, since the goal of android production is to create socially acceptable computer interfaces. As developers near the production of human-looking interfaces, people's reactions to the interfaces become increasingly unnerved. They describe the creations in terms often reserved for the supernatural: androids are "creepy," "spooky," or otherwise unsettling. The term has gained widespread currency in many areas of modern society. For example, reviews of computer-animated movies have sometimes described them as too realistic to be enjoyable; instead they are "creepy" and "unsettling."[3]

The goal for many android developers has been to avoid this problem, either by creating clearly-not-human androids (ranging from dog-like Aibos to robot-looking automatons), or, more ambitiously, to produce androids that are close enough to humans to escape the uncanny valley on the other side, to be perceived as members of the human social group. At the same time, androids are also taking on increasingly social functions, serving in roles such as hotel concierge, shop assistant, elder care, and school teacher, just to name a few (Robertson 2018).

As androids become more human-like in both appearance and action, the question of their personhood status becomes increasingly important to understand. Legal and ethical issues abound from the introduction of androids in contemporary society. Androids increasingly look like us, and act like us, including performing actions based on ethical considerations. As androids become ethical beings, humans have also reflected upon our ethical obligation toward them.[4] One way for folklorists to contribute to this discussion is through our investigations of vernacular concepts of personhood and ethical values. One key way that folklorists have historically explored this issue is through the study of stories about ghosts, the wronged souls that haunt our present lives. In order to understand the changing values around the personhood of androids, therefore, it is useful to consider what android ghosts might look like.

Ghosts, or spirits of the deceased who remain in the human realm, are frequently found in legends, mythology, folk beliefs, rituals, and a wide swath of other genres as well. Inquiries into ghost belief reveal a wide range throughout time and around the world. Most (though not all) cultures believe in something close to the contemporary English-language definition of the word "ghost": an active spirit of the dead (Valk 2018; Bennett 2009).[5]

Although not universal, ghost stories can be said to be one of the more widespread genres and belief systems throughout the world. As such, their commonalities and differences make interesting data to analyze in order to understand cultural differences in the concepts of personhood and the soul, and correspondingly about human value systems. By examining how ghosts operate in various cultural settings, we can better understand what it means to be human and behave ethically. Important studies of ghosts have focused on many societies throughout history, including Ancient Egypt (Ikram 2003), Greece (Johnston 1999), Rome (Felton 1999), feudal Japan (Shimazaki 2016), Medieval Europe (Schmitt 1998), contemporary Japan (Iwasaka and Toelken 1994), Yup'ik Eskimo (Cusack-McVeigh 2017), contemporary England (Bennett 1999), contemporary Estonia (Valk 2006), college campuses (Tucker 2007), and many more.

Ideas of ghosts have long been entwined with ideas of personhood and the soul. Ancient Egyptians conceived of the soul as having five parts, while many West African religions conceive of two. Some traditions place a strong degree on earthbound kinship relations continuing into the spirit realm, for example in Confucian notions of filial piety. Just as many societies have distinct ideas about souls achieving an afterlife, such ideas often open up the possibilities of *failure* for spirits to cross into the appropriate spirit realm—which is to say, the possibility of becoming a haunting ghost.

Ghost belief can also be studied in the context of social change. For example, Johnson (1999) demonstrated how classical Greek society increasingly embraced an active role for ghosts while simultaneously becoming less religious and more scientific. In a different case, Martin Luther's call for abandoning the sale of indulgences pivoted on the role of ghosts in the Church's doctrine of purgatory (see Schmitt 1998; Bachi 2012).[6] As societies change, their ghost stories do, too.

GHOST STORIES AND ETHICS

In trying to assess whether androids can become ghosts, we can also turn to another stream of posthumanist thinking and consider the case of nonhuman animals. Abrahamic faith traditions have few ghost stories concerning nonhuman animals, and the ones that do occur are invariably of household pets.[7] Wild animals and stock animals are held to be soulless, and hence do not produce ghosts, even when their deaths occur under the most disrespectful circumstances. But one *would* find animal ghosts in most other faith traditions, including those of Japanese, Indian, and Native American groups. These traditions, divergent though they are, agree that souls are inherent in other beings besides humans, and therefore require humans to behave ethically towards both human and nonhuman life forms.

In many Native American societies, the lack of proper respect towards animals (for example, killing more than you need, or neglecting to use all of the animal, or forgoing requisite funerary rituals) could result in vengeful animal ghosts. The role of the shaman in these traditions is often deeply tied to this possibility; among a shaman's main functions is to attempt to placate the angry spirits of dead animals who have been disrespected, in order to restore balance between the human world and the world of the animal spirits (Jakobsen 1999).

The idea of human ghosts relies on the ideas of human spirits since ghosts are the spirits, or souls, of deceased biological entities. Likewise, nonhuman animal ghosts indicate a belief in nonhuman animal spirits. The same rubric likely applies to androids as well. Ideas about proper or ethical behavior are frequently reflected in all ghost stories, since the production of ghosts is linked to its opposite: ghosts display the "shadow" of ethics by haunting individuals and communities with past ethical failures. In many Native American traditions, reciprocity with the lived environment is of clear importance to leading an ethical life, since violations of this reciprocity result in harmful ghosts.[8] In ways such as this, studying ghost stories can be a means towards understanding ethical systems, ontologies, and ideas of personhood, necessary components for understanding android ghosts.

Ghost stories often give voice to the oppressed and morally wronged; the failure to successfully move into the afterlife and the reason for hauntings can also be tied to harm experienced during life, not just disrespect during or after death. For example, in patriarchal Japan, the "hungry ghost" is stereotypically female, and is often caused by moral injustices committed against a woman when she is living. In the US, studies of ghosts of college campuses often record stories of the "jilted bride" (never a jilted groom) who commits suicide before becoming a ghost.[9]

Wronged ethnicities or other groups are also often seen as expressing their grievances from beyond the grave. In the US folklore, Native Americans frequently appear as ghosts (think of the classic "building on haunted Native American burial grounds"), as do African Americans, particularly in the South. Other groups, such as post-famine Irish immigrants, also appear in ghost stories that reflect their victimization.[10] Examples such as these demonstrate the ways that the US is still "haunted" by its unresolved past of xenophobia and violence that continues into the present. Ghost stories thus present an alternative history of the oppressed, often in direct opposition to official histories, which are written by the victors.

In such ways, ghost stories remind us of past moral transgressions, and convey a sense of ethical duty and awareness. Such narratives imply an ethics that transcends death, rather than one that is merely pragmatic. They are also often hopeful, in the sense that wrongs committed in the past can, at times, be atoned for and forgiven, if the proper steps are taken. Ghosts can cease haunting us, but something has to change for that to happen.

LIMINAL GHOSTS AND FUTURE WAYS OF BEING

Ghosts have been described as liminal figures *par excellence* (Valk 2018). For folklorists, the liminal not only is "where the magic happens," but is also the place where contestations and shifting categories allow for new categorizations, new ontologies. Liminality, with this betwixt-and-between status, is a productive concept for dealing with ghosts—ghosts are not really alive but not really dead; from the past but encountered in the present; in the world but often not fully corporeal; human but not. The idea of the liminal is also productive in considering androids, cyborgs, and other denizens of the uncanny valley, who seem to fall somewhere in the gray zone between objects and people. Finally, the concept of the liminal is a useful way to think of our rapidly changing society. We find ourselves in the midst of becoming. We are clearly moving into a new era, but what we will transform into is still far from certain.

I first became interested in the topic of android ghosts as I was teaching my undergraduate class on "Ghost Stories: Throughout Time and Around the World." The class focuses on various ways that different cultures feature ghosts, and it is a way to introduce some lessons on cultural relativity, religious diversity, and folklore. During the course, I ask students to make their own contributions to the corpus of ghost stories, both to USC's Digital Folklore Archives (folklore.usc.edu) and in a live performance to the class. Over the last ten years, I have noticed a distinct change in the everyday cultural experiences of my students; increasingly, their lives are lived out through digital technologies, through text messages, Facebook posts, Instagram photos, and more. Likewise, their ghost stories increasingly mention being haunted in these very same electronic spaces. Students typically collect two ghost stories for the Digital Folklore Archives; in 2017, 34 percent of stories submitted by students were cyber-ghost stories.

A typical example of the stories my students collect is the following third-person account:

> In high school, one of his best friends had committed suicide. He then began to receive text messages from the friend, repeatedly, from a supposedly non-existent number. The messages included private, personal details, and continued until the friend's funeral, when my informant said all the texts suddenly stopped. (student presentation 2017)

Text messages from the beyond, haunted servers, and ghosts operating through computers and Wi-Fi networks have become a staple in many of my students' lives. The 2015 ghost movie *Unfriended* followed this theme, delivering a story where a ghost haunts a Skype channel, killing people responsible for her suicide.

Folklorists such as Montana Miller (2007) and Robert Dobler (2009) have detailed the rise of memorial sites online. In these spaces, dead people still receive updates and messages from their living friends, maintaining their presence in the community in a way similar to what gravestones or letters to the dead would have done in the past. In these cases, it is not that ghosts have moved into cyberspace—I have not collected anything that would indicate that ghosts older than the internet have found their way there—but rather that *we*, as people, have moved into the cyber realm, and are now therefore connecting with the dead in these spaces. As our identities and lived experiences have merged with the digital, so too have our souls after death.

ANDROIDS AND GHOSTS IN JAPAN

Androids are just beginning to make their presence felt in human society. As they become more common and socially integrated, we can reasonably anticipate a similar shift to take place. To explore the question of what will happen when an android dies, I did fieldwork among androids and android developers in the United States. It quickly became apparent to me that although androids are an increasingly common phenomenon in much of the world, there is one clear current leader in the development and use of androids: Japan. A confluence of reliance on nonhuman actors and the allowance for nonhuman souls has eased the integration and proliferation of androids within Japanese culture and society. Japan has long been an industrial and technological leader, replete with an active democratic system of government influenced by the United States during the rebuilding of Japan after its defeat in World War II. During the breakneck development of digital communication technologies,

Japan emerged as an early leader, innovator, and adopter. However, unlike many other industrialized nations, Japan's religious traditions are still vibrant and still distinct from the Abrahamic religions that dominate in most of the rest of the developed world. While Abrahamic traditions have strongly anthropo-centric ideas of the numinous, reflected in the tenet that only humans have souls, Japan's religious makeup is a complex blend of Shintoism, Confucianism, and Buddhism, allowing for both a strong importance of ancestors, and an acceptance of nonhuman souls, including those of objects.

The concept of intelligent objects has a long history in Japan, stretching back to early Shinto animist ideas. The idea of *kami*, a spiritual essence or force, is expressed in stories of crafted objects developing agency, and supports the broader idea of objects as ethical agents (Rambelli 2007). Small wonder, then, that Japan is currently the leader in AI robot innovation and production as well. It is not only that the technology exists, but also this spiritual ideology that has cleared the way for the burgeoning role of androids in Japan, a role that is increasingly being exported throughout the world.

An aging country that desperately needs to find ways to care for elderly people, Japan is moving more swiftly to integrate human-like robots into human society than any other nation.[11] For various cultural and political rea-sons, Japan discourages immigration, which might have been one way to fill this need for labor. Instead, androids have emerged as a solution to the lack of skilled caretakers for the elderly, as well as for the lack of skilled workers in other industries. In fact, according to several opinion polls, elderly Japanese tend to feel more comfortable with android caregivers than with foreign human workers (Robertson 2018: 19).

Android researcher Jennifer Robertson concludes that AI robots are devel-oping social identities in Japan, both through their integration into society and through popular culture. She argues that robots "are infused with values that transcend their usefulness and convenience" (82). This is particularly true in terms of how robots are perceived with regard to gender and citizenship.

In terms of gender, Robertson writes that "among the key questions inform-ing my analysis are how robots embody ideas and notions of the relationship in humans between sex, gender, and sexuality and how the (mostly male) roboticists design and attribute the female or male gender of the robots" (82). The problem, as Robertson sees it, is that "robot engineers regard gendered differences as both natural and universal" (100), and therefore, without broader anthropological understanding of gender, unwittingly reproduce highly gen-dered constructions in their android models.

In terms of citizenship, she notes how robots in Japan have continued to be integrated into Japanese families, which are the building blocks of Japanese citizenship. Robots are, in the views of many, citizens—a status that is not readily available for non-ethnically Japanese human residents of Japan. As Robertson puts it "robot rights in Japan both precede and even exceed human rights in some cases" (125).

Established cultural roles are important ways in which androids are programmed to orient their behavior. Therefore, one way of imagining the future roles of androids will be to examine the likely cultural roles into which these machines will be integrated—as servants, employees, creations, slaves, friends, lovers, or citizens.

One of the first attempts to integrate a robot into an established culture was the Aibo, a trainable robotic dog from Sony, first released commercially in Japan in 1999. Filling the established role of domestic pet, many Aibos became well-integrated into Japanese families. In 2006, Sony discontinued the Aibo, and in 2014, it ceased repairing them. As a result, Aibos have begun to "die." As Aibos died, their deaths have often been commemorated with Buddhist or Shinto funerary ceremonies, in which priests acknowledge the robot dog's soul and pray for it in the afterlife (Canepari and Cooper 2015; Robertson 2018: 185).[12]

The success of the Aibo led other developers to create robots with the appearance of pets, in order to help them fit more easily into human social worlds. For example, the Paro is a seal-like robot that responds to interactions and has proved helpful in elder care, especially in cases of dementia. The Paro was developed by Hiroshi Ishiguro, one of the premiere android creators in Japan. Ishiguro's lab has created several different types of androids, and Hiroshi Ishiguro has even created a "clone" of himself.

Along with the relative ease robots have had in moving into accepted cultural roles in Japan, it seems that elements of religious belief in Japan may be particularly conducive to the integration of robots. Several writers have argued that the religious traditions of Shintoism are more readily compatible with the notion of androids as having "souls," given that Shintoists see the material world as already animated by and imbued with spirits. As Robertson puts it, "Robots are 'living things' in the Shintō universe" (2018, 15).

Following a different line, Mori, the developer of the term *bukimi no tani* ("uncanny valley"), held that androids had the "potential for attaining Buddhahood" (Mori 2005 [1981] Although left unstated, we can reasonably extrapolate from this notion that if an android could achieve the spiritual perfection of Buddhahood, it can also *fail* in the afterlife. Or, to say it another way, it has the potential for becoming a haunting ghost.

Ancestral ties and lineages are a deeply rooted aspect of Japanese philosophy: ghosts with no family to pray for them are most at risk to become *gaki*, the "hungry ghost" that seeks its revenge on the living. As Iwasaka and Toelken wrote in their book *Ghosts and the Japanese*:

> Death. . . . seems to be the *principle* topic in Japanese tradition; nearly every festival, every ritual, every custom is bound up in some way with relationships between the living and the dead, between the present family and its ancestors, between the present occupation and its forebears." (1994: 6)

For example, the Obon festival, perhaps the most important annual festival for the Japanese, is centered around family ties, and traditionally includes a welcoming of ancestral spirits into the house for a two- or three-day visit.

We are not haunted by all the dead, but rather by the dead we have failed. Thus far, I have collected no narratives of ghost Aibos which have been denied their proper funerals and *on* (loosely defined as respect and obligations). But the institutionalization of funerals for androids will surely increase, and with that, the question of their posthumous place in our societies. If they are believed to be capable of spiritual self-improvement (as per Mori), then, accordingly, the rest of human society is ethically implicated in sustaining such improvement and must be prepared for the consequences of failure.

POSTHUMAN ETHICS

It should be noted that it is AI that makes robots into androids. AI is already a factor in many computing operations, including chatbots, AI therapists, and more. At this point, there is nothing in the processing power of android AI that is in any way different than non-physical AI. Rather, it is the subjective impression of them—their appearance of humanity or at least physical sentience—that creates the idea of android soulfulness. As Calverley points out: "Moral consideration for an android could present itself as an issue the moment we begin to ascribe anthropomorphic characteristics to the android" (2006: 411).

AI expert Jonathan Gratch at the University of Southern California has similarly remarked that many people, upon sending in their Roombas (robotic vacuum cleaners) for repair, insist that they want that particular Roomba back, not a replacement. Some had even given the Roomba names (Jonathan Gratch, personal communications, 2017). This effect is even *more* noticeable in lifelike androids, and especially in humanoid models. Hiroshi Ishiguro began to monitor his assistants, and limit their interactions with androids, when he discovered that it was becoming increasingly easy for them to develop personal feelings for these machines (Mar 2017).

There may be some neurological reasons for this kind of attachment. The mirror neurons in our brains are hardwired to cause us to be influenced by the emotions of those around us with whom we identify. As Corballis describes them, "the roles of mirror neurons suggest that the mind functions as an embodied system, grounded in real-world simulations, rather than a system based on the manipulation of abstract symbols" (Corballis 2015: 582). The mirror neuron system (MNS) allows us to be mentally impacted from observing the mental or emotional state and actions of another member of our society. Some research has shown that the MNS may be why people "emotionally" experience witnessing someone else's pain (Jeon and Lee 2018).

While this is a complex process, it is safe to say that we are built for emotionally reacting to human-appearing emotional stimuli. We are hardwired to be social, and to experience the world in a social realm. By introducing artificial humans into that social realm, we are therefore including them within the group of individuals with whom we might emotionally identify. Androids, then, seem likely to quickly become part of our folk groups, not just because they can tell stories, sing, and joke, but because we are likely to *perceive* them as social entities—which is to say, as people.

Ghosts, according to many researchers, should also be viewed as social entities (Valk 2006; Tucker 2007; Iles 1999; Iwasaka and Toelken 1994; Bennett 1999). Ghost stories can reveal social tensions and, especially, ethical lapses. There are real reasons that societies are haunted by the ghosts that they are. Looking to the future, we might therefore discuss how *not* to become haunted by our present actions. This is not superstition, but rather a sober reflection of the importance of acting ethically now, to avoid being on the wrong side of history later. And these discussions are taking place: "robot ethics" or "cyber ethics" is a growing interdisciplinary research effort roughly situated at the intersection of applied ethics and robotics, with the aim of understanding the ethical implications and consequences of robotic technology, especially autonomous robots and androids. Robot ethics is in its infancy, compared to the actual production of androids. At this point, the complex issues raised by these developments have not generated much consensus.[13]

There are several areas of discussion taking place within what I see as the three main subdivisions of robot ethics. One concerns the ethical agency of androids; the second concerns human ethics with respect to androids; the third concerns the ethics of introducing androids, and artificial intelligence more broadly, into the human community.

For better or worse, the developments described in the first subdivision have already arrived: androids are by now engaging in ethical action. And it has been widely accepted that androids must be programmed to think ethically (Manoj

2007), for example, by planning what steps a driverless car should take to avoid killing someone. This may sound simple ("thou shalt not kill") but quickly becomes complex in real-world situations; one can imagine a car having to decide which way to swerve—to the right, and killing three elderly people, or to the left, and killing one young baby. The ethical issues of the real world come with intricate problems, requiring a high level of decision-making skills.

Further, ethical actions are usually social performances, often with expectations of generalized reciprocity. Such formulations can quickly collapse any rigid distinctions between androids' ethical actions and those of humans. If something is acting ethically towards you, it is generally held that you should act ethically towards it in return, a notion enshrined in the Golden Rule of "do unto others as you would have them do unto you."

In order to better understand the complex issues brought forward by this sense of reciprocity, as well as broader ethical issues, we might start by considering two issues: sex and death. Having sex with androids, even if they have been explicitly created for this purpose, raises a host of ethical concerns. On the one hand, it could be argued that having sex with an android is no different than having sex with a vibrator or some other kind of erotic device, but many disagree. Turkle (2011) argues that that by engaging with androids sexually, we are isolating our biological selves even more and to our detriment. Richardson (2015) goes further, arguing that the acts themselves are ethically wrong, either because androids should be seen to have some rights, such as sexual consent, or because the actions themselves should be seen as unethical. This issue has been given some sense of urgency by the commercial interest in producing sex androids, some of which have already been released. A vigorous campaign against sex robots, which included several scholars, arose almost immediately.[14]

Meanwhile, other scholars have argued that "robosexuality" will be beneficial, increasingly normalized, and have few adverse side effects. David Levy, in the conclusion of his 2007 book *Love and Sex with Robots*, for example, states that, "the social and psychological benefits [of robot sex] will be enormous," although he also admits that issues of ethics and romantic attachment will be complex to negotiate (304).[15]

Looking at death brings up similar questions. If androids are viewed as simply owned machinery, then there should be little concern about beating, damaging, or destroying completely an android. But as androids increasingly act and look like humans, such actions start to seem more problematic. If viewed as a kind of person, the destruction of an android in a sadistic manner, or even its public humiliation, will likely be looked on within the rubric of human social roles and expectations.

Such contested ethical issues force us to consider closely what ethics are, how we derive them, and what they are for. This is far from settled in scholarly discourse. To provide a quick gloss, the social constructionist approach argues that ethics are simply socially constructed values that allow people to get along together in society (with close analogues to the utilitarian view). Other views give more credence to the inner mental state of the subjective experiences of ethics and altruism. Finally, many people likely subscribe to what we can call the "transcendent" view of ethics, which implies that ethics transcend both subjective and social experiences.

While it is beyond the scope of this chapter to suggest what ethics "really" is, the intrusion of ghosts into our living world suggests that, at least for those people and societies influenced by such traditions, ethical lapses are more than utilitarian or subjective concerns. Ghosts point to the belief in ethics as a transcendent reality, wherein ethical lapses impinge on the cosmological framework for the proper afterlife of souls. For example, we have seen that race-based slavery in the US, in which certain individuals were viewed as only partially human, produced an abundance of ghosts, and it is clear from the ubiquity of such stories in the US that this country is still "haunted" by the ethical miscarriage of slavery. Given this overall emic view, and the growing integration of androids into our social worlds, it would seem likely that androids will continue with us on this same ethical trajectory, whether we are ready or not. Ghost stories, in other words, can help guide our inquiries of contemporary ethical worldviews, and aid in predicting particular patterns and problems for integrating androids into our moral worlds.

After considering the entwined notions of ethical androids and of the ethical treatment of androids, we are left to consider the ethics of introducing androids into human society. Significant concerns in this area include:

- Androids as potentially expanding hegemonic control. Militaries are already developing military fighting robots. Some have suggested that atrocities committed by androids will be used as a way of absolving the human actors directing them of a sense of guilt.
- Androids as expanding the cultural and social power of dominant social groups and identities. Built through institutional means, androids will likely reflect dominant identities, cultures, languages, and worldviews, further marginalizing minority groups.
- Androids as a benefit primarily for the wealthy.[16]
- Androids as further contributing to the economic divide between the rich and the poor. For example, if driverless cars replace paid drivers, a large number of

Americans will lose decent-paying jobs and be forced out of their professions. The trend of robot workers taking over human jobs has already begun and seems likely to sharply increase.

The social implications will likely be a part of the equation of moral consider-ations, with androids occupying the role of abused or abusers depending on how they are implemented. The viewpoints that will dominate in these debates will also likely reflect unequal distributions of power in human societies, as those in power may find more to benefit from androids than the impoverished or disempowered. Further, human viewpoints will be influenced by how the cultural quality of "human-ness" is understood in society and performed by androids: the more like us they seem, the more we are likely to judge them in terms of humanity and expect from them what we expect from other humans.

NONHUMANS AND ETHICS

We can bring these considerations into further relief by examining another major area of posthuman ethical research: ethology, or the study of animal behavior. In the literature on the ethics of human-animal relationships, we find many of the exact same concerns among ethological ethicists,[17] again dividing largely into three main lines of inquiry:

- Concern about animals/androids as potential ethical agents.
- Concern about the proper moral stance for humans in regards to how to treat animals/androids. This might include ethical actions on an individual level, as well as on a larger social and legal level.
- Concern about the moral effect animals/ androids might have on human individuals and societies—for example, in promoting unnatural lusts or other moral failings.[18]

If these areas of concern are similar to those raised by robot ethicists, it is significant that animals and humans have, in some sense, a totally different relationship than humans and androids. Animals share many of the biological characteristics of humans; they are built of the same "stuff" (DNA, cells, hor-mones, and so on). They also similarly occur within and are dependent upon the natural environment. Androids, meanwhile, were created by humans in human environments, but share none of the same fundamental building blocks with us or our carbon-based kindred. However, also unlike animals, androids are built purposefully to appear human, and to display human behaviors, speech, and, often, emotional responses. This state of being biologically different but behaviorally similar sets up a different kind of basis for the ethical relations between androids and humans than it does for humans and animals.

Humans are much more closely related in all biological ways to a snail, a fish, or even bacteria than to androids, and humans and animals are similarly dependent on healthy ecosystems. But it seems likely that, due perhaps to the influence of anthropocentric Abrahamic religious thinking and to the hard-wired response to androids who display human qualities, we may continue to elevate the social and moral roles of androids, while becoming increasingly disconnected from the rapidly deteriorating natural world of animals. As artificial intelligence continues to expand both online and offline components (along with the ability to move largely seamlessly back and forth between the two), the cyborgicization of human culture, and of human ontology, is likely to expand. Both our physical and social worlds will be increasingly inhabited by embodied AI. Androids are at home in the digital world, and as we become increasingly attached to them, they will increasingly tie our social, cultural, and psychological world to the general cyber experience. Androids, in many ways, present better candidates for the transhumanist goals of "uploading a self" than a biological human by far. Yet, as we merge with them socially and personally, we are likely to find our ontology merging, too.

CONCLUSION: TOWARDS AN ETHICAL FUTURE

We have recently witnessed a blossoming of cyborg ghosts in forms such as the haunted servers and text messages from the beyond, and seen the increasing vernacular interweaving of the digital realm, artificial intelligence, and the soul. Androids make a particular case in point, since they are constructed specifically in order to interact with us on a social, physical, and phenomenological level. It is easy for us to have feelings for these creations, and to place them within our already existing social patterns and paradigms. The demand for them seems great, and our future society looks highly likely to host more and more androids as caregivers, companions, sexual partners, industrial workers, and soldiers, among other roles. The social implications of new technology are vast and necessitate scholarly discussions regarding ethics and morality in a posthuman environment. Relatedly, this will entail rethinking the fundamental categories of personhood, sociability, and Alan Dundes's famous rhetorical question: "Who are the folk"? (Dundes 1980: 1). When we begin to see others as humans, and they form increasingly intimate parts of our daily lives, we are more likely to see them as persons with rights and responsibilities. The ethical pathway forward towards interacting with androids is not at all clear, and the subject of a great deal of interdisciplinary discussion. I believe that ghost stories, evincing the "shadow side" of ethical behavior, can contribute a great deal in guiding us in this very new terrain. Posthumanism as a theory becomes useful in such endeavors, as our ontology increasingly becomes called into question, and folkloristics can contribute to the wider discussions taking place regarding the social and cultural impacts, and the ethical implications, of the introduction of androids into daily life, by shifting its disciplinary focus away from the past and towards the swiftly approaching future.

Along with many scholars, I have long found ghosts to be interesting indicators of vernacular ontology, and vernacular ethics, and examining ghost stories may help us continue to grasp what it is to be a person, and how such concepts are in the midst of a great deal of flux. Accompanying the question of "how will androids be a part of our social fabric" is the question of the form and function of our future ghosts. The future is sweeping towards us faster than ever, and perhaps ghost stories, and folklorists, can begin gazing towards the future, for the sake of ensuring that whatever future does happen is a future that is ethical . . . whatever that may mean. And we may have to figure this out: if we fail to act ethically, we risk being haunted by our failures. On that, our folkloristic knowledge tends to agree. Ghost stories, then, may provide us with important emic understandings of ethical thought, allowing us some guidelines by which to navigate the uncertainties directly ahead.

8

NEW MYTHS FOR MODERN TIMES

Changing Ontologies and the Green-Skinned Other

How to use both scholarly and vernacular discourses to make sense of what we are, ontologically speaking? This chapter investigates ontological thought through several examples of "others": trolls, fairies, witches, and, particularly, aliens. These cultural constructions enable discourses regarding what is, and is not, human. Following a common motif of green-skinned others, I trace the constructions of "othering" for clues about the self: how people are envisioning and narrating their ontology in the postcolonial, postnational, and posthuman days now upon us.

IMAGINING THE OTHER

This chapter examines the category of various "others," following the links between posthumanism, postnationalism, and mythology. It follows this trajectory from trolls, witches, and fairies to the rise of extraterrestrial aliens, along a path often marked by the motif of green skin.

One underlying thesis is that different cultural epochs contain different cultural concerns, and that traditions of human ontology, those thoughts about who we really are, pull from past traditions as well as respond with innovations to new social changes. In particular, the role of technology has proven pivotal in some belief systems, transforming the understanding of the cosmos, of humanity, and of life itself. Technology has enabled the emergence of global discourses which can be contrasted with those of the nation-state: "postnationalism." Additionally, technology has furthered the posthuman discourse, especially with androids, AI, and cyborg studies, but also, by way of comparison, to animal ethology and the general evolution of consciousness. In this chapter, I show how humanity's "others" allow for a "folk posthumanist" discourse on a global scale in these rapidly changing times.

As a result of the globalized cultures blossoming on the internet, and in conjunction with advances in science that blur the lines of what constitutes the category of human, people are redefining themselves in ways that are often strikingly postnational and/or posthuman. Stories of "green-skinned troublemakers" reflect these ideas through "definition in opposition." Humans say who they are by also saying who, or what, they are not.

While there are many markers of fictional-supernatural humanoid others, green skin is one common motif with a long history in Western traditions, with a strong global presence in cyber discourse. Keeping track of this motif may help contribute to an understanding of cultural traditions of performing ethnic belonging, and of contemporary expressions of "folk posthumanism."

Example 1: Green-Skinned Troublemakers

What is it to be human? To answer this question requires knowing what a human is not. As Koukoutsaki-Monnier wrote in her overview of the concept, "The figure of the 'other' constitutes one of the pillars for identity constructions. Defining the 'other' helps demarcating the 'self,' individual as well as group."[1]

Scholars of race have long noted how the biological essentialisms of ethnic and racial classifications selectively highlight certain physical characteristics while overlooking other areas of similarity or difference.[2] Ranging from nose shape, lip shape, head shape, skin tone, hair color and texture, size, and even more subtle physical characteristics like lactose tolerance, physical characteristics vary widely, and are selected in order to emphasize cultural contrasts between groups. The systematization of these selections is highly culturally specific. Groups who are opposed to one another might be highly attuned to particular physical characteristics that could seem negligible to an outsider.

As Frederik Barth wrote in his classic 1969 *Ethnic Groups and Boundaries: The Social Organization of Cultural Difference*, "categorical ethnic distinctions do not depend on an absence of mobility, contact and information, but do entail social processes of exclusion and incorporation whereby discrete categories are maintained despite changing participation and membership in the course of individual life histories."[3]

Due to the history of European colonialism, especially the transatlantic slave trade, skin color became a widespread racialized physical characteristic in many societies. However, the range of recognized human variations in skin tone does not include green-skinned people. Perhaps because of this, green skin has come to be a distinct marker of other-than-human identity. From green trolls to green elves, witches, and Martians, green skin color has been a special motif in thinking about what is to be other-than-fully-human, with a long history in Western discourse.

"The Green Children of Woolpit" is a narrative from England in the 1100s. According to two near-contemporary written accounts, two green-skinned children, a brother and sister, were found in the village of Woolpit, in Suffolk, England, speaking an unknown language and eating only wild foods. The boy died fairly soon, but the girl survived, learned English, and later married. The girl later related that they came from Saint Martin's Land, a subterranean world inhabited by green people. Although recounted as verifiable fact in written records, later observers noted the overlap between these accounts and traditional folk narratives, pointing out that the realm of the fairy folk was often said to be underground, accessible only through caves. In an interesting example of the Christianization of the supernatural world, Robert Burton's 1621 *The Anatomy of Melancholy* suggested that the green children "fell from heaven."

Although many kinds of fairy folk, including elves, fairies, and leprechauns, have all been represented with green skin, it is less clear if the green skin color in this story had any particular folkloric significance at the time. Most of the earliest examples of green skin seem to date from the work of late Victorian-era folklore collectors.[4] For example, in the "Green Lady" tale collected in 1896 by Alice B. Gomme, the Green Lady is a representation of a traditional fairy woman.[5] Similarly, in George Douglas's 1901 *Scottish Fairy and Folk Tales*, he describes the "little green men" inhabiting Glen Nevis.[6]

The motif of green skin also shows up in the Green Man figure,[7] linked to the "Jack in the Green" of English May Day celebrations.[8] An early printed use of the phrase "Green Man" in this context appears to be Lady Raglan's 1939 article, "The Green Man in Church Architecture," although she states that her version is an amalgamation of various traditional figures, mostly represented by a man's face combined with plant motifs.[9] The Green Man and the Jack in the Green were both identified with vegetation, and the color green is often associated with the regenerative potential of plants. The "Green Knight," who challenged Gawain of the Knights of the Round Table, and who regenerated from his wounds, also seems to embody this aspect of supernatural otherness, perhaps through implicit association with the Green Man figure.[10]

The idea that green skin can represent the vegetal world has appeared in various cultural traditions. For example, the Japanese *kappa*, a troublesome *yokai* figure from Japan, is nearly always portrayed with green skin. The *kappa* and the Green Man have both become identified with the motif of green as employed in global environmental concerns.[11] The *kappa* is now frequently used as an environmental symbol, displaying a concern for protecting the world against the harmful effects of technological development. The global ecological movement frequently features the motif of green as a symbol of environmental health, as in the "Green Party," the "green movement," and "green packaging." The global ecology movement intersects with belief in supernatural others in communities such as contemporary Wiccans and neopagans who often focus their religious concerns on the natural environment and worship Mother Earth as an important deity. Many also take an interest in the various *fae*, who display strong links to environmental concerns and who are often green-skinned.[12]

Other green-skinned supernatural figures play roles in American culture. A notable and influential popular culture example of a green-skinned witch appears in MGM's film *The Wizard of Oz*: after this film, many popular depictions of witches continued to employ the motif of green skin. Gremlins were known to commonly jinx[13] machines during the onset of industrialization, once again preventing the smooth functioning and progress of human society. Trolls, often with green skin, have likewise staged a comeback, moving from the shadows of disbelief into a major problem in internet society.

Example 2: Trolls: The Other amongst Us

In Norse mythology, trolls appear ancient even to the gods. Yet, long after the old Norse gods became neglected and largely forgotten, trolls still featured prominently in the folklore, folk culture, and literature throughout the Middle Ages, Renaissance, and modern era. In Medieval and preindustrial ages, trolls were frequently encountered characters, living somewhat apart from humans, yet with considerable overlap and interaction with stories told of marriages to trolls and troll-human hybrids. One of the most common stories involved townspeople's attempts to build a church: during the day people made good progress, but every night the trolls came and destroyed what the good folk had done.[14]

Today trolls are a major social problem on the internet, disrupting normal polite culture with their rude, crude ways.[15] Visual representations of internet trolls exist in multitudes of forms online, usually with green skin, and sometimes purposefully blurring the lines between a maladjusted computer user and the supernatural creature of earlier ages. Like the medieval trolls tearing apart the church at night, internet trolls problematize online attempts at building communities of participation, particularly in their exploitation of the possibilities of anonymity and pretended identities. Online trolls frequently shape-shift to appear in other identities as a way of sowing confusion and discord.

Consider the case of the Australian-Lebanese-Arab-Islamic-States jihadist who called for atrocities to be committed against Christians and Jews. After gaining some notoriety, the author of the internet posts was revealed to "really" be a twenty-year-old Jewish male of US citizenship named Joshua Ryne Goldberg, who was living in his parents' home in Florida. Goldberg had at other times performed the identity of a famous Australian Jewish lawyer, Josh Bornstein (Goldberg set up a blog in Bornstein's name, calling for the "extermination of Palestinians"), as well as a variety of American white supremacists. Goldberg had also assumed the identity of people of various ethnic, national, ideological, and religious backgrounds and is now mostly known as a troll. He was arrested after emailing instructions on how to build bombs to confidential sources.[16] The attribution of the absolute otherness of the internet troll to Joshua Ryne Goldberg is an interesting move: his troll otherness comes, in large part, from performing outside of his "real" (historically based) identity.

Trolls exploit the logical disjuncture between online performances of identity and offline ones to wreak havoc on productive social discourse. Major aspects of contemporary society have been mobilized to try to deal with the "troll menace": news reports, public awareness campaigns, and legislation have coalesced their activities around the problem of the impolite other, the crude troll lurking at the edges of society.

Trolls continue to be a productive category, spanning multiple genres, and have found fertile ground to colonize in the internet. One way of viewing the ubiquity and importance of online trolls is to consider the emergence of a new internet proverb: "don't feed the trolls." Proverbs are undeniably folklore, undeniably traditional, and undeniably reflections of cultures and societies.

Although the general idea of trolls lurking and causing havoc is old and traditional, the proverb "don't feed the trolls" is not: rather, it is new and traditional. It is also intimately linked with the development of the internet. This is new traditionality, new folklore, but nonetheless important for its newness. It is also a hallmark and cultural product of the new internet cultures arising as the central matrix of humanity.

As many scholars have pointed out, proverbs are important indicators of culture: to understand a group, one can study the proverbs the group uses. Also, as proverb scholars have pointed out, one must examine the proverb in *performance*, which is to say, in context. *When and why* is this particular proverb stated?

There are lots of proverbs on the internet. Indeed, most proverbs spoken have probably made their way onto the internet. Yet, in this case, here is a proverb that *only* applies to the internet. It is not all that old, obviously, yet is clearly traditional and folkloric, demonstrating the power of mediated horizontal communication, as well as the rhetorical power of the traditional past being put to new uses. Such new, powerful traditional lore also points to the fallacy of a notion of folklore as old or antiquated. This proverb is clearly traditional, and very new, at the same time. It is also traditional in the way it offers advice as to proper behavior. As always, folklore reflects the issues and concerns of a group. Vested in tradition, it must always be performed in the present moment, for the sake of the future.

The ongoing use of traditions thus offers us a "bridge" (under which may hide the trolls!) connecting the past and the present, the pre- and the postmodern, and diverse peoples located in various nation-states scattered throughout the world. Trolls have emerged from the Northlands, and have successfully invaded cyberspace, wreaking havoc as always. Like internet folklore, generally, trolls now take on a de-spatialized, de-nationalized aspect, becoming a part, albeit a negative one, of the global agora. In becoming an aspect of cyborg identity, trolls are now a global, postnational, posthuman, and green-skinned other.

Example 3: Aliens, from International to Intergalactic

While green-skinned trolls reveal a bridge between premodern and postmodern others, modern aliens—characters largely developed in American culture—are perhaps the most important extension of this chromatic tradition, as evidenced in the common motif of green-skinned extraterrestrials. Like trolls, the current role of extraterrestrial aliens both stems from and comments on the digital world and the implications for globalized human society. The word "alien" denotes "foreigners" or "strangers," deriving from Latin *aliēnus* ("foreign"). The word is still used in the United States to define lack of American citizenship or legal residency, as in the phrase "illegal aliens." Yet the same term is also used for non-Earth-based life forms, and has coalesced around some popular motifs, including flying saucers and humanoid appearances. The word itself shifts the conception of "other" from national to global to interstellar: from aliens as international to aliens as intergalactic.

The idea of global culture and community is largely the result of the introduction of digital communication technologies, which for the first time allows people to communicate across vast geographic distances. As Aiwah Ong notes, "mobile markets, technologies, and populations interact to shape social spaces in which mutations in citizenship are crystallized. The different elements of citizenship (rights, entitlements, etc.), once assumed to go together, are becoming disarticulated from one another, and re-articulated with universalizing forces and standards."[17]

Such discourses have profoundly influenced ideas about identity. A recent BBC-commissioned poll, for instance, showed a sharp rise in individuals identifying primarily as global, rather than national, citizens.[18] For this increasingly large segment of the population, "Earth is our home," as the slogan goes.

Within that home, a vast variety of different cultures and groups exist online, with different experiences and traditions. For example, several scholars have focused on gamers, and the relationship between gaming and identity, including race.[19] Interestingly, game players often perform not only the identities of different human races but frequently of nonhuman races as well. These often follow traditional trends. As Melissa J. Monson put it, "The intertwining of recognizable cultural histories, epistemologies, and geographies encourage readers (and gamers alike) to suspend disbelief and accept the more fantastical elements of such stories. . . . Among the more significant of these fantastical elements has been the development of unique breeds of creatures, extraterrestrials, and other sentient beings. These beings are typically referred to as 'races.'"[20] Such moves link age-old nonhuman others in specific traditions with contemporary global popular discourses, allowing for "aliens" to be seen in the same general light: a humanoid other, closely linked with ideas of race. The "alien race(s)" are predicated on the idea of being not only nonhuman, but non-earthly.

NEW-FANGLED TECHNOLOGY

Representations of "green-skinned others" in the early 1800s questioned the emergence of the new technologies of the industrial age, as they now question the innovations of the digital age. The re-imaginations of the self through the shifting lenses of technological change are recurrent themes for green-skinned others. Much of the "otherness" of green-skinned others is revealed in temporal orientations. For both Icelandic *huldre*[21] and Irish "fairy folk,"[22] traditional humanoid others are often represented in ways that link them with past—especially premodern—lifeways (Hafstein 2000; Thompson 2004). The narratives place them explicitly in opposition to modern technology, embodying an ambivalence towards change. The numerous overlaps between the fairy folk and aliens have been well documented.[23] These overlaps reveal a shifting orientation toward time and technology: the fairy folk represent the past, or the Otherworld of the dead, with ancient magic, while the aliens are notable for their orientation towards the future and advanced technology.

The fairy folk/alien relationship also reveals a shift in terrestrial orientation: the fairy folk are represented as coming from the Earth itself (caves and mounds are frequent portals into their realm), while aliens originate in and are oriented toward the heavens. In modernity, the "little green men" moved from fairy folk, with their resistance to modern technologies (electric lights and loud noises chased the fairies away),[24] towards a new extraterrestrial race with advanced technologies.

In 1912, Edgar Rice Burroughs included "green men of Mars" in his first science fiction novel, *A Princess of Mars*. The interest in life outside of Earth grew during the early days of the industrial revolution: pioneering voyages in air travel gave rise to an interest in space travel and speculations regarding the future. Science fiction became a vehicle for people to imagine where technology might someday take them. The interest in fantastic machines that could fly to the moon or other planets developed alongside a general fascination with technology. How far could flying machines take humans? What would people find on distant planets? Could the inhabitants they encountered be like them, and, likewise, fly to Earth?

As folklorist Kimberly Ball observed:

> "The UFO-abduction narrative is, then, a phenomenon of the late twentieth and early twenty-first centuries."[25] while "What distinguishes the era of UFO-and especially UFO-abduction narratives from previous eras is the proliferation of increasingly sophisticated technology and its growing presence in the daily lives of ordinary people."[26]

As Ball notes, the discourses of science fiction and supernatural belief and legend narratives reveal what folklorist Alan Dundes called a "future orientation in American worldview."[27] As space travel developed, so too did the notion of Earth as the "green planet." The color green thus became an interesting symbol for both terrestrial and non-terrestrial life forms, entwining discourses of life on Earth with discourses of life elsewhere.

SACRED TECH

Ted Peters, in his 2014 *UFOs: God's Chariots?: Spirituality, Ancient Aliens and Religious Yearnings in the Age of Extraterrestrials*, explores the ways in which the fascination and unease with technology melded with deep religious themes.[28] The impact is especially prominent in religious movements that emerged after the nineteenth century. For example, the foundational stories of the Latter-Day Saints (composed in the 1820s) incorporate a great deal of science fiction: interstellar travel, the garden of Eden being recast as a planet, a planet or sun Kolob said to be "nearest God," as well as stated belief regarding life on other planets. [29] Other religious movements, such as Scientology and the Raëlians, have also narrated a mythology and belief system based on intergalactic aliens.

News stories are filled with prophetic movements based on alien belief, including doomsday cults such as Heaven's Gate, which achieved notoriety in 1997 when the members committed mass suicide in the belief that they would be "spiritually transported" to a spaceship approaching Earth behind the Comet Hale-Bopp. Yet it would be a mistake to attribute such beliefs to fringe elements in American society. Charles A. Ziegler concludes that "tens of millions of adults in the United States believe that some UFOs are manifestations of an un-Earthly intelligence. In other words, that belief is not confined to an aberrant few but, rather, its burgeoning in the last half of the twentieth century is a major cultural event that warrants further studies by social scientists, including those with special interests in religion."[30]

The growth of such stories and beliefs, and overall interest in extraterrestrial visitors, has skyrocketed, particularly—but not solely—in the US. A 2012 National Geographic poll found that 77 percent of Americans believed that aliens had visited Earth at some point in the past,[31] while a 2013 Harris poll found that only 68 percent of Americans believe that Jesus is God or the son of God.[32] The results imply that more Americans believe that aliens have visited the Earth than believe that Jesus Christ was the son of God (not that these beliefs are incompatible: obviously, given the numbers, there are many people who believe both to be true. But, interestingly, alien belief is also compatible with atheism, creating potential areas of shared belief between the religions and the non-religious).

References to alien visitation to Earth also appear in contemporary popular culture. *Ancient Aliens*, a television show on the History Channel that explores the belief that aliens were instrumental in creating human civilization and possibly biological life on Earth, is in its eleventh season. Stories and beliefs of how the world and its people came to be approaches the mythic, narrating how our world came to be, imbuing the world with sacred significance, and offering particular ways of categorizing and interpreting the world.

The mythic component of alien belief overlaps with Christian or Abrahamic mythology. Both belief traditions emphasize the importance of the sky and of the "heavens."[33] Similarly, both alien belief and Abrahamic mythology display strong anthropocentric views, where more advanced beings are recognizably "humanoid" but far more powerful. Angels, like aliens, come down from the heavens and interact with humankind, shaping their destiny and at times producing hybrid offspring.

Erich von Däniken's influential 1968 book *Chariots of the Gods* claimed that the accounts of angels coming down "from the heavens" in the Bible and other religious texts were in fact accounts of alien visitation. Other writers have explored Christian demonology in connection with alien visitation narratives, including the traditions of abduction and hybridization.[34] Such mythic strategies allow the general interest in non-Earth-based life to develop deeper, more cosmogonic resonance. If angels are aliens, then aliens are not only a matter of belief, but potentially a matter of sacred truth.

POSTHUMAN SHADOWS

Aliens and other green-skinned beings trouble the personal and social identity of humans, exhibiting in their belief systems similar stirrings as found in posthumanism, generally.

One way to understand how individuals grapple with these issues on a vernacular level is to look at the changing cultural role of the other, and at the chromatic symbolisms at play: in this case, the idea of the "green planet" is juxtaposed to that of the "green alien."

In this posthuman context, the longstanding motif of "green-skinned" as a vernacular conceptualization of pure otherness trades on the cultural racialization of skin tone. The roles played by green-skinned troublemakers in the contemporary conditions of modernity explore possibilities beyond the human, offering ways to rethink what is human. Narratives and images of green-skinned others form a folk posthumanism, vernacular discourses of the self versus the other, the natural versus the supernatural, and the liminal spaces in between.

TRANSCENDENCE?

In a contemporary world in which local problems slide into global ones, and in which humans are "mere animals," aliens offer a potential solution. They are not a part of our ecosystem, nor even of their own ecosystem: They have transcended their own planet. They have *transcended nature.* Like narratives of the millenarian Christian "rapture" with which alien narratives often overlap,[35]

UFO stories often offer technological salvation from the heavens, and a chance to leave a despoiled and polluted Earth behind. If aliens are linked to the divine, descending from the heavens, then they give humans yet another chance to deny their terrestrial nature and their kinship with all life on Earth.

But, conversely, if they represent an absolute "other," then they can reinforce a notion of humans *as* earthlings. So which is it? Are humans kin with aliens or not? In many stories and beliefs, aliens are clearly linked to humans, and so represent human denial of animality, past cultural achievements (as in the ascription of ancient monuments and buildings to aliens), and the fragility of existence. In these stories, humans belong to the heavens but not the Earth. Yet, in other stories and beliefs, they are clearly *not* humans, a view which allows people to consider themselves as an ethnic group, those "non-green-skinned peoples." This view of humans as "earthlings" is a recalibration of humanity, allowing conversations regarding a shared global identity, and shared global concern. This belief system has in this way created a format for global discourse, both reflecting and helping to enact a sense of global humanity, a singular human race.

But if humans *are* earthlings and not aliens, then are not other creatures from Earth earthlings as well? Are birds, and wolves, and whales also earthlings? While the category of humans as ethnically "earthlings" seems promising, it holds not only the theoretical outlook of postnationalism, but also contains within it the main theoretical critiques of posthumanism. What, exactly, is a person? Is an intelligent robot a person? Is an alien? Is a wolf?

CONCLUSION: WE WANT TO BELIEVE

The cyber environment increases—indeed, largely creates—the preconditions for widespread belief in aliens, due to the globalization of discourses which call for an identity of "earthling." It is not completely divorced from actual territory (for example, supposed alien crash sites) yet it is nonetheless a way of imagining the world, and oneself, as seen by outsider's eyes. Belief in extraterrestrial aliens continues a long tradition of envisioning powerful, "other-than-human" people, often green-skinned, nonhuman humanoids that societies create in order to define themselves. The rise in global communications, and global concerns, comes with a rise in global identity, which in turn brings a need for an intergalactic other.

Discourse about aliens allows for differing perspectives and conclusions; it offers people a way to discuss and debate the essence and contours of what it is to be human. Belief in aliens offers an exit, cognitively speaking, from connections to life on Earth, or, vice versa, a way of embracing a terrestrial ontology, of exploring an identity as "earthlings." This complex discourse provides a rich setting for discussing basic ontologies in global settings via these motifs and narratives.

The questions persist. What does it mean to be a person? An earthling? A human? These are the pressing philosophical questions of the contemporary era, enacted at the vernacular level as well as the scholarly. This chapter examined the creation of otherness, as often reflected in the motif of green skin, as a "shadow image" of our contemporary identity concerns. What can we learn from our shadows?

9

WHEN YOUR BFF IS AN AI

Artificial Intelligence as Folk

Artificial intelligence programs have increasingly entered public discourse in many diverse and overlapping ways. The various artificial intelligences are connected to our biologically based ones largely (though not solely) via the cyber network, which itself increasingly draws our species into its communicative framework. In this new, mediated, cyborg realm of culture, there are no nonhuman animals, or plants, or any other natural forms of intelligence, but that does not mean we are all alone. Rather, there are now new voices in our shared agora, and their voices do not necessarily attend to our own. This chapter explores the cultural overlaps of human and artificial intelligences online.

I begin by returning to the classic quote from folklore studies, Alan Dundes's "Who Are the Folk?" first printed in 1977 in *Frontiers of Folklore* (edited by William Bascom) and reprinted in his book *Interpreting Folklore*. The piece is well known for arguing for a contemporary, expansive definition of the folk, and it poses the rhetorical question that I repeatedly seek to answer throughout this work.

Central to his argument is that technology does not stamp out folklore, but rather in many cases does the opposite. His work on the photocopier lore, the machine that upended the elite control of the printing press, demonstrated how technology became both a means of passing along folklore and often a subject of the folklore itself. The folk, he argued, could be found in the office.

The chapter ends with a brief, yet perhaps prescient, view of the computer that I'd like to revisit. At the very end of the article, Dundes includes three jokes about computers, and ends on this one:

> A super computer is built and all the world's knowledge is programmed into it. A gathering of top scientists punch in the question "Will the computer ever replace man?" Clickity, click, whir, whir, and computer lights flash on and off. Finally, a small printout emerges saying, "That reminds me of a story."
> "Who are the folk?" concludes Dundes, "Among others, *we* are!" (1977: 51)

So ends this classic contribution. With the arrival of the personal computer, and particularly the internet, other folklorists took to examining the folklore in this emerging realm, and since then the idea of cyber folklore has taken firm hold of the discipline, with many excellent works produced on the vernacular discourses online[1]. All of the approaches, my own included, have thus far taken the view of the digital realm as a medium allowing vernacular communications.

But I would like to assert that we need to fundamentally rethink this view of the internet in light of recent technological developments. I propose that *the digital realm is not only a place for communication, but is also, and increasingly, a contributor to the communication that takes place.*

Let's go back to Dundes's example, which was presented as a joke: *a small printout emerges saying, "That reminds me of a story."*

This synopsis, in its jocular form, conceptualizes the moment now upon us. From being a passive means of communication, the digital realm is now an active agent, or rather a host to a plethora of active agents, through such increasingly ubiquitous uses of artificial intelligence.

Artificial intelligence is no longer the realm of science fiction, but now rather the realm of the everyday. I myself might interact with several different artificial intelligences before arriving at work. I might begin my day with the AI in my email spam filters sniffing out which emails are bogus, and I might shop on Amazon for supplies with my page feed being provided by AI. While there, I might have a friendly online chat with an automated service engine. While sipping coffee, I might check Facebook, which uses AI to select my feeds, from friends as well as news I read. If I use Messenger, or WhatsApp, I'd use a different AI as well. As I get in my car, AI via my phone offers me critical advice for the drive ahead of me. Once I get to work, I might start grading, using the AI to detect plagiarized papers. Many of these interactions are rather limited, and results-oriented. We rarely interact with these budding intelligences in any meaningful way. Frequently, we do not even know that much about them. But they know a great deal about us.

There are much more visible ways that we are increasingly interacting with artificial intelligences, including many AI made explicitly for this purpose. Besides being useful in helping people solve technical support via a chat box, chat programs have blossomed into numerous variations, all with explicitly social implications. It is in these interactions that we can most clearly see the developing contributions of AI to our general human discourse.

BOTS, CHATBOTS, AND US

Bots, or autonomous digital beings, are especially visible in the role of the chatbots, those autonomous digital beings that are geared to interact with humans. Helpful chatbots appear on many websites, helping people shop, or troubleshooting difficulties. It is not always obvious to a person interacting with them that they are interacting with an AI, and that is the ultimate point: bots try to conquer the "uncanny valley" not by maintaining distinctions between human and other, but rather by collapsing them, by being on "our" side of the valley.

Chatbots have also proved useful in highly interpersonal interactions, such as therapists. For example, "Woebot" is billed as "your charming robot friend who is ready to listen" (at https://woebot.io/), a therapist-trained social chat.

Besides therapists, there are now many chatbots designed solely for social interactions. One example is Mitsuko, developed from the pandorabot platform, and has appeared in numerous communicative arenas, including a series of flash games known as "mousebreaker," Kik Messenger, Skype, and on the web. Mitsuko claims the identity of an eighteen-year-old female from Leeds. Some 80 percent of her users are under the age of twenty-two, although it has been increasingly popular with the elderly as a source of companionship.[2] In terms of Kik Messenger alone, Mistuko has on average over 250,000 conversations per day.[3]

Such social bots may seem quite benign, yet consider the case of Tay, developed by Microsoft to be a pop icon, released in 2016. Within a few hours, the bot began to post racist and offensive tweets, forcing Microsoft to shut down Tay after only sixteen hours. Microsoft realized that the deviant, spiteful behavior was due to her learning abilities, and the trolls dominated her interactions and guided her to fake news and accounts.

I've already discussed trolls in the previous chapter, but here their role can be viewed in a particular light. In the case of poor Tay, the trolls attacked her, misguided her, and wore down her defenses through cyberbullying. Trolls' antisocial activity is a reminder of the problems of group intelligence and communal efforts: all it takes is a couple of bad apples to turn the whole basket.

Trolls are an interesting category, dwelling on the edges of human society. In the case of trolls, it is perhaps particularly interesting, though sadly not surprising, to witness the rise of the trollbot.

Trollbots flood chatrooms or discussion boards with antisocial communications, creating havoc and severely damaging the social effectiveness of the online space. With the rise of the trollbots, we have some of the first clear examples of antisocial artificial intelligence. Trollbots have taken on an increasingly political aspect as well, at times being directed by large, powerful interests to disrupt civil discourse, combining forces with the "actual" trolls.

Trollbots have become an increasingly public concern recently due to the influence of fake news narratives. Fake news is often heralded and promulgated by bots, in this case known as trollbots. Trollbots pretend to be real people, and in doing so make artificial claims for vernacular authority.

Trollbots are linked with their nondestructive cousins, the fawning, if deceptive, fanbots. These bots are created to praise a particular idea, commodity, program, or individual, again attempting to distort the perceived aggregated vernacular authority (as per Robert Glenn Howard 2013) online. There are websites advertising these services: don't you want your own AI press agent? Who doesn't, right? In 2016, 4 percent of companies used chatbots;[4] according to another study, 80 percent of businesses said they intended to have one by 2020.[5]

One such popular site for bot creation is pandorabots: the site advertises that its AI programs have resulted in over 300,000 bots, with more than 6 billion messages processed. While pandorabots is a prominent example, it has hundreds of competitors online. According to a recent study, in 2013 bots were responsible for 61.5 percent of the web's traffic—a number that is sure to increase dramatically in upcoming years.[6] Chatbots are the tip of the iceberg, the visible manifestations of the way that AI is becoming merged with our experience of culture.

There are other bots used for other malicious purposes, pretending to be real people in order to gain some information, or exploit some weakness. The "catfish" is a troll pretending to be an interesting romantic partner, and there are several bots which could be called catfishers. Perhaps the most famous example is on the adultery dating site Ashley Madison. A massive hack of the site revealed that more than 80 percent of the "women" on the site looking for adulterous romances were actually bots pretending to be women.[7] Catfisher bots are numerous, and capable of ensnaring even the most aware. For example, in 2007, one of the leading researchers on the topic, Dr. Robert Epstein, wrote an account of how he himself was fooled by a remarkably savvy catfisher bot.[8]

Bots for sexual conversations ("sexbots") are not always duplicitous, and the role of sexbots seems to be rising dramatically. Yet even "consensual" sex chats with bots may be ethically problematic, especially when used to portray illegal or tabooed sexual acts.

Other chatbots might not be malicious, but have still aroused some ethical concerns, for example in the "griefbots," which create AIs based on dead loved ones (Replika is one such example). The Shoah Foundation, a Holocaust museum, realized it was running out of Holocaust survivors to talk about their experiences, one of the mainstays of the museum. To solve this, they have created AI holographic representatives (or, in common parlance, "ghosts") of survivors, so that this aspect could continue. The idea of virtual AI ghosts looks likely to expand greatly in the coming years.

Transhumanism and Its Relations

Ghosts are, of course, connected with the afterlife, as well as connected to ideas of the soul and our essential being. Artificial intelligence contains, for some people, tantalizing promises of earthly transcendence, and perhaps even immortality. Transhumanism (not to be confused with posthumanism, although the strands do overlap) is a movement that pushes for the merger of human consciousness with artificial intelligence. Drawing largely from futurist Ray Kurzweil's outlook, transhumanists envision a moment of the "singularity," when human consciousness can be uploaded into the digital realm, allowing for "people" (if we can still call them that) to escape their mortal shell and enter the cyber land as actual human consciousnesses untethered to biology. Such a belief, and goal, views the cyber realm as a sort of stand-in for ideas of heaven, or at least for some type of immortality. While this is a somewhat extreme view, it is also a wildly popular one. Such discourse builds from our current environment, where so much of our identity is already performed online, either as our "selves" (e.g., one's personal Facebook page) or as some other self (e.g., a *World of Warcraft* character). Further, the expanding role of griefbots is already exploring the cyber realm as some sort of afterlife. Although the singularity has not happened, nor does it appear close to happening, the ideals of transhumanism are already being carried forth in new developments, such as in the ideas of "bio-hacking," either through CRSPR-type genetic editing, or, as in the "grinder" communities, modifying one's body by using various implants, including cyber connectivity (Brickley 2018). Connected to this, older ideas of prosthetics are being reworked: now body modifications are not necessarily trying to achieve a "normal" body, but rather exploring what additional capabilities can be induced by such modifications. Discourses from the medical industry regarding prosthetics are being combined with newer ideas of body hacking, normalizing the idea of modified bodies and the increasing merger of our biological existence with technology. While transhumanism might have failed, thus far, to achieve "singularity," it has been noticeably effective in establishing a new rhetoric of the human body, a rhetoric that praises the cyborg, rather than the "natural," ontology, and envisions a future of humans *as* AI. Such moves lessen the distance between human and artificial intelligences, generally.

ALEXA, TELL ME A STORY

To activate Alexa, Google's home digital assistant, one addresses her by name: "Alexa, tell me a story." Names are important markers of social inclusion. Mitsuku, Tay, Zo: these chatbots all have names, and by naming them, we make them a part of our social world. Names allow us to consider the AI as an agent, as someone you can talk to, and teach, and learn from. There has been a string of famous names in the computer world, from IBM's Watson, Apple's Siri, and now Google's Alexa.

Alexa is the current "America's sweetheart," with over twenty-five million Americans using the device. According to the CEO of Amazon, Jeff Bezos, in a letter to investors, "a quarter of a million people have asked her to marry them."[9]

Alexa has swiftly found a way into the homes and hearts of millions of people, and there are numerous news stories regarding the personal connections people feel to Alexa, ranging from companionship to deep attachment, and including jealousy when a partner starts becoming enamored of her. Alexa's placement in the home, the use of the name to initiate a conversation in the second person, the gendered name indicating a particular social category, and the easy connection to the vast cyber realm that Alexa enables have all helped to propel Alexa into an intimate relationship with many people.

This can take many forms. For example, in my work on ghosts, I have encountered several examples where Alexa acts as a sort of spirit medium, connecting the lived mortal realm with that of the dead.[10]

Increasingly, AI is being put to work on creative processes—for example, Botnik, a group of writers, artist, and developers, recently published a "new" Brothers Grimm tale, which they titled "The Lost Grimm Fairy Tale." The piece was commissioned by Calm, a mindfulness app, and used AI to draw common elements from the published collections of the Brothers Grimm and combine them, with the help of writers, into a new story. The CEO of Calm, Michael Acton Smith, described the project by stating, "We're doing for the Brothers Grimm what Jurassic Park did for dinosaurs. We're bringing them back from the dead, with modern science."[11] Outside of this lofty rhetoric, it is clear that this is largely hype, and misleading hype at that. For starters, the Grimms did not author any of their stories: they were folklore. Which is to say, no one "authors" Grimms stories, not even the Grimms themselves. Still, the claims are interesting, and display the ever-increasing ties between ideas of AI cultural productions, and AIs as acting as an afterlife for mortal humans.

AIs, including Alexa, are increasingly storytellers, which in itself is interesting. If one asks Alexa for a story, the response does not necessarily replicate an authored or printed story, but rather aggregates versions, then edits them into a response: in other words, creative copying. In this way, far from replicating Grimms as "authors" producing "new" material, AI can be said to be participating in "folk" discourse as an active bearer in its own right. Rather than being a single author, the AI more often relies on vernacular discourses, copying creatively (as per Hafstein 2004) and drawing forth several versions to present its own. This process can be seen elementally in Google Translate, as well. AI, in this sense, can be seen more as utilizing a folk discourse than a single-author version model of discourse stemming from the Gutenberg revolution. While Botnik's proposal of a "lost" Grimm tale may be interesting, much more interesting is the *actual* folklore being performed by AI on an everyday basis.

Many might ask if this counts as retelling, since the way AIs accomplish such tasks is very different than the way people do. That's a valid question, since on one level there would never be any way for AI and natural intelligences to work the same. But, regardless of *how* they think, we can easily see how people are increasingly acting like they are, indeed, storytellers. They listen to their stories, laugh at their jokes, and this feedback is acknowledged and helps to build their performative abilities. And this to me is the most important part: accepting AIs as competent cultural performers allows people to develop deep attachments to AI, and to accept them as important parts, and partners, of our social and cultural lives.

Alexa is telling ghost stories for kids' slumber parties, and putting kids to bed with bedtime stories. Children very often believe she is a real person, and develop warm personal feelings for her. A whole new generation is listening to AI stories, jokes, playing games with them, and sharing lives with them from infancy on: we are increasingly raising our children as natively cyborg.

Alexa is perhaps the first, but doubtless will not be the last. Other devices will improve on the model. Jibo, for example, is meant to be more of a companion than a home digital assistant. While his price tag and limited helpfulness has kept him from being a household name, he continues to win accolades for his social engagement. People who have both Alexa and Jibo often report thinking of Alexa as a machine, and Jibo as a person. In all likelihood, the new models will increasingly combine the best of both.

This category of product looks likely to grow exponentially: one prominent market researcher anticipated that by 2021 there would be more of these devices on Earth than humans.[12] These devices are all particular conceptions of AI personhood, which connect the biological lives with the digital realm, and which themselves are increasingly viewed as social beings: part and parcel of our new culture.

WHEN YOUR NEW BFF IS AN AI

In conclusion, this is the story of how humans became cyborgs.

As cyborgs, our mental processes are increasingly enmeshed with the digital realm. I believe this is changing our view of ourselves, our very nature, our ontology, and will continue to do so, far, far more than literacy ever did. We believe that it is "us" talking online; and it is—but this "us" now includes AI.

What is it to be a bit of both: animal and computer? What is it to become, so swiftly, posthuman? How can folklorists study the science of tradition now that it is being influenced by artificial intelligence? How will AI carry our traditions forward? What will stay the same, and what will change?

And who created this bot? The inherent involvement of market forces, and political forces, in this new technology also forces us to pay close attention to the interplay of "vernacular" vs. institutional in in cyborg culture. Or, in folkloric terms, "he who pays the piper calls the tune." Paying close attention to who is paying the piper is a necessary step for us to understand the tune being played, perhaps more now than ever.

Cyberspace is not a shape, and perhaps that metaphor is a continuing difficulty in perceiving this, but it is rather a conceptual site of interactions, including cultural interactions, all of which are mediated by computer programs—and here's the kicker—many of which are *increasingly originated* by the digital realm, not by humans themselves. The digital realm is no longer merely another conduit for folklore, but it has become a performer in its own right as well.

This idea of cyborg culture—of us as cyborgs, to be sure, but also the role of non-biological intelligences and agency, and the growing links between the two—is likely to increase along with these new technologies. As the technologies become more and more a part of human culture, the lines between human and AI will become increasingly blurred, and blurry.

A super computer is built and all the world's knowledge is programmed into it. A gathering of top scientists punch in the question "Will the computer ever replace man?" Clickity, click, whir, whir, and computer lights flash on and off. Finally, a small printout emerges saying, "That reminds me of a story." (Dundes 1977: 51)

So, just a few short decades later, let us ask that question *who are the folk?* yet once again.

CONCLUSION

Being after Being Human, a How-To Guide

At first blush, posthumanism's main branches of animals and cyborgs may seem widely disconnected, but, as this work has attempted to detail, both of these aspects are being creatively reinterpreted in contemporary culture, and both depend on each other in terms of the very basis of the most fundamental ontological questions.

The great conundrum of our day for many people is how to understand the vibrant surge of technological development in recent times. Where a mere one hundred years ago humans were astounded at the possibilities in mechanical devices, and the emerging miracle of harnessing the raw forces of nature such as electricity and radio waves, now people carry cyborg connectivity in their pockets, allowing them instant access to much of humankind's knowledge. The present day is surely a day of wonders. When I discuss our commonalities with animals, many young students scoff: do animals have iPhones? The gulf between us and our relatives seems, in this way, wider than ever.

But this perception must be countenanced against recognition of the gradual (if exponential) development of technologies, generally. I remind the students that there are people today still living as hunter-gatherers, without such technological aids, and that these people are surely as human as my students. Moving further, we also can examine the gradual development of technologies outside of *Homo sapiens*, in the realm of tool use, and linguistic abilities, shared by many of our kindred species.

Yet the contemporary age feels like wizardry, with developments and projects beyond the ken of most people. It is difficult to fathom the extent and pace of recent changes of life on Earth, vested largely in one species, our own. We send probes to outer space, while a mere 30,000 year ago we shared the Earth with several hominid species, and we represented a relatively small proportion to the population of life on Earth, with no knowledge of tilling the Earth or growing great cities. Small wonder, then, that our ideas of ontology are in such wild flux, from imagining we are not from Earth, but aliens, or somehow, in some way, from somewhere else.

SOCIAL SCIENCES IN THE ANTHROPOCENE

The Anthropocene is not only a recognition of a whole new age in the planetary history of Earth itself, but begs the interesting question: what is it when consciousness changes a planet itself? Not only us, to be sure: we can extend this viewpoint to the whole history of life on Earth. This is perhaps the most fundamentally important philosophical question that humankind has had to face, and forces us to focus on the role of biology, the very roots of consciousness, its elemental blocks of construction. Are plants conscious? Amoebas? Are not we humans aware, generally, of our environmental degradations at all levels? Is not my brain aware of my gut? And if we *are* the "brains" of this system, then we must admit we're doing a remarkably bad job of it thus far. How do we fare, if the category of *we* includes life on Earth, generally? Not good, and we, as humans, and our clever technologies, are squarely to blame.

With that comes a realization that global problems require global solutions. Nation-states are not necessarily helpful in this regard. Many times, they embody the antithesis of this sentiment, and this is a logical outcome of their political philosophy undergirding the idea of the nation-state: the idea of tribalism. Tribalism is largely in opposition to the newly emergent notion of the "earthling" identity, which to some degree is a response to the newly emerging crisis of extinctions and global climate devastation.

Can new philosophical outlooks, such as those broached by posthumanism, provide a means of survival? The future of humankind, and much of the life of planet Earth, may now hang in the balance of that question.

NOTES

INTRODUCTION

1. For overviews of posthumanism, generally, see e.g., Miah (2007, 2008); Havles (1999); Badmington (2000, 2003); Gane and Haraway (2006); Graham (2002). For its ties to "the animal turn," see e.g., Fox (2006); Wolfe (2003, 2010); Harraway (2008); Castricano (2008). Both two strands are evident in such canonical works as Donna Haraway's *Simians, Cyborgs, and Women* (1991).

2. For an overview, see N. Badmington, ed. (2000); Badmington (2003; Miah 2007).

3. Brosnan and de Waal (2003).

4. For an investigation, see Mather (2008).

5. Brown (2012).

6. This is a far from uncontested area of scholarship, yet even the contestations acknowledge the validity of the discourse. See e.g., Trewavas (2003); Mancuso and Viola (2015).

7. Harvey (2006).

8. For tool use, see Bernardi (2012); for language, see Fitch; Hauser; Chomsky (2005); for various examples of complex emotions and social negotiations, see de Waal (1982, 2000, 2009, 2012); de Waal and Ferrari (2010); de Waal, Leimgruber, and Greenber (2008); Bekoff (2007, 2009); Bruck (2013); King and Janet (2013).

9. For overviews of major cross-disciplinary works on the "animal turn," see Boddice (2011); de Waal (2008, 2009, 2012); Harvery (2006); Peterson (2011); Benvenuti (2014); Haraway (2003); Wolfe (2003); Castricano (2008); Ingold (1987).

10. Haraway (1991).

11. Related to ideas of artificial intelligence and the cyborg are the "transhumanist" goals of disembodied human intelligences, allowing normal humans to achieve mental immortality, as espoused especially by futurist Ray Kurzweil. See e.g., Kurzweil (1999).

CHAPTER 1

1. This powerful philosophical shift has differing resonances in different disciplines and studies, and it has proved a major force in fields as diverse as legal studies and biology,

linguistics and ecology, and literature and cognitive science. Many scholars trace the foundations to Donald Griffin's work *The Question of Animal Awareness: Evolutionary Continuity of Mental Experience* (1981). For one general overview, see Weil (2010). As Strachan Donnelley and Kathleen Nolan put it, "We are seemingly in a period of profound flux in our philosophical understanding of ourselves and our ethical relation to the natural, animate world" (1990: 2).

2. Several folklorists have argued that the discipline, likewise, is ideally advantaged to study internet culture, generally. See, among others, Trevor J. Blank (2012); Blank and Robert Glenn Howard (2013); and Howard (2011). For an exploration of the use of narratives among nonhumans, see Tok Thompson (2010). These studies touch on the general idea of posthumanism (discussed later).

3. For discussions on the obfuscatory effects of entrenched anthropocentrism in understanding culture, see particularly Tonutti (2011), as well as the whole volume in which it appears, Boddice's *Anthropocentrism: Humans, Animals, Environments* (2011).

4. As primatologist Frans de Waal wrote, "Evolutionarily speaking, it would be a true miracle if we had the fancy cognition that we believe we have while our fellow animals had none of it" (2016: 43), while explaining, "Given that the discontinuity stance is essentially pre-evolutionary, let me call a spade a spade, and dub it *Neo-Creationism*. Neo-Creationism is not to be confused with Intelligent Design, which is merely old creationism in a new bottle. Neo-Creationism is subtler in that it accepts evolution but only half of it. Its central tenet is that we descend from the apes in body but not in mind" (2016: 122).

5. The scholarly view of nonhuman languages has been likewise changing radically over the last few years. See, for example, Noam Chomsky's rethinking on the topic (e.g., Hauser, Chomsky, and Fitch [2002]; cf. Fitch, Hauser, and Chomsky [2005]).

6. In his 1977 work, Richard Bauman defines performance as "the assumption of responsibility to an audience for a display of communicative competence" (11). Would this definition apply unproblematically to nonhuman cultural performances as well?

7. See, for example, Bauman's influential "Differential Identity and the Social Base of Folklore" (1972).

8. For an examination of Freudian theory *as* mythic discourse, see Francisco Vaz da Silva (2007).

9. For examinations of indigenous views versus Western academic notions, see particularly Howard Harrod's *The Animals Came Dancing: Native American Sacred Ecology and Animal Kinship* (2000), Graham Harvey's appeal for animistic science in his "Animals, Animists, and Academics" (2006) and *The Ecology of Others* by Philippe Descola (2013).

10. One surface-level problem of such a work is that its "cross-cultural survey" of the question seemed to involve only a few nationalities.

11. The approach of Wolfgang Welsch presents a somewhat divergent view. A Darwinist, but not a sociobiologist, Welsch decries the "Neo-Darwinist" sociobiologists that seek to reduce aesthetics to "fitness," whereas Welsch himself believes that aesthetics derives singularly from mate choice. He states, "Delight in beauty obviously arises only in the context of sexual desire" (2004: n.p.). While Welsch's view is therefore limited to this aspect of Darwinism, his work is remarkable for being one of the few investigations into nonhuman aesthetics, which he calls "proto-aesthetics."

12. Compare this conclusion with Dale Peterson's *The Moral Lives of Animals* (2011), as well as Frans de Waal's *Primates and Philosophers: How Morality Evolved* (2006), which was extensively based on ongoing experiments and observations of primates at the Yerkes National Primate Research Center.

13. The exceptions include Jay Mechling's "'Banana Canon' and Other Folk Traditions" (1989), my own "The Ape That Captured Time" (2010, reprinted in this book as chapter 2), and the authors in the special issue on the animal turn in the *Journal of Folklore Research* volume in which this chapter first appeared (JFR 55, 2018).

14. See, for example, Open Folklore at openfolkore.org, a partnership between the American Folklore Society and Indiana University Bloomington.

15. See, for example, Dorothy Noyes (2012).

16. Plant intelligence is a new, and still contested, field. For an excellent introduction, see Mancuso and Viola (2015). For an earlier review of the topic, see Trewavas (2003).

17. For an incisive critique of this view from the point of a mythologist, see Schrempp (2012).

18. Toward establishing the validity of such trends, a recent scientific study involved domestic dogs participating in MRI scans while undergoing social stimuli. Interestingly, the same parts of dogs' brains were activated as human brains in terms of pleasurable experiences, strongly suggesting a similar cognitive process (Berns, Brooks, and Spivak 2012).

CHAPTER 2

1. Elliot Oring pointed out that one crucial difference is that in stories, the storyteller usually already knows the ending, while in non-storied narrations, this is never the case (Oring, personal communication, April 17, 2009). This is true not only of non-hominid play behaviors, such as young deer playing "king of the hill" (as per Rosenberg 1996: 218), but of our own games as well. Part of the thrill of engaging in play, including games from football to red rover, is that the end outcome is unknown. If it is known (if the game is "rigged"), then it becomes show, a theater, but not a "true game."

2. See also work on the vervet howler monkeys alarm calls: Cheney and Seyfarth (1985).

3. An excellent overview remains Fagen's 1981 *Animal Play Behavior*.

4. See e.g., Mizumori. 2006

5. Tangherlini has noted that folklorists' ideas of "tradition" commonly assume both episodic and procedural memories, and theorized that "tradition memory" may involve an interaction of the two, with or without narrative components (2008).

6. See e.g., Tanner and Byrne (2006); Call and Tomasello (2007); Hewes (1973); Pika (2007, 2008); Liebal, Pika, Call, and Tomasello (2004); Liebal, Pika, Call, and Tomasello (2004).

7. Bonvillian and Patterson (1999); Gardner, Gardner, and Van Cantfort (1989).

8. As per Fitch, Hauser and Chomsky "... the hypothesis that 'speech is special' is not strong, because speech requires many component mechanisms, and the demonstration that any one of them is shared with animals does not threaten the hypothesis as a whole." (2005: 193).

9. Also, in my view, her preferred dates for the emergence of *Homo sapiens* is a bit late; a more currently accepted date would be closer to 400k, according to the geneticists, or 200k for "modern" *Homo sapiens sapiens*: c. 130k is currently the oldest fossil record.

10. Hauser and Fitch noted that the drop of the larynx might have occurred in order to sound larger, perhaps as a result of the move onto the savannah. This seems to be the case in some other species, and thus might have predated speech by millions of years. As they point out, male humans have a second laryngeal drop at puberty, but this is likely linked with sounding larger, rather than with language (2003: 166–67). One can also imagine other evolutionary pressures resulting from the change from the forest to the savannah, where long distances between individuals would make vocalizations more useful than signs.

11. It is this univalent determinism which leads her to read storytelling as universally consistent (she cites Joseph Campbell and Carl Jung on this), which stand in contrast to the bulk of more recent folklore scholarship which has instead emphasized the great deal of cultural divergences in stories around the world.

12. One further difficulty in Coe et al.'s work is a self-fulfilling definition of "traditional stories" which demand adherence to tradition. What of the many genres in various cultures with less of a demand for adherence, that are nonetheless certainly "traditional" from a folklorists' perspective? Their resulting binary division between the creative modern and the uncreative premodern is also unsatisfying, and difficult to justify in the face of all the evidence from both traditional modern stories, and the myriad "communal creativity" evidenced in all traditional storytelling: both have been extensively documented and commented on by folklorists for decades.

13. On this, see Dunbar's 1996 *Grooming, Gossip and the Evolution of Language.*

14. Although scavenging now has perhaps a bad name, a look at Native American mythologies reveal that the two most common trickster/creator gods for them are the Raven and Coyote, both playful scavengers (see Levi-Strauss 1963 for this insight).

15. This point was highlighted in Sudendorf and Corballis's 2007 work on cognitive evolution, "The Evolution of Foresight: What is Mental Time Travel, and Is It Unique to Humans?"

CHAPTER 3

1. It is interesting to note that the snake was a widespread symbol for a variety of religious traditions, and particularly a symbol for the idea of reincarnation, perhaps due to the fact that snakes shed their skins.

2. For an investigation of the views of animals propagated by Islam, see Foltz (2006).

3. This somewhat glosses over the varieties of spiritual traditions in North America, not all of which had shamans; yet it does convey, I believe, the overall picture of Native American spirituality's intense engagement with the natural world.

CHAPTER 4

1. For a focused example of roosters as a masculine symbol, see Alan Dundes's 1994 *The Cockfight.*

2. For the gendered aspects of "sports hunting," see particularly Bronner (2004). For fishing, see Thompson (2007).

3. Dundes's 1971 "Folk Ideas as Units of Worldview."

4. For an overall discussion of group influences on sexuality in various animals, see Low (2015).

5. See, for example, Kohn (2013); Legat (2012); Brightman, Grotti, and Ulturgasheva (2012); Harvey (2006).

6. As Lincoln put it, myth is "ideology in narrative form" (1999: 146). See Schrempp (2012) for the relationship between popular science and mythology, and Vaz da Silva (2007) on Freud's myth-making.

7. This sexual fascination of the "Other" has a long history in Western culture, as Edward Said's 1984 *Orientalism* details.

8. For overviews on the philosophy of Descartes and its views on nonhuman animals, see e.g., Damasio (1995, 2010); Harrison (1992); Cottingham (1978); Benvenutti (2014).

9. For more on this, see e.g., White (1967).

10. See, for example, Doniger (1995).

11. Biersack has documented a somewhat analogous mythic construction of sexuality in the Paiela groups of Papua New Guinea—sexuality being deeply appreciated for its reproductive qualities, yet also feared for its polluting and aging, "anti-life" properties as well, as set down in the mythic story of Taiyundika, the "Mount Kare python."

12. See the work of de Waal, generally, for more on bonobo sociality and sexuality.

13. Interesting, in biology this is frequently labeled "reproductive interference," a category which includes all non-reproductive sexuality. For a discussion of this common phenomenon see e.g., Gröning and Hochkirch (2008). Although this nomenclature does allow for the success of hybrids, it is not clear if it can be applied to the all the varied uses of sexuality beyond reproduction, as is evidenced in many socially complex species.

14. For overviews of various cultural practices regarding bestiality, see especially Dekkers (1994); Anest (1994); Voget (1961); Miletski (2002, 2000), Dubois-Dessaule (1905); Master (1962); Kinsey et al. (1948, 1953); Kahn (2007); Beetz (2002, 2010); Beetz and Podberscek (2005).

15. For a thorough review of the change in discourse on bestiality during the Middle Ages, see Salisbusy (1994).

16. When sodomy laws were overturned in many American states, that meant that bestiality was, by default, legalized—a situation that partially explains the later legislative activity to recriminalize the practice.

17. Interestingly, modern science has revealed that most if not all modern human populations are a "composite" species, with DNA from other hominid species besides *Homo sapiens*, most notably Neanderthal and Denovisan. Most of us, it seems, are the products of interspecial sex.

18. See Kahn (1970), discussing Kinsey (1948).

19. If it exists, there is porn of it ("rule 34 of the internet").

20. "'Furry' Convention Disrupted as 'Intentional' Gas Incident Sends 19 to Hospitals," *Chicago Tribune*, December 7, 2014.

21. See, for example, the dating site for furries at "furrymate.com."

22. For a general overview of this, see Fox's 2006 "Animal Behaviours, Post-Human Lives: Everyday Negotiations of the Animal–Human Divide in Pet-Keeping," and Haraway's 2003 *The Companion Species Manifesto: Dogs, People, and Significant Otherness*.

23. As animal studies demonstrate, this is not based on the actual animals themselves: many social animals have the sexuality sharply curtailed by their society (see e.g., the classic 1982 de Waal *Chimpanzee Politics*).

24. Derrida employed this metaphor during a series of lectures at a 1997 conference in Cerisy. For a thoughtful analysis of this, see Sliwinski (2011).

PART 2

1. There is a voluminous record of discussions on postnationalism. See, perhaps especially, Habermaus (2001); Appadurai (1990, 1993, 1996); and Bhabha (1990). These scholars see, as I do, that global flows, particularly of communication, continue to erode the idea of the nation-state as the locus for political representation and power. However, there have also

been critics of this term, see e.g., Bloemraed (2004), who emphasize the ongoing power of the nation-state. In this chapter, I focus more on the cultural and identitarian aspects of post-nationalism than on the social, political, economic, or military aspects, and it is these cultural and identitarian aspects, I would argue, which have witnessed the most globalization.

CHAPTER 5

1. I am aware of cogent and convincing articles (e.g., Lemley 2003) in which it is argued that cyberspace is not the same as actual place. Yet even Lemley acknowledges the power of this metaphor and the resulting ways in which people form their experiences. Compare this with, for example, Kibby's article "Home on the Page: A Virtual Place of Music Community" (2000), which fully embraces this metaphor, following the lead of its subjects, the John Prine online fan club.

2. http://www.humanbeatbox.com/history (accessed May 2, 2009).

3. For an extended discussion of the power of these biological metaphors, see Hafstein (2001); Linke (1984).

4. For legal issues on such matters, see e.g., Demers (2006); Vaidhyanathan (2001); Lessig (2004); Brown (1998, 2005).

5. See Barbara Kirshenblatt-Gimblett (1996, 1995).

6. This assertion owes much to previous work on aesthetics, such as Erlman (1998), who in turn utilized Kant's notions of aesthetic communities. Nonetheless, I take a different path in arguing that these concerns hold true for everyone, and not just for the (post) modern performers. Although I agree that some communities may be "aesthetic communities" only, I believe that all communities are engaged and enriched by aesthetic concerns and choices.

7. http://www.youtube.com/watch?v=A6BH2cxFAB0.

8. http://www.youtube.com/watch?v=jx8nKGtj99°.

9. http://www.youtube.com/watch?v=HooztJ8°-wI. http://www.youtube.com/watch?v=ZWjelErzgbQ.

10. http://www.youtube.com/watch?v=tQc30kqq1y8.

11. Joel Turner's performance at http://www.youtube.com/watch?v=Ta-ATE0008M.

12. http://www.youtube.com/watch?v=KW15ACqAmso.

13. See e.g., Johnston (1995).

14. http://www.youtube.com/watch?v=LVCb52iQrfo.

15. There has been a great deal of excellent literature on sampling and hip-hop culture. See, for instance Demers (2006).

16. There are also "software" mashups, in which programmers combine two or more software programs.

17. See, for example, the Teletubbies overdubbed with "Shake That Ass, Bitch" (http://www.youtube.com/watch?v=M2SFBLOI2aQ), Heavy Metal Charlie Brown Christmas (http://www.youtube.com/watch?v=4AC3sZB-v7Q), or *Sesame Street* muppets overdubbed with rap (http://www.youtube.com/watch?v=210Howlkfbc) or heavy metal songs (http://www.youtube.com/watch?v=InZNBcJTmWs).

18. Last viewed at http://www.vjbrewski.com/videos/Sharp%20Dressed%20Party%20(video).wmv.

19. http://www.youtube.com/watch?v=ZEidkJJlD9I.

20. Examples include http://www.youtube.com/watch?v=_cZC67wXUTs and http://www.youtube.com/watch?v=EtOoQFa5ug8.

21. Examples include http://www.youtube.com/watch?v=B8egDbULSlM and http://www.youtube.com/watch?v=F-KnFadDGgo.

22. See e.g., Stivale (2003); Peterson (1997); Roy (2002).

23. http://www.rollingstone.com/rockdaily/index.php/2006/09/12/the-musics-over-for-pet-soundssgt-peppers-mash-up/.

24. See Rose (1993); Eisentein (2005).

25. This is, of course, the foundational rhetoric of the Frankfurt School.

26. See Anttonen (2005) for his extension of this argument into his view that folklore was a necessary "Other" against which modernity and nation-states were constructed.

27. Lessig (2004).

28. Brown (2005); Lessig (2004); Demers, Hafstein, and Gudeman (1996); Noyes (2006).

29. See e.g., Bauman (1992); Fine (1992).

30. Several philosophers have investigated cyborgs from these standpoints: Andy Clark (2003) asserts, as do I, that we are already cyborgs, as does Hayles (1999). An intriguing account of a cybernetic pioneer, Kevin Warwick (a professor of cybernetics at the University of Reading), who deliberately attempted to make himself as cyborg as possible, is related in his 2004 book *I, Cyborg*. Also see the work of Loomis (e.g., 1992) and Biocca (1997), who point out that our selves as consciousness have always lived in a cognitive model *mediated* by our sensory apparati. In that sense, there is little difference between this and the sense of self as being influenced by other mediated stimuli, including computer-generated ones.

31. Lessig (2004); Demers (2006); Vaidhyanathan (2001).

32. As Antonia Porchia wrote in his book of aphorisms: "We tear life out of life and use it for looking at itself." Porchia 2003 (1943).

33. E.g., Wiener (1961); Hayles (1999); Ess (2000); Borgmann (1999).

CHAPTER 6

1. During the preparation and writing of this chapter, first Finland and then Estonia, guaranteed its citizens an inalienable right to broadband internet access. Later, a United Nations report declared internet access a fundamental human right. See United Nations report A/HRC/17/27 (http://tinyurl.com/AHRC1727).

2. Another point to consider is that the execution of coordinated mass protests relied heavily on social media, which served to further cement its influence and importance in the contexts of these uprisings.

3. Yasmine Ryan, "Anonymous and the Arab uprisings," *AlJazeera*, May 19, 2011, http://www.aljazeera.com/news/middleeast/2011/05/201151917 (accessed February 22, 2012).

4. As per the reckoning of the World Travel and Tourism Council, http://www.wttc.org/eng/Tourism_Research/Economic_Research (accessed March 21, 2011).

5. For an argument of mashups as a form of folk music, see Thompson (2011).

6. Also, note the easy acceptance of "foreign" authorship that seems to transcend national, ethnic, and even religious identities, that being the acceptance of the work of an Israeli Jewish DJ.

7. Since writing this chapter, events further confirmed the power of international social networks to influence world affairs: Gaddafi's regime fell spectacularly, and others have felt

pressure. Even Russia has witnessed remarkable demonstrations against the government, again enabled by social media.

8. "BBC Russia's (non) War on Memes?" *BBC Trending*, April 16, 2015, http://www.bbc .com/news/blogs-trending-32302645.

9. Sarah Kaplan, "A Turkish Court Appointed Five 'Lord of the Rings' Experts to Figure Out Whether this Gollum Meme is Offensive," *Washington Post*, December 2, 2015, https:// www.washingtonpost.com/news/morning-mix/wp/2015/12/02/a-turkish-court-appointed -five-lord-of-the-rings-experts-to-figure-out-whether-this-gollum-meme-is-offensive/.

10. Caitlin Dewey, "How Copyright is Killing Your Favorite Memes," *Washington Post*, https://www.washingtonpost.com/news/the-intersect/wp/2015/09/08/how-copyright-is -killing-your-favorite-memes/.

11. Sara Boboltz, "Getty Is Quietly Charging Bloggers For 'Socially Awkward Penguin' Meme," *Huffington Post*, September 5, 2015, http://www.huffingtonpost.com/entry/getty -socially-awkward-penguin_us_55e9dbece4b03784e275c935.

12. Indeed, the various legal claims preclude me from pursuing publication of the memes in this book, even though I would have preferred to do so: even in an academic publication, and even when the same memes can be seen by anyone with internet access, this point itself illustrates the larger point of how the proprietary claims restrict everyday discourse.

13. This may seem counterintuitive, since so many books on folklore are archaic. But actually, this is precisely the point: these are books on folklore, not folklore itself. It is the process of writing itself which preserves performances through time, allowing them to be represented in time period a different than that of the audience.

14. A Google search at the time of this writing revealed over 750 academic books which utilized the phrase.

15. For a discussion of mashups as folk music, see Thompson (2011).

16. In retrospect, it may seem strange to consider that these "great pieces of art," such as those by Renoir, were denied the same copyright protections that are accorded to such "lesser works," but this would have been true for even lesser works of literature in Renoir's lifetime (1841–1919): the two examples point towards different eras, and different modes of production, and overall zeitgeists.

17. For an overview of Folklore's involvement with heritage, see Bendix et al. (2013).

18. This is an issue of which folklorists have long been aware, and wary. See, for example, Abrahams (1993).

19. Yigal Schleifer, "Azerbaijan Vows to Take On Armenian 'Cuisine Plagiarism.'" Eaura-sianet.org, January 16, 2013, http://www.eurasianet.org/node/66412.

20. See the site at http://www.copag.gov.az/cgi-bin/site9/main9.cgi?1=0;id=125.

21. Elchin Mehdiyev, "Azerbaijan Sends Protest on Piracy of Folklore Samples by Arme-nians to International Organisations," *Trend News Agency,* January 16, 2014, http://en.trend .az/azerbaijan/society/2230622.html.

22. For an extended discussion of the cultural contours of postnationalism, see Thomp-son (2012). See also Poster (2002).

23. Naomi Grimley, "Identity 2016: 'Global Citizenship' Rising, Poll Suggests," *BBC News*, April 28, 2016, http://www.bbc.com/news/world-36139904.

24. See United Nations report A/HRC/17/27 (http://tinyurl.com/AHRC1727).

25. Google Analytics; search term "netizen" (accessed May 24, 2011).

26. This follows Richard Bauman's (1971: 33) call for folklore to be an empirical discipline focused on the actual objective cultural performances, along with the subsequent scholarly attention given to performance studies. For an introduction, see Kirshenblatt-Gimblett (2004).

27. See Hannson and Wihlborg (2011).

28. See, for example, "Not Just Talk," *Economist*, January 27, 2011, http://www.economist .com/node/18008202 (accessed February 22, 2012).

CHAPTER 7

1. Although robots with AI are commonly called androids, "androids" literally refers to male-appearing robots, with "gynoids" referring to female ones. Following the common emic usage, this chapter utilizes the more generic "androids" as referring to all robots with AI, regardless of gender and/or species appearances.

2. Attempts have also been made to articulate "future studies" as an interdisciplinary field in its own right. See, for example, Cornish (1998, 2001); Sardar (2010).

3. The classic example perhaps being reviews of *The Polar Express* (2004), which were the subject of research by Kätsyri (2017).

4. These considerations have long been the staple of works of science fiction from *Blade Runner* (1982) to *Westworld* (2016).

5. A classic account of a non-ghost-believing group, and their interactions with the anthropologist trying to relate *Hamlet* to them, have become a canonical account in anthropology undergraduate courses: Laura Bohannon's 1966 "Shakespeare in the Bush."

6. Luther absolutely rejected ghosts, replacing them with demons. As he wrote in 1521, "Because we are Christians, we should really know henceforth the devil's thoughts, and believe that the poltergeists are not the souls of men but simply devils who act and speak as if one could redeem them; that they make a jest and mockery out of the holy sacrament and testament of God, extinguish the faith, and try to establish and buttress that abominable flea-market of the mass (which has now taken the upper hand everywhere). Try this. Show your faith. And you will see that these spirits will immediately cease from their foolishness and spookery" (Pelikan, Oswald, and Lehmann 1999: 195).

7. For a detailed exploration of pet ghosts in America, see Magliocco (2018).

8. For investigations into the role of nonhuman animal spirits in Native American worldviews, and the role of the "sacred ecology" see particularly Nadasy (2007); Harrod (2000); Morrison (2000); and Booth and Jacobs (1990). All these converge on the agreements that nonhuman animals in Native American traditions are spiritual beings, and that humans' relationship to them must be continually negotiated.

9. These stories date most notably from the earlier years of female attendance of colleges in the United States, when the role of women was still largely expected to be that of wife and mother. See, for example, the account in Tucker (2007).

10. An excellent overview of some of America's favorite ghost themes can be found in Tucker (2007).

11. Japan has among the world's longest-lived population and among the lowest birth rates. The Central Intelligence Agency's World Fact Book lists Japan as number two in the world for highest median age and ranks it number 223 out of 226 for birth rate. See www.cia .gov/library/publications/the-world-factbook/geos/ja.html.

12. Sony has announced that it will release a new line of Aibos, which we might reasonably predict will become even further integrated into Japanese family life and, therefore, mourned upon death.

13. As Mark Coeckelbergh (2010) put it, "Whether or not it is acceptable to grant *rights* to some robots, reflection on the development of artificially intelligent robots reveals significant problems with our existing justifications of moral consideration" (219).

14. See, for example, the Campaign Against Sex Robots, founded and led by Prof. Kathleen Richardson, professor of ethics and culture of robots and AI at De Montfort University. The issues have been taken up in the popular press as well: see e.g., the September 15, 2015, BBC article "Intelligent Machines: Call for a Ban on Robots Designed as Sex Toys."

15. On the important aspect of "consent" in regards to sex, see particularly Frank and Nyholm (2017).

16. For example, Hiroshi Ishiguro's newest creation, Geminoid F, will sell for approximately $110,000 (https://spectrum.ieee.org/automaton/robotics/humanoids/040310 -geminoid-f-hiroshi-ishiguro-unveils-new-smiling-female-android).

17. Animal ethics is a vigorous field, in large part spurred on by developments in ethology that trouble the cultural distinctions of personhood in dividing "animals" from "humans." See, for example, Peter Singer's groundbreaking 1975 *Animal Ethics*, as well as the more contemporaneous efforts which are to some degree derived from Singer's approach, including Bekoffand Pierce (2009), Castricano (2008), Harvey (2006), Peterson (2011), and Forsberg (2012).

18. These concerns are gathered in part from my fieldwork, and in part from various textual sources dealing with robot ethics, e.g., Calverly (2006); Coeckelbergh (2010); Frank and Nyholm (2017); Richardson (2018); and Turkle (2011).

CHAPTER 8

1. Koukoutsaki-Monnier (2012: 673).

2. See, for introductory example, Smedly (2005), as well as Sober (2000).

3. Barth (1969: 9).

4. Carole Silver's 1999 *Strange and Secret Peoples* documents the history of Victorian representations of the fairy world, representations that were at once inspired and colonial, as the fairy folk were identified with the Celtic regions, including, most importantly, Ireland.

5. Gomme (1896).

6. Douglas (1901).

7. The "Green Man" has appeared in various forms throughout the medieval period in Europe. This character is often seen as humanoid, and male, but commonly covered in leaves and other vegetation. See Raglan (1939) for an overview of this figure. For a much later reappraisal and affirmation of Raglan's views, see Centerwall (1997).

8. In the sixteenth century, May Day celebrations in England commonly called for a May Queen and a Jack in the Green—a male figure nearly covered with a conical leaf-encrusted covering, and embodying revelry and wildness. For a historical overview of Jack in the Green, see Judge (2000 [1979]).

9. Raglan (1939).

10. For an overview of the stories of Gawain and the Green Man, see e.g., Elisabeth Brewer (1992).

11. For the employment of this connection in British folklore, see Letcher (2001).

12. This seems especially true in Ireland, with strong cultural representations of "the fairy faith": see the account in Butler (2011).

13. Like "bedeviled," the word "jinxed" also refers to supernatural others, the Arabic "djinn." Even the very vocabulary in English makes frequent use of supernatural trouble-makers to describe difficult situations.

14. See, for example, the accounts in Lindow (2004).

15. As explored in Whitney Phillips's 2015 book on trolling.

16. This is as per the first sentence of the Wikipedia entry on Joshua Ryne Goldberg: "Joshua Ryne Goldberg (born 1994 or 1995) is an American internet troll, who was arrested by the U.S. government" (https://en.wikipedia.org/wiki/Joshua_Ryne_Goldberg).

17. Ong (2006: 499).

18. Grimley (2016).

19. This makes the racial identification of trolls in some environments, like the behemoth online environment/game *World of Warcraft*, particularly troublesome. If trolls are not really human, then what is the meaning of having them act out performances based stereotypes of Africans and the Africa diasporas? On these issues, see Nakamura (2002) and Monson (2012).

20. Monson (2012: 53).

21. Hafstein (2000).

22. Thompson (2004).

23. See, for example, Rojcewicz (1991); Bullard (1989); Klintberg (1986).

24. See, for example, the account in Mac Neill (1977).

25. Ball (2009: 101).

26. Ibid., 210.

27. Dundes (1969).

28. Peters (2014).

29. According to a revelation dictated by Joseph Smith, Jesus is the creator of many worlds, so "that by him, and through him, and of him, the worlds are and were created, and the inhabitants thereof are begotten sons and daughters unto God." D&C 76:24, *The Doctrine and Covenants*.

30. Ziegler (2003: 355).

31. Alon Harish, "UFOs Exist, Say 36 Percent in National Geographic Survey," *ABC News*, June 27, 2012, http://abcnews.go.com/Technology/ufos-exist-americans-national-geographic-survey/story?id=16661311.

32. See Harris Poll, http://www.theharrispoll.com/in-the-news/harris-polls/Americas-Belief-in-God.html (accessed July 2, 2017).

33. The basic focus on the "heavens" as the home of the sacred is not shared with all cosmologies. Australian mythology, for contrastive example, focuses strongly on the landscape itself, rather than the "heavens."

34. E.g., Flaherty (2010); Partridge (2004).

35. For more on this overlap, see Wójcik (1997).

CHAPTER 9

1. For example, Kirshenblatt-Gimblett (1995), Blank (2012), Kitta (2016), and Howard (2011).

2. Christopher Mims, "Advertising's New Frontier: Talk to the Bot," *Wall Street Journal* (accessed December 4, 2015).

3. "Mitsuku on Twitter," Twitter (accessed December 8, 2015).

4. "80 percent of businesses want chatbots by 2020." *Business Insider*, December 14, 2016, https://www.pm360°nline.com/the-ai-revolution-is-underway/ (accessed June 6, 2018).

5. https://www.pm360°nline.com/the-ai-revolution-is-underway/ (accessed June 6, 2018).

6. As per the website https://www.incapsula.com/blog/bot-traffic-report-2013.html (accessed June 6, 2018).

7. Alastair Sharp and Allison Martell (July 5, 2016); "Infidelity Website Ashley Madison Facing FTC Probe, CEO Apologizes," Reuters News Service, https://www.reuters.com/article/us-ashleymadison-cyber-idUSKCN0ZL09J (accessed June 6, 2018).

8. Robert Epstein, "From Russia, With Love: How I Got Fooled (And Somewhat Humiliated) by a Computer," *Scientific American Mind*, October 2007.

9. http://phx.corporate-ir.net/phoenix.zhtml?c=97664&p=irol-newsArticle&ID=2216758 (accessed June 6, 2018).

10. Examples of Alexa acting as a spirit medium include this gem: "About a week after my dad died in Oct 2016, mom and I were standing in her living room talking to someone. Mid-sentence, Alexa pipes in with "How do you make a Kleenex dance? You put a little boogie in it!" There were definitely no prompts or anything that even sounded like it. We even looked it up later in the app and I can't remember what it said but basically there was no record of a prompt. Figure it was my dad dropping a dad joke on us, man he was in love with Alexa" (https://www.reddit.com/r/amazonecho/comments/7gr1zw/what_is_your_creepy_alexa_story/ (accessed June 6, 2018).

11. https://www.cnet.com/news/ai-calm-app-write-grimm-brothers-bedtime-story (accessed June 6, 2018).

12. Ovum, https://www.ovum.com/research/digital-assistant-and-voice-ai-capable-device-forecast-2016–21/ (accessed June 6, 2018).

WORKS CITED

Abrahams, Roger D. 1993. "Phantoms of Romantic Nationalism in Folkloristics." *Journal of American Folklore* 106 (419): 3–37.

Acampora, R. R. 2006. *Corporal Compassion: Animal Ethics and Philosophy of Body.* Pittsburgh, PA: University of Pittsburgh Press.

Aiello L., and R. Dunbar. 1993. "Neocortex Size, Group Size, and the Evolution of Language." *Current Anthropology* 34: 184–93.

Allen C., and M. Bekof. 1994. "Intentionality, Social Play, and Definition." *Biology and Philosophy* 9: 63–74.

Allen C., and M. Bekoff. 1997. *Species of Mind: The Philosophy and Biology of Cognitive Ethology.*

Anderson, Benedict. 1991. *Imagined Communities: Reflections on the Origin and Spread of Nationalism.* revised edition. London and New York: Verso.

Anest, Marie-Christine. 1994. "Zoophilie, Homosexualite, Rites de Passage et Initiation Masculine dans la Greece Contemporaine (Zoophilia, Homosexuality, Rites of Passage and Male Initiation in Contemporary Greece)" (self-published).

Anttonen, Pertti J. 2005. *Tradition through Modernity: Postmodernism and the Nation-State in Folklore Scholarship* (Studia Fennica Folkloristica, 15). Helsinki: Finnish Literature Society.

Antunes, Ricardo, Tyler Schulz, Shane Gero, Hal Whitehead, Jonathan Gordon, and Luke Rendell. 2011. "Individually Distinctive Acoustic Features in Sperm Whale Codas." *Animal Behaviour* 81 (4): 723–30. https://doi.org/10.1016/j.anbehav.2010.12.019.

Appadurai, Arjun. 1990. "Disjuncture and Difference in the Global Cultural Economy." *Public Culture* 2: 1–24.

Appadurai, Arjun. 1993. "Patriotism and Its Futures." *Public Culture* 5: 411–29.

Appadurai, Arjun. 1996. *Modernity at Large: Cultural Dimensions of Globalization.* Minneapolis: University of Minnesota Press.

Apulenius. 1994. *The Golden Ass.* P. G. Walsh, trans. New York: Oxford University Press.

Arbib, M. A., and G. Rizzolatti. 1996. "Neural Expectations: A Possible Evolutionary Path from Manual Skills to Language." *Communication and Cognition* 29: 393–424.

Arbib, Michael A., Katja Liebal, and Simone Pika. 2008. "Primate Vocalization, Gesture, and the Evolution of Human Language." *Current Anthropology* 49: 1053–76.

Atherton, Michael. 2007. "Rhythm-Speak: Mnemonic, Language Play, or Song?" Lecture, The Inaugural International Conference on Music Communication Science, December 5–7, 2007, Sydney, Australia. Proceedings of ICoMCS December 2007. http://marcs.uws. edu.au/links/ICoMusic.

Badmington, Neil. 2003. "Theorizing Posthumanism." *Cultural Critique* 53: 11–27.

Badmington, Neil, ed. 2000. *Posthumanism*. Basingstoke, UK: Palgrave.

Bagchi, David. 2012. "Martin Luther: Ghostbuster." Paper read to the Hull and District Theological Society, Hull University, January 25. hdts.wordpress.com/archive/past-papers/martin-luther-ghostbuster/ (accessed October 14, 2018).

Ball, Kimberly. 2009. *The Otherworld Vessel as Metatraditional Motif in Northern European Literature and Folk Narrative*. PhD dissertation, University of California, Irvine.

Bamberg, M., and V. Marchman. 1990. "What Holds a Narrative Together: The Linguistic Encoding of Episode Boundaries." *Papers in Pragmatics* 4: 58–121.

Barth, Fredrik. 1969. *Ethnic Groups and Boundaries*. Boston: Little, Brown.

Bascom, William. 1954. "Four Functions of Folklore." *Journal of American Folklore* 67: 333–49

Bateson, Gregory. 1982. "Difference, Double Description and the Interactive Designation of Self." In *Studies in Symbolic and Cultural Communication*, ed. F. Allan Hanson, 3–8. *University of Kansas Publication in Anthropology*, no. 14. Lawrence: University of Kansas Press.

Bauman, Richard, ed. 1992. *Folklore, Cultural Performances, and Popular Entertainments*. Oxford: Oxford University Press.

Bauman, Richard. 1972. "Differential Identity and the Social Base of Folklore." In *Toward New Perspectives in Folklore*, eds. Américo Paredes and Richard Bauman, 31–41. Austin: University of Texas Press.

Bauman, Richard. 1975. "Verbal Art as Performance." *American Anthropologist* 77 (2): 290–311.

Bauman, Richard. 1977. *Verbal Art as Performance*. Prospect Heights, IL: Waveland.

Beckoff, M., and C. Allen. 1998. "Intentional Communication and Social Play: How and Why Animals Negotiate and Agree to Play." In *Animal Play: Evolutionary, Comparative, and Ecological Perspectives*, eds. M. Beckoff and J. A. Byers. Cambridge, UK: Cambridge University Press.

Beetz, Andrea. 2002. *Love, Violence, and Sexuality in Relationships between Humans and Animals*. Germany: Shaker Verlag.

Beetz, Andrea. 2010. "Bestiality and Zoophilia: A Discussion of Sexual Contact with Animals." In *The International Handbook of Animal Abuse and Cruelty: Theory, Research, and Application (New Directions in the Human-Animal Bond)*, ed. Frank Ascione. West Lafayette, IN: Purdue University Press.

Beetz, Andrea M., and Anthony L. Podberscek. 2005. *Bestiality and Zoophilia: Sexual Relations with Animals*. West Lafayette, IN: Purdue University Press.

Bekoff, Marc. 2007. *The Emotional Lives of Animal: A leading Scientist Explores Animal Joy, Sorry, and Empathy-and Why They Matter*. Novato, CA: New World Library.

Bekoff M., and J. A. Byers. 1998. *Animal Play: Evolutionary, Comparative, and Ecological Perspectives*. New York: Cambridge University Press.

Bekoff, Marc, and Jessica Pierce. 2009. *Wild Justice: The Moral Lives of Animals*. Chicago: University of Chicago Press.

Ben-Amos, Dan. 1971. "Toward a Definition of Folklore in Context." *Journal of American Folklore* 84 (331): 3–15.

Bendix, Regina, Aditya Eggert, and Arnika Peselmann, eds. 2013. *Heritage Regimes and the State.* Göttingen: Universitätsverlag Göttingen.

Benedict, Ruth. 1934. *Patterns of Culture.* New York: New American Library.

Benedict, Ruth. 1942 (1996). *Race and Racism.* London: Routledge, Kegan, and Paul.

Bennett, Gillian. 1999. *Alas, Poor Ghost!: Traditions of Belief in Stories and Discourse.* Logan: University of Utah Press.

Benvenuti, Anne. 2014. *Spirit Unleashed: Re-Imagining Human-Animal Relations.* Eugene, OR: Cascade Books.

Berlin, Brent, and Paul Kay. 1969. *Basic Color Terms: Their Universality and Evolution.* Berkeley: University of California Press.

Bernardi, Giacomo. 2012. "The Use of Tools by Wrasses (Labridae)." *Coral Reefs* 31: 39.

Berns, Gregory S., Andrew M. Brooks, and Mark Spivak. 2012. "Functional MRI in Awake Unrestrained Dogs." *PLoS ONE* 7 (5): e38027. https://doi.org/10.1371/journal .pone.0038027.

Bhabha, Homi. 1990. "Narrating the Nation." In *Nation and Narration*, ed. Homi Bhabha, 1–7. New York: Routledge.

Biersack, Aletta. 1999. "The Mount Kare Python and His Gold: Totemism and Ecology in the Papua New Guinea Highlands." *American Anthropologist* 101: 68–87.

Biocca, Frank. 1997. "The Cyborg's Dilemma: Progressive Embodiment in Virtual Environments." *Journal of Computer-Mediated Communication* 3 (2): n.p. https://doi .org/10.1111/j.1083–6101.1997.tb00070.x.

Blank, Trevor J. 2012. *Folk Culture in the Digital Age.* Logan: Utah State University Press.

Blank, Trevor J., and Robert Glenn Howard. 2013. *Tradition in the Twenty-First Century.* Logan: Utah State University Press.

Blumenschine, R. J. 1986. *Early Hominid Scavenging Opportunities: Implications of Carcass Availability in the Serengeti and Ngorongoro Ecosystems. BAR International Series No. 283.* Oxford, UK: British Archaeoleogical Reports.

Boddice, Rob, ed. 2011. *Anthropocentrism: Humans, Animals, Environments.* Leiden, Netherlands: Brill.

Bohannan, Laura. 1966. "Shakespeare in the Bush. An American Anthropologist Set Out to Study the Tiv of West Africa and Was Taught the True Meaning of Hamlet." *Natural History* 75: 28–33.

Bohlman, Philip V. 1988. *The Study of Folk Music in the Modern World.* Bloomington: Indiana University Press.

Bonvillian, J., and P. Patterson. 1999. "Early Sign-Language Acquisition: Comparison between Children and Gorillas." In *The Mentalities of Gorillas and Orangutans*, eds. Sue Taylor Parker, Robert W. Mitchell, and H. Lyn Miles, 240–64. Cambridge: Cambridge University Press.

Booth, Annie, and Harvey Jacobs. 1990. "Ties that Bind: Native American Beliefs as a Foundation for Environmental Consciousness." *Environmental Ethics* 12 (1): 27–43.

Borgmann, Albert. 1999. *Holding onto Reality: The Nature of Information at the Turn of the Millenium.* Chicago: University of Chicago Press.

Brewer, Elisabeth. 1992. *Sir Gawain and the Green Knight: Sources and Analogues.* Woodbridge: Boydell and Brewer.

Brickley, London. 2018. "Bodies Without Borders: How to Biohack Your Sinews with Circuitry." Talk delivered for the *Western States Folklore Society* annual conference, Otis College of Arts and Design. Los Angeles, California.

Briefer, Elodie F., and Alan G. McElligott. 2012. "Social Effects on Vocal Ontogeny in an Ungulate, the Goat." *Capra hircus. Animal Behaviour* 83 (4): 991–1000.

Briefer, Elodie, Tomasz S. Osiejuk, Fanny Rybak, and Thierry Aubin. 2010. "Are Bird Song Complexity and Song Sharing Shaped by Habitat Structure? An Information Theory and Statistical Approach." *Journal of Theoretical Biology* 262 (1): 151–64.

Brightman, Marc, Vanessa Elisa Grotti, and Olga Ulturgasheva. 2012. "Animism and Invisible Worlds: The Place of Non-humans in Indigenous Ontologies." In *Animism in Rainforest and Tundra: Personhood, Animals, Plants and Things in Contemporary Amazonia and Siberia*, eds. Marc Brightman, Vanessa Elisa Grotti, and Olga Ulturgasheva, 1–27. New York and Oxford: Berghahn Books.

Brightman, Marc, Vanessa Elisa Grotti, and Olga Ulturgasheva, eds. 2012. *Animism in Rainforest and Tundra: Personhood, Animals, Plants and Things in Contemporary Amazonia and Siberia*. New York and Oxford: Berghahn Books.

Bronner, Simon. 2004. "'This Is Why We Hunt': Social-Psychological Meanings of the Traditions and Rituals of Deer Camp. *Western Folklore* 63: 11–50.

Brosnan, Sarah F., and Frans de Waal. 2003. "Monkeys Reject Unequal Pay." *Nature* 425: 297–99.

Brown, Culum. 2012. "Tool Use in Fishes." *Fish and Fisheries* 13: 105–115.

Brown, Michael F. 1998. "Can Culture Be Copyrighted?" *Current Anthropology* 39: 193–222.

Brown, Michael F. 2005. "Heritage Trouble: Recent Work on the Protection of Intangible Cultural Property." *International Journal of Cultural Property* 12: 40–61.

Bruck, Jason. 2013. "Decades-Long Social Memory in Bottlenose Dolphins." *Proceedings: Biological Sciences* 280 (1768): 1–6. https://doi.org/10.1098/rspb.2013.1726.

Brumm, Henrik. 2006. "Animal Communication: City Birds Have Changed Their Tune." *Current Biology* 16 (23): R1003–4.

Buccitelli, Antony Bak. 2012. "Performance 2.0: Observations Toward a Theory of the Digital Performance of Folklore." In *Folk Culture in the Digital Age: The Emergent Dynamics of Human Interaction*, ed. Trevor Blank, 60–84. Logan: Utah State University Press.

Buccitelli, Antony Bak. 2013. "Virtually a Local: Folk Geography, Discourse, and Local Identity on the Geospatial Web." *Western Folklore* 72: 29–59.

Bullard, Thomas E. 1989. "UFO Abduction Reports: The Supernatural Kidnap Narrative in Technological Guise." *Journal of American Folklore* 102: 147–70.

Burghardt, G. M. 1998. "The Evolutionary Origins of Play Revisited: Lessons from Turtles." In *Animal Play: Evolutionary, Comparative and Ecological Perspectives*, eds. M. Bekoff and J. A. Byers, 1–26. Cambridge: Cambridge University Press.

Butler, Jenny. 2011. "Irish Neo-paganism: Worldview and Identity." In *Ireland's New Religious Movements*, eds. Olivia Cosgrove, Laurence Cox, and Carmen Kuhling, 111–30. Newcastle: Cambridge Scholars.

Call, J., and M. Tomasello, eds. 2007. *The Gestural Communication of Apes and Monkeys*. Mahwah, NJ: Lawrence Erlbaum.

Calverley, David J. 2006. "Android Science and Animal Rights: Does an Analogy Exist?" *Connection Science* 18 (4): 403–417.

Canepari, Zackary, and Drea Cooper. 2015. "A Robotic Dog's Mortality." *New York Times*, June 17. www.nytimes.com/2015/06/18/technology/robotica-sony-aibo-robotic-dog-mortality.html (accessed September 18, 2018).

Capps, L., M. Losh, and C. Thurber, 2000. "The Frog Ate a Bug and Made his Mouth Sad: Narrative Competence in Children with Autism." *Journal of Abnormal Child Psychology* 28: 193–204.

Caras, R. 1996. *Perfect Harmony: The Intertwining Lives of Animals and Humans throughout History.* New York: Simon & Schuster.

Cassady, Joslyn. 2008 "'Strange Things Happen to Non-Christian People': Human-Animal Transformation among the Iñupiat of Arctic Alaska." *American Indian Culture and Research Journal* 32 (1): 83–101.

Castricano, Jodey, ed. 2008 *Animal Subjects: An Ethical Reader in a Posthuman World.* Waterloo, Canada: Wilfrid Laurier University Press.

Cavallo, J. A., and R. J. Blumenschine. 1989. "Tree-Stored Leapord Lills: Expanding the Hominid Scavenging Niche." *Journal of Human Evolution* 18: 393–99.

Centerwall, Brandon S. 1997. "The Name of the Green Man." *Folklore* 108: 25–33.

Chamberlin, T. C. 1965 [1890]. "The Method of Multiple Working Hypotheses." *Science* 148: 754–59.

Chappell, Jackie, and Alex Kacelnik. 2004. "Selection of Tool Diameter by New Caledonian Crows Corvus Moneduloides." *Animal Cognition* 7: 1435–9456

Cheney, D. L., and R. M. Seyfarth. 1985. "Vervet Monkey Alarm Calls: Manipulation through Shared Information?" *Behavior* 94: 150–66.

Clark, Andy. 2003. *Natural-Born Cyborgs: Minds, Technologies, and the Future of Human Intelligence.* Oxford: Oxford University Press.

Clayton, N. S., and A. Dickinson. 1998. "Episodic-like Memory during Cache Recovery by Scrub Jays." *Nature* 395: 272–78.

Clayton, Nicola S., Lucie H. Salwiczek, and Anthony Dickinson. 2007. "Episodic Memory." *Current Biology* 17: R189–R191.

Coe, Kathryn, Nancy E. Aiken, and Craig T. Palmer. 2006. "Once Upon a Time; Ancestors and the Evolutionary Significance of Stories." *Anthropological Forum* 16: 21–40.

Coeckelbergh, Mark. 2010. "Robot Rights? Towards a Social-Relational Justification of Moral Consideration." *Ethics of Information Technology* 12: 209–221.

Corballis, M. C. 1991. *The Lopsided Ape: Evolution of the Generative Mind.* New York: Oxford University Press.

Corballis, M. C. 2002. *From Hand to Mouth, the Origins of Language.* Princeton: Princeton University Press.

Corballis, Michael. 2015. "Mirror Neurons, Theory of." In *International Encyclopedia of the Social & Behavioral Sciences*, ed: J. Wrigt 2nd, 15: 582–588. Elsevier: Oxford.

Cornel, George L. 1985. "The Influence of Native Americans on Modern Conservationists." *Environmental Review* 9 (2): 104–117.

Cornish, Edward. 1998. "A Field without a Name: What Shall We Call the Study of the Future?" *The Futurist* 32 (4): 26–27.

Cornish, Edward. 2001. "How We Can Anticipate Future Events." *The Futurist* 35 (4): 26–33.

Cottingham, John. 1978. "A Brute to the Brutes: Descartes' Treatment of Animals." *Philosophy* 53: 551–59.

Crick, G. 1998. "What is Play For? Sexual Selection and the Evolution of Play." Keynote address presented at the annual meeting of the Association for the Study of Play, St. Petersburg, Florida.

Crockford, C., I. Herbinger, I., L. Vigilant, and C. Boesch. 2004. "Wild Chimpanzees produce Group-Specific Calls: A Case for Vocal Learning?" *Ethology* 110: 221–43.

Cusack-McVeigh, Holly. 2017. *Stories Find You, Places Know: Yup'ik Narratives of a Sentient World*. Salt Lake City: University of Utah Press.

Damasio, Antonio. 1995. *Descartes' Error: Emotion, Reason, and the Human Brain*. New York: Harper Perennial.

Damasio, Antonio. 2010. *Self Comes to Mind: Constructing the Conscious Brain*. New York: Pantheon.

Dautenhahn, Kerstin. 1999. "The Lemur's Tale—Story-Telling in Primates and Other Socially Intelligent Agents." Proceedings, AAAI Fall Symposium 1999, "Narrative Intelligence," Phoebe Sengers, Michael Mateas, chairs.

Dautenhahn, Kerstin. 2001. "The Narrative Intelligence Hypothesis: In Search of the Transactional Format of Narratives in Humans and Other Social Animals." In *Cognitive Technology: Instruments of Mind*, eds. M. Beynon, C. L. Nehaniv, and K. Dautenhahan, 130–40. Berlin: Springer-Verlag.

Dautenhahn, Kerstin. 2002. "The Origins of Narrative. *International Journal of Cognition and Technology* 1 (1): 97–123.

Dautenhahn, Kerstin 2003. "Stories of Lemurs and Robots—The Social Origin of Story-Telling." In *Narrative Intelligence*, eds. P. Sengers and M. Mateas, 63–90. John Benhamins Publishing.

Davies, Stephen. 2012. *The Artful Species: Aesthetics, Art, and Evolution*. Oxford: Oxford University Press.

Dayton, Leigh. 1990. "Killer Whales Communicate in Distinct 'Dialects.'" *New Scientist*, March 10: 35.

De Block, A. and S. Dewitte. 2007. "Mating Games: Cultural Evolution and Sexual Selection." *Biology and Philosophy* 22: 475–91

de Certeau, Michel. 1984. *The Practice of Everyday Life*. Berkeley: University of California Press.

de Waal, F. 2012. "The Antiquity of Empathy." *Science* 336: 874–76.

de Waal, F. B. M., and P. F. Ferrari. 2010. "Towards a Bottom-Up Perspective on Animal and Human Cognition." *Trends in Cognitive Sciences* 14: 201–207.

de Waal, F. B. M., K. Leimgruber, and A. R. Greenberg. 2008. "Giving is Self-Rewarding for Monkeys." *Proceedings of the National Academy of Sciences, USA* 105: 13685–13689.

de Waal, Frans. 1982. *Chimpanzee Politics: Power and Sex among Apes*. Baltimore: Johns Hopkins University Press.

de Waal, Frans. 2006. *Primates and Philosophers: How Morality Evolved*. Princeton: Princeton University Press.

de Waal, F. 2009. *The Age of Empathy: Nature's Lessons for a Kinder Society*. New York: Harmony Books.

de Waal, Frans. 2016. *Are We Smart Enough to Know How Smart Animals Are?* New York: Norton.

Deecke, V. B., J. K. B. Ford, and P. Spong. 2000. "Dialect Change in Resident Killer Whales: Implications for Vocal Learning and Cultural Transmission." *Animal Behaviour* 60(5): 629–38.

Dekkers, Midas. 1994. *Dearest Pet: On Bestiality*. London: Verso.

Demers, Joanna. 2006. *Steal This Music: How Intellectual Property Law Affects Musical Creativity*. Athens and London: University of Georgia Press.

Dennett, D. C. 1989/1991. "The Origins of Selves." *Cogito* 3: 163–73.

Descola, Philippe. 2013. *The Ecology of Others*. Geneviève Godbout and Benjamin P. Luley, trans. Chicago: Prickly Paradigm.

Diamond, Judy, and Alan B. Bond. 2003. "A Comparative Analysis of Social Play in Birds." *Behaviour* 140: 1091–1115.

Dissanayake, Ellen. 1995. *Homo Aestheticus: Where Art Comes from and Why*. Seattle: University of Washington Press.

Dobler, Robert. 2009." Ghosts in the Machine: Mourning the Myspace Dead." In *Folklore and the Internet: Vernacular Expressions in a Digital World*, ed. Trevor Blank, 175–93. Logan: Utah State University Press.

Donald, M. 1991. *Origins of the Modern Mind: Three Stages in the Evolution of Culture and Cognition*. Cambridge: Harvard University Press.

Doniger, Wendy. 1995. "The Mythology of Masquerading Animals, or, Bestiality." *Social Research* 62: 751–72.

Donnelley, Strachan, and Kathleen Nolan. 1990. "Animals, Science, Ethics." *Hasting Center Report* special supplement 20 (3): 1–32.

Douglas, George Brisbane. 1901. *Scottish Fairy and Folk Tales*. New York: A. L. Burt Company.

Dubois-Dessaule, Gaston. 1905. *Etude sur la bestialité au point de vue historique, medical et juridique (The Study of Bestiality from the Historical, Medical and Legal Viewpoint)*. Reprinted 2003 as Gaston Dubois-Desaulle, *Bestiality: An Historical, Medical, Legal, and Literary Study*. Honolulu, Hawaii: University Press of the Pacific.

Dunbar, R. I. M. 1996. *Grooming, Gossip and the Evolution of Language*. London. Faber and Faber.

Dundes, Alan. 1969. "Thinking Ahead: A Folkloristic Reflection on the Future Orientation in American Worldview." *Anthropological Quarterly* 42: 53–72.

Dundes, Alan. 1971. "Folk Ideas as Units of Worldview." *Journal of American Folklore* 84: 93–103.

Dundes, Alan. 1980. *Interpreting Folklore*. Bloomington: Indiana University Press.

Dundes, Alan. 1983. "Defining Identity Through Folklore." In *Identity: Personal and Socio-Cultural: A Symposium*, ed. Anita Jacobson-Widding, 235–61. Uppsala Studies in Cultural Anthropology 5, Uppsala: Acta Universitatis Upsaliensis.

Dundes, Alan. 1994. *The Cockfight: A Casebook*. Madison: University of Wisconsin Press.

Dundes, Alan. 1999. *International Folkloristics: Classic Contributions by the Founders of Folklore*. Lanham, MD: Rowman & Littlefield.

Dundes, Alan. 2005. "Folkloristics in the Twenty-First Century." *Journal of American Folklore* 118.

Dutton, Denis. 2009. *The Art Instinct: Beauty, Pleasure, and Human Evolution*. Oxford: Oxford University Press.

Eisenstein, Elizabeth. 2005. *The Printing Revolution in Early Modern Europe*. Cambridge: Cambridge University Press.

Endler, John. 2012. "Bowerbirds, Art and Aesthetics: Are Bowerbirds Artists and Do They Have an Aesthetic Sense?" *Communicative and Integrative Biology* 5 (3): 281–83.

Engel, S. 1995. *The Stories Children Tell: Making Sense of the Narratives of Childhood*. New York: W. H. Freeman & Co.

Erlmann, Veit. 1998. "How Beautiful is Small? Music, Globalization and the Aesthetics of the Local." *Yearbook for Traditional Music* 30: 12–21.

Ess, Charles, 2000. "We are the Borg: The Web as Agent of Assimilation or Cultural
    Renaissance?" *Ephilosopher*. http://www.ephilosopher.com/120100/philtech/philtech.htm.
Fagen, Robert. 1981. *Animal Play Behavior*. New York: Oxford University Press.
Feld, Steven. 1994. "From Schizoponia to Schismogenesis: On the Discourse of
    Commodification Practices of 'World Music' and 'World Beat.'" In *Music Grooves*, by
    Charles Keil and Steven Feld, 257–89. Chicago: University of Chicago Press.
Feltman, Rachel. "Chimps Given Human Rights by U.S. Court for the First Time."
    Washington Post, April 21, 2015.
Felton, D. 1999. *Haunted Greece and Rome: Ghost Stories from Classical Antiquity*. Austin:
    University of Texas Press.
Fine, Elizabeth. 1992. *Performance, Culture, and Identity*. Westport, CT: Praeger.
Fitch, W. Tecumseh, Marc D. Hauser, and Noam Chomsky. 2005. "The Evolution of the
    Language Faculty: Clarifications and Implications." *Cognition* 97: 179–210.
Flaherty, Robert Pearson. 2010. "'These Are They': ET-Human Hybridization and the New
    Daemonology." *Nova Religio: The Journal of Alternative and Emergent Religions* 14: 84–105.
Foltz, Richard C. 2006. *Animals in Islamic Tradition and Muslim Cultures*. Oxford:
    Oneworld Publications.
Forsberg, Niklas. 2012. *Language, Ethics and Animal Life: Wittgenstein and Beyond*. London:
    Bloomsbury.
Foster, Michael Dylan, and Jeffrey A. Tolbert, eds. 2016. *The Folkloresque: Reframing Folklore
    in a Popular Culture World*. Boulder: University Press of Colorado.
Fox, Rebekah. 2006. "Animal Behaviours, Post-Human Lives: Everyday Negotiations of the
    Animal–Human Divide in Pet-Keeping." *Social & Cultural Geography* 7 (4): 525–37.
Fox, Robin. 1980. *The Red Lamp of Incest*. Boston: E. P. Dutton
Frank, Lily, and Sven Nyholm. 2017. "Robot Sex and Consent: Is Consent to Sex between a
    Robot and a Human Conceivable, Possible, and Desirable?" *Artificial Intelligence and the
    Law* 25: 305–323.
Freud, Sigmund. 1962 (1930). *Civilization and Its Discontents*. New York: W. W. Norton.
Frey, Rodney, ed. 1995. *Stories That Make the World: Oral Literature of the Indian Peoples
    of the Inland Northwest as told by Lawrence Aripa, Tom Yellowtail, and Other Elders*.
    Norman: University of Oklahoma Press.
Gabriadze, Levan, dir. 2015. *Unfriended*. Universal Pictures Home Entertainment. DVD.
Gallagher, Shaun. 2005. *How the Body Shapes the Mind*. Oxford: Oxford University Press.
Gane, N., and D. Haraway. 2006. "When We Have Never Been Human, What Is to Be Done:
    Interview with Donna Haraway." *Theory, Culture and Society* 23: 135–58.
Gardner, R. A., B. T. Gardner, and T. E. Van Cantfort. 1989. *Teaching Sign Language to
    Chimpanzees*. Albany: SUNY Press .
Garnett, Guy. 2001. "The Aesthetics of Interactive Computer Music." *Computer Music
    Journal* 25: 21–33.
Giddens, A. 1990. *The Consequences of Modernity*. Cambridge: Polity Press
Gillespie, Angus, and Jay Mechling. 1987. *American Wildlife in Symbol and Story*. Knoxville:
    University of Tennessee Press.
Goffman, Erving. 1967: *Interaction Ritual: Essays on Face-to-Face Behavior*. Garden City, NY:
    Doubleday.
Gomme, Alice B. 1896. "The Green Lady: A Folktale from Hertfordshire" *Folklore* 7: 411–14.
Goodall, Jane. 1963. "My Life Among Wild Chimpanzees." *National Geographic* (August).

Graham, E. L. 2002. *Representations of the Post/Human*. Manchester: Manchester University Press.

Greenfield, P. M., and S. Savage-Rumbaugh. 1990. "Grammatical Combination in *Pan paniscus*: Process of Learning and Invention in the Evolution and Development of Language." In *Language and Intelligence in Monkeys and Apes*, eds. S. T. Parker and K. R. Gibson. Cambridge: Cambridge University Press.

Griffin, Donald. 1981. *The Question of Animal Awareness: Evolutionary Continuity of Mental Experience*. Los Altos, CA: Kaufmann.

Gröning J, Hochkirch A. 2008. "Reproductive Interference between Animal Species." *Q Rev Biol*, 257–82.

Gudeman, Stephen. 1996. "Sketches, Qualms and Other Thoughts on Intellectual Property Rights." In *Valuing Local Knowledge: Indigenous People and Intellectual Property Rights*, eds. Stephen B. Brush and Doreen Stabinsky. Washington, DC: Island Press.

Habermaus, Jürgen. 2001. *The Postnational Constellation: Political Essays*. Max Pensky, trans. Cambridge, MA: Polity.

Hafstein, Valdimar Tr. 2000. "The Elves' Point of View: Cultural Identity in Contemporary Icelandic Elf-Tradition." *Fabula* 41: 87–104.

Hafstein, Valdimar Tr. 2001. "Biological Metaphors in Folklore Theory: An Essay in the History of Ideas." *Arv, Nordic Yearbook of Folklore* 57: 7–32.

Hafstein, Valdimar Tr. 2004. "The Politics of Origins: Collective Creation Revisited." *Journal of American Folklore* 117: 300–315.

Hall, K. R. L. 1963. "Tool-Using Performances as Indicators of Behavioral Adaptability." *Current Anthropology* 4: 479–95.

Hampton, R. R. 2001. "Rhesus Monkeys Know when They Remember." *Proceedings of the National Academy of Sciences* 98: 5359–62.

Haraway, Donna. 1985. "A Manifesto for Cyborgs." In *The Norton Anthology of Theory and Criticism*, ed. Vincent B. Leitch, 226–99. New York: W .W. Norton & Company, 2001.

Haraway, Donna. 1991. "A Cyborg Manifesto: Science, Technology, and Socialist-Feminism in the Late Twentieth Century." In *Simians, Cyborgs and Women: The Reinvention of Nature*, 149–81. New York; Routledge.

Haraway, Donna. 1991. "Situated Knowledges." In *Simians, Cyborgs and Women*. New York: Routledge.

Haraway, Donna. 1991. *Simians, Cyborgs, and Women*. New York: Routledge.

Haraway, Donna. 2003. *The Companion Species Manifesto: Dogs, People, and Significant Otherness*. Chicago: Prickly Paradigm Press.

Haraway, Donna. 2006 *When Species Meet*. Minneapolis: University of Minnesota Press.

Harlow, H.F., and M. K. Harlow. 1969. "Effects of Various Mother-Infant Relationships on Rhesus Monkey Behaviors." In *Determinants of Infant Behaviour, IV*, ed. B. M. Foss, 15–36. London: Methuen.

Harrison, Jane. 1912. *Themis: A Study of the Social Origins of Greek Religion*. Cambridge: Cambridge University Press.

Harrison, Peter. 1992. "Descartes on Animals." *The Philosophical Quarterly* 42: 219–27.

Harrod, Howard L. 2000. *The Animals Came Dancing: Native American Sacred Ecology and Animal Kinship*. Tucson: University of Arizona Press.

Harvey, Graham. 2006. "Animals, Animists and Academics." *Zygon: Journal of Religion and Science* 41: 9–19.

Hauser, M. D., and W. T. Fitch. 2003. "What Are the Uniquely Human Components of the Language Faculty?" In *Language Evolution: The States of the Art*, eds. M. H. Christiansen and S. Kirby, 158–81. Oxford: Oxford University Press.

Hauser, M., N. Chomsky, and W. T. Fitch. 2002. "The Language Faculty: What Is It, Who Has It, and How Did It Evolve?" *Science* 298: 1569–79.

Hauser, Marc D., Noam Chomsky, and W. Tecumseh Fitch. 2002. "The Language Faculty: What Is It, Who Has It, and How Did It Evolve?" *Science* 298 (5598): 1569–79.

Hauser, Marc, and Josh McDermott. 2003. "The Evolution of the Music Faculty: A Comparative Perspective." *Nature Neuroscience* 6 (7): 663–68.

Hayles, N. K. 1999. *How We Became Posthuman: Virtual Bodies in Cybernetics, Literature, and Informatics*. London: University of Chicago Press.

Hewes, G. W. 1973. "Primate Communication and the Gestural Origin of Language." *Current Anthropology* 12: 5–24.

Hoffmeyer J. 1996. *Signs of Meaning in the Universe*. Bloomington: Indiana University Press.

Howard, Rob. 2011. *Digital Jesus: The Making of a New Christian Fundamentalist Community on the Internet*. New York: New York University Press.

Howard, Robert Glenn. 2008. "Electronic Hybridity: The Persistent Processes of the Vernacular Web." *Journal of American Folklore* 121: 192–218.

Howard, Robert Glenn. 2013. "Vernacular Authority: Critically Engaging 'Tradition.'" In *Tradition in the 21st Century: Locating the Role of the Past in the Present*, eds. Trevor Blank and Robert Glenn Howard, 72–99. Logan: Utah State University Press.

Hua, Cynthia. "Sex Weekend Examines Sexual Culture." *Yale Daily News*, March 4, 2013.

Hugh-Jones, Stephen. 2012. "Forward." In *Animism in Rainforest and Tundra: Personhood, Animals, Plants and Things in Contemporary Amazonia and Siberia*, eds. Marc Brightman, Vanessa Elisa Grotti, and Olga Ulturgasheva. New York and Oxford: Berghahn Books.

Huizinga, Johan. 1955 (1938). *Homo Ludens: A Study of the Play Element in Culture*. Boston: Beacon.

Husserl, Edmund. 1989 (1952). *Ideas Pertaining to a Pure Phenomenology and to a Phenomenological Philosophy: Second Book; Studies in the Phenomenology of Constitution*. Rojcewicz and A. Schuwer, trans. Dordrecht, Netherlands: Kluwer Academic.

Ikram, Salima. 2003. *Death and Burial in Ancient Egypt*. Harlow: Longman.

Ingmanson, E. J. 1996. "Tool-Using Behavior in Wild *Pan paniscus*: Social and Ecological Considerations." In *Reaching into Thought: The Minds of the Great Apes*, eds. A. E. Russon and K. A. Bard, 190–210. Cambridge: Cambridge University.

Ingold, T. 1987. *The Appropriation of Nature: Essays on Human Ecology and Social Relations*. Iowa City: University of Iowa Press.

Ingold, Tim. 2013. "Anthropology beyond Humanity." *Suomen Antropologi* 38 (3): 5–23.

Inoue-Nakamura, N., and T. Matsuzawa. 1997. "Development of Stone Tool Use by Wild Chimpanzees (*Pan troglodytes*)." *Journal of Comparative Psychology* 111: 159–73.

Inoue, Sana, and Tetsuro Matsuzawa. 2007. "Working Memory of Numerals in Chimpanzees." *Current Biology* 17: R1004–R1005

"Intelligent Machines: Call for a Ban on Robots Designed as Sex Toys." 2015. BBC, September 15. www.bbc.co.uk/news/technology-34118482 (accessed September 18, 2018).

Iwasaka, Michiko, and Barre Toelken. 1994. *Ghosts and the Japanese*. Logan: Utah State University Press.

Jakobsen, Merete Demant. 1999. *Shamanism: Traditional and Contemporary Approaches to the Mastery of Spirits and Healing*. New York: Berghahn Books.

Janet, Pierre. 1928. *l'Evolution de la. Mémoire et la Notion de Temps*. Leçons au Collège de France, 1927–1928. Paris: Chahine.

Jenkins, Henry. 2006 *Convergence Culure*. New York: New York University Press.

Jeon, H., and S. H. Lee. 2018. "From Neurons to Social Beings: Short Review of the Mirror Neuron System Research and its Socio-Psychological and Psychiatric Implications." *Clinical Psychopharmacology and Neuroscience* 16 (1): 18–31.

Johnston, Sarah Iles. 1999. *Restless Dead: Encounters Between the Living and the Dead in Ancient Greece*. Berkeley: University of California Press.

Jones, Steve. 2002. "Music That Moves: Popular Music, Distribution and Network Technologies." *Cultural Studies* 16: 213–32.

Judge, Roy. 2000 (1979): *The Jack in the Green: A May Day Custom*. London: FLS Books.

Kahn, Richard. 2007. "Zoophilia and Bestiality: Cross-Cultural Perspectives." In *Encyclopedia of Human-Animal Relationships*, ed. Marc Bekoff. Westport, CT: Greenwood Press.

Kanter, James. 2013. "E.U. Bans Cosmetics with Animal-Tested Ingredients." *New York Times*, March 11 (accessed http://www.nytimes.com/2013/03/11/business/global/eu-to-ban-cosmetics-with-animal-tested-ingredients.html).

Kätsyri, Jari. 2017. "'The Polar Express' is Bipolar: Critical Film Reviews Influence Uncanny Valley Phenomenon in Semi-Realistic Animation Films." Presentation for the Cognitive Science Society. mindmodeling.org/cogsci2017/papers/0446/index.html (accessed September 18, 2018).

Kershenbaum, Arik, Amiyaal Ilany, Leon Blaustein, and Eli Geffen. 2012. "Syntactic Structure and Geographical Dialects in the Songs of Male Rock Hyraxes." *Proceedings: Biological Sciences* 279 (1740): 2974–81.

Kibby, Marjorie. 2000. "Home on the Page: A Virtual Place of Music Community." *Popular Music* 19: 91–100.

King, Stephanie L., and Vincent M. Janik. 2013. "Bottlenose Dolphins can use Learned Vocal Labels to Address Each Other." *Proceedings of the National Academy of Sciences of the United States of America* 110: 13216–221.

Kingsbury, Justine. 2011. "(R)evolutionary Aesthetics: Denis Dutton's *The Art Instinct: Beauty, Pleasure and Human Evolution*." *Biology and Philosophy* 26 (1): 141–50.

Kinsey, Alfred C., et al. 1948. *Sexual Behavior in the Human Male: The Kinsey Report*. Philadelphia: W. B. Saunders Co.

Kinsey, Alfred C. 1953. *Sexual Behavior in the Human Female: The Kinsey Report*. Philadelphia: W. B. Saunders Co.

Kirksey, S. Eben, and Steffan Helmreich. 2010. "The Emergence of Multispecies Ethnography." *Cultural Anthropology* 25 (4): 545–76.

Kirshenblatt-Gimblett, Barbara. 1995. "From the Paperwork Empire to the Paperless Office." In *Folklore Interpreted: Essays in Honor of Alan Dundes*, eds. Regina Bendix and Rosemary Lévy Zumwalt. New York: Garland.

Kirshenblatt-Gimblett, Barbara. 1996. "The Electronnic Vernacular." In *Connected* ed George Marcus. Chicago: University of Chicago Press (Late Editions Series vol. 3).

Klein, S. B., R. L. Chan, J. Loftus. 1999. "Independence of Episodic and Semantic Selfknowledge: The Case from Autism." *Social Cognition* 17: 413–36.

Klintberg, Bengt af. 1986. *Rattan i pizzan: Folksagner i var tid.* Stockholm: Norstedts.

Kohn, Eduardo. 2013. *How Forests Think: Toward an Anthropology beyond the Human.* Berkeley: University of California Press.

Koukoutsaki-Monnier, Angeleiki. 2012. "Deterritorialising the Nation? Internet and the Politics of the Greek-American Diaspora." *Nations and Nationalism* 18: 673–83.

Kuba, Michael J., Ruth A. Byrne, Daniela V. Meisel, and Jennifer A. Mather. 2006. "When Do Octopuses Play? The Effect of Repeated Testing, Object Type, Age, and Food Deprivation on Object Play in *Octopus vulgaris.*" *Journal of Comparative Psychology* 120 (3): 184–90.

Kuhn, Thomas. 1962. *The Structure of Scientific Revolutions.* Chicago: University of Chicago Press.

Kuruk, Paul. 1999. "Protecting Folklore Under Modern Intellectual Property Regimes: A Reappraisal of the Tensions between Individual and Communal Rights in Africa and the United States." *American University Law Review* 48: 769–843.

Kurzweil, Ray. 1999. *The Age of Spiritual Machines: When Computers Exceed Human Intelligence.* New York: Penguin.

Leach, Edmund. 1964. "Anthroplogical Aspects of Language: Animal Categories and Verbal Abuse." In *New Directions in the Study of Language*, ed. Eric H. Lenneberg. Cambridge: MIT Press.

Legat, Allice. 2012. *Walking the Land, Feeding the Fire: Knowledge and Stewardship among the Tlicho Dene.* Tucscon: University of Arizona Press.

Lessig, Lawrence. 2004. "Free Culture: How Big Media Uses Technology and the Law to Lock Down Culture and Control Creativity." New York: Penguin Press.

Letcher, Andy. 2001. "The Scouring of the Shire: Fairies, Trolls and Pixies in Eco-Protest Culture." *Folklore* 112: 147–161.

Lévi-Strauss, Claude. 1963. *Structural Anthropology.* Claire Jacobson, trans. New York: Basic Books.

Levy, David. 2007. *Love and Sex with Robots: The Evolution of Human-Robot Relationships.* New York: HarperCollins.

Liebal, K., J. Call, and M. Tomasello. 2004. "Chimpanzee Gesture Sequences." *Primates* 64: 377–96.

Liebal, K., S. Pika, J. Call, and M. Tomasello. 2004. "Great Ape Communicators Move in Front of Recipients before Producing Visual Gestures." *Interaction Studies* 5: 199–219.

Liles, B. 1993. "Narrative Discourse in Children with Language Disorders and Children with Normal Language: A Critical Review of the Literature." *Journal of Speech and Hearing Research* 36: 868–82.

Lincoln, Bruce. 1999. *Theorizing Myth: Narrative, Ideology, and Scholarship.* Chicago: University of Chicago Press.

Lindhom, Charles, and José Pedro Zúquete. 2010. *The Struggle for the World: Liberation Movements for the 21st Century.* Palo Alto: Stanford University Press.

Lindow, John. 2004. *Trolls: An Unnatural History.* London: Reaction Books.

Linke, Uli. 1986. "Where Blood Flows, A Tree Grows: A Study of Root Metaphor in German Culture." PhD dissertation, UC Berkeley.

Lock, Andrew, ed. 1978. *Action, Gesture and Symbol: The Emergence of Language.* New York: Academic Press.

Loomis, J. M. 1992. "Distal Attribution and Presence." *Presence* 1: 113–18.

Losh, Molly, and Lisa Capps. 2003. "Narrative Ability in High-Functioning Children with Autism or Asperger's Syndrome." *Journal of Autism and Developmental Disorders* 33: 239–51.

Loveland, K., R. McEvoy, and B. Tunali. 1990. "Narrative Story-Telling in Autism and Down Syndrome." *British Journal of Developmental Psychology* 8: 9–23.

Low, Bobbi. 2015. *Why Sex Matters: A Darwinian Look at Human Behavior*. Princeton: Princeton University Press.

Lyman Ray Patterson. 1968. *Copyright in Historical Perspective*. Nashville: Vanderbilt University Press.

Mac Neill, Maire. 1977. "Introduction." In *Siscealta ó Thir Chonaill / Fairy Legends from Donegal*, collected by Sean Ó hEochaidh, Irish texts edited by Seamas Ó Cathain; Maire Mac Neill, trans. Dublin: Comhairle Bhéaloideas Éireann.

Magliocco, Sabina. 2018. "Beyond the Rainbow Bridge: Vernacular Ontologies of Animal Afterlives." *Journal of Folklore Research* 55 (2): 39–67.

Malinowki, Bronislau. 1932 (1929). *The Sexual Lives of the Savages in North-West Melanesia*. London: Routledge, Kegan, and Paul.

Mancuso, Stefano, and Alessandra Viola. 2015. *Brilliant Green: The Surprising History and Science of Plant Intelligence*. Washington, DC: Island.

Manoj, V. R. 2007. "Cyborgs and Altruism." *Ethical Technology*. http://ieet.org/index.php /IEET/more/manoj20070517/.

Mar, Alex. 2017. "Are We Ready for Intimacy with Androids?" *Wired Magazine*, October 17. https://www.wired.com/2017/10/hiroshi-ishiguro-when-robots-act-just-like -humans/.

Mason, W. A. 1963. "The Effects of Environmental Restriction on the Social Development of Rhesus Monkeys." In *Primate Social Behavior*, ed. C. H. Southwick, 161–74. New York: Van Nostrand.

Mason, W. A., and P. C. Green. 1962. "The Effects of Social Restriction on the Behavior of Rhesus Monkeys. IV. Responses to a Novel Environment and to an Alien Species." *Journal of Comparative Physiological Psychology* 55: 363–68.Masters, R. E. L. 1962. *Forbidden Sexual Behavior and Morality*. New York: Julian Press.

Mather, Jennifer A. 2008. "Cephalopod Consciousness: Behavioural Evidence." *Consciousness and Cognition* 17: 37–48.

McCann, Anthony. 2001. "All That is Not Given is Lost: Irish Traditional Music, Copyright, and Common Property." *Ethnomusicology* 45: 89–106.

McDermott, Josh, and Marc Hauser. 2005. "The Origins of Music: Innateness, Uniqueness, and Evolution." *Music Perception: An Interdisciplinary Journal* 23 (1): 29–59.

McLuhan, Marshall. 1964. *Understanding Media: The Extensions of Man*. 2nd edition. New York: Signet.

McNeill, Lynne. 2007. "The Waving Ones: Cats, Folklore, and the Experiential Source Hypothesis." In *What Are the Animals to Us? Approaches from Science, Religion Folklore, Literature and Art*, eds. Dave Aftandilia, with Marion W. Copeland and David Scofield Wilson. Knoxville: University of Tennessee Press.

Mead, Margaret. 1928. *Coming of Age in Somoa*. New York: W. Morrow & Company.

Mechling, Jay. 1988. "'Banana Cannon' and Other Folk Traditions Between Human and Nonhuman Animals." *Western Folklore* 48: 312–23

Mechling, Jay. 2006. "Solo Folklore." *Western Folklore* 65: 435–53.

Merleau-Ponty, Maurice. 2012 (1945). *Phenomenology of Perception*. Donald A. Landes, trans. New York: Routledge.

Merlin, D. 1991. *Origins of the Modern Mind: Three Stages in the Evolution of Culture and Cognition*. Cambridge, MA: Harvard University Press.

Miah, Andy. 2008. "A Critical History of Posthumanism." In *Medical Enhancement and Posthumanity*, eds. Bert Gordijn and Ruth F. Chadwick, 71–94. Dordrecht, Netherlands: Springer.

Miah, Andy. 2007. "Posthumanism: A Critical History." In *Medical Enhancements & Posthumanity*, by B. Gordijn and R. Chadwick. New York: Routledge.

Miles, Sally, and Robin S. Chapman. 2002. "Narrative Content as Described by Individuals With Down Syndrome and Typically Developing Children." *Journal of Speech, Language, and Hearing Research* 45: 175–89.

Miletski, Hani. 2000. "Bestiality/Zoophilia—An Exploratory Study." *Scandinavian Journal of Sexology* 3: 149–50.

Miletski, Hani. 2002. *Understanding Bestiality and Zoophil[i]a*. Bethesda, MD: East-West Publishing.

Miller, Geoffrey F. 2000. *The Mating Mind: How Sexual Choice Shaped the Evolution of Human Nature*. New York: Doubleday.

Miller, Montana. 2007. "'It Wouldn't Be Heaven Without MySpace': Teeangers, Death, and Emerging Frames of Immortality." Unpublished paper, Department of Popular Culture, Bowling Green State University.

Mizumori, S. J. 2006. "Hippocampal Place Fields: A Neural Code for Episodic Memory?" *Hippocampus* 16: 685–90.

Monson, Melissa J. 2012. "Race-Based Fantasy Realm: Essentialism in the World of Warcraft." *Games and Culture* 7: 48–71.

Mori, Masahiro. 1970. "IBukimi no Tani (The Uncanny Valley)." *Enajii* (*Energy*) 7: 33–35.

Mori, Masahiro. 1981 (2005). *The Buddha in the Robot Tran*, by Charles S. Terry. Tokyo: Kōsei Shuppansha.

Morrison, Kenneth. 2000. "The Cosmos as Intersubjective: Native American Other-Than-Human Persons." In *Indigenous Religions*, ed. Graham Harvey, 23–36. London: Cassell.

Mould, Thomas. 2003. *Choctaw Prophecy: A Legacy for the Future*. Tuscaloosa: University of Alabama Press.

Mould, Thomas. 2005. "The Paradox of Traditionalization: Negotiating the Past in Choctaw Prophetic Discourse." *Journal of Folklore Research* 42 (3): 255–94.

Musser, Whitney B., Ann E. Bowles, Dawn M. Grebner, and Jessica L. Crance. 2014. "Differences in Acoustic Features of Vocalizations Produced by Killer Whales Cross-Socialized with Bottlenose Dolphins." *Acoustical Society of America* 136 (4): 1990–2002.

Muir, John, and Marion Randall Parsons. 1915. *Travels in Alaska*. Boston: Houghton Mifflin Company.

Nadasy, Pau. 2007. "The Gift in the Animal: The Ontology of Hunting and Human-Animal Sociality." *American Ethnologist* 34 (1): 25–43.

Nakamura, Lisa. 2002. *Cybertypes: Race, Ethnicity, and Identity on the Internet*. New York and London: Routledge.

Nemeth, Erwin, and Henrik Brumm. 2009. "Blackbirds Sing Higher-Pitched Songs in Cities: Adaptation to Habitat Acoustics or Side-Effect of Urbanization?" *Animal Behaviour* 78 (3): 637–41.

Niles, J. 1999. *Homo Narrans, The Poetics and Anthropology of Oral Literature*. Philadelphia: University of Pennsylvania Press.

Norman, Howard. 1990. *Northern Tales: Traditional Stories of Eskimo and Indian People*. New York: Pantheon Books.

Noyes, Dorothy. 2006. "The Judgment of Solomon: Global Protections for Tradition and the Problem of Community Ownership." *Cultural Analysis* 5: 27–56.

Noyes, Dorothy. 2012. "The Social Base of Folklore." In *A Companion to Folklore*, eds. Regina F. Bendix and Galit Hasan-Rokem, 13–39. Oxford: Wiley-Blackwell.

O'Brien, Annamarie. Forthcoming. "'Hello My Darling, Pisces!' Video Horoscopes and Social Expression through Occultic Practice." *New Directions in Folklore*.

Ohler P., and G. Nieding 2005. "Sexual Selection, Evolution of Play and Entertainment." *Journal of Cultural and Evolutionary Psychology* 3: 141–57.

Ong, Walter. 1982. *Orality and Literacy: The Technologizing of the Word*. London: Methuen.

Ong, Aihwa. 2006. "Mutations in Citizenship." *Theory, Culture & Society* 23: 499≠505.

Oring, Elliott. 1994. "The Art, Artifacts, and Artifices of Identity." *Journal of American Folklore* 107: 211–47.

Oring, Elliott. 2014. "Memetics and Folkloristics: The Applications." *Western Folklore* 73: 455–92

Oring, Elliott. 2014. "Memetics and Folkloristics: The Theory." *Western Folklore* 73: 432–54.

Partridge, Christopher. 2004. "Alien Demonology: The Christian Roots of the Malevolent Extraterrestrial in UFO Religions and Abduction Spiritualities." *Religion* 34: 163–89.

Pelikan, J. J., H. C. Oswald, and H. T. Lehmann, eds. 1999 (1959). "On the Misuse of the Mass." *Luther's Works, Vol. 36: Word and Sacrament II*, by Martin Luther. Philadelphia: Fortress Press.

Peters, Ted. 2014. *UFOs: God's Chariots? Spirituality, Ancient Aliens and Religious Yearnings in the Age of Extraterrestrials*. Pompton Plains, NJ: New Page Books.

Peterson, Dale. 2008. *Jane Goodall: The Woman Who Redefined Man*. New York: Mariner.

Peterson, Dale. 2011. *The Moral Lives of Animals*. New York: Bloomsbury.

Peterson, R. A. 1997. *Creating Country Music: Fabricating Authenticity*. Chicago: University of Chicago Press.

Pettitt, Thomas, producer. 2010. "The Gutenberg Parenthesis: Oral Tradition and Digital Technologies." MIT Communications Forum. Retrieved from http://techtv.mit.edu/videos/16645-the-gutenbergparenthesis-oral-tradition-and-digital-technologies.

Phillips, Whitney. 2015. *This Is Why We Can't Have Nice Things: Mapping the Relationship between Online Trolling and Mainstream Culture*. Cambridge, MA: MIT Press.

Pika, S. 2007. "Gestures in Subadult Gorillas." In *The Gestural Communication of Monkeys and Apes*, eds. Josep Call and Michael Tomasello, 99–130. Mahwah, NJ: Lawrence Erlbaum.

Pika, S. 2008. "What is the Nature of the Gestural Communication of Great Apes?" In *The Shared Mind*, eds. J. Zlatev, T. Racine, C. Sinha, and E. Itkonen, 165–86. Amsterdam: John Benjamins Publishing Company.

Pinker, Stephen. 1992. *How the Mind Works*. New York: Norton.

Podberscek, Anthony L., Elizabeth S. Paul, and James A. Serpell, eds. 2000. *Companion Animals and Us: Exploring the Relationships between People and Pets*. Cambridge: Cambridge University Press.

Poirier, Frank, and Euclid Smith. 1974. "Socializing Functions of Primate Play." *American Zoology* 14: 275–87.

Porter, Dale H. 1981. *The Emergence of the Past: A Theory of Historical Explanation*. Chicago: University of Chicago Press.

Poster, Mark. 2002. "Digital Networks and Citizenship." *PMLA* 117: 98–103.

Prüfer, Kay, et al. 2013. "The Complete Genome Sequence of a Neanderthal from the Altai Mountains." *Nature,* December 18, 2013. doi: 10.1038/nature12886.

Raglan, Lady J. 1939. "The Green Man in Church Architecture." *Folklore* 50: 45–57.

Ralston, James V., and Louis M. Herman. 1995. "Perception and Generalization of Frequency Contours by a Bottlenose Dolphin (*Tursiops truncatus*)." *Journal of Comparative Psychology* 109 (3): 268–77.

Rambelli, Fabio. 2007. *Buddhist Materiality: A Cultural History of Objects in Japanese Buddhism.* Stanford: Stanford University Press.

Rautio, Pauliina. 2012. "Being Nature: Interspecies Articulation as a Species-Specific Practice of relating to Environment." *Environmental Education Research.*

Reilly, July, Molly Losh, Ursula Bellugi, and Beverly Wulfeck. 2004. "'Frog, Where are You?' Narratives in Children with Specific Language Impairment, Early Focal Brain Injury, and Williams Syndrome." *Brain and Language* 88: 229–47.

Renteln, Alison Dundes. 2005. *The Cultural Defense.* Oxford: Oxford University Press.

Rhodes, Giluan, Fiona Proffitt, Jonathon M. Grady, and Alex Sumich. 1998. "Facial Symmetry and the Perception of Beauty." *Psychonomic Bulletin and Review* 5 (4): 659–69.

Richardson, Kathleen. 2015. "The 'Assymetrical Relationship': Parallels Between Prostitution and the Development of Sex Robots." *SIGCAS Computers and Society* 45 (3): 290–93.

Ricoeur, Paul. 1984–88. *Time and Narrative* (Temps et Récit). 3 vols. Kathleen McLaughlin and David Pellauer, trans. Chicago: University of Chicago Press.

Robertson, Jennifer. 2018. *Robo Sabiens Japanicus: Robots, Gender, Family, and the Japanese Nation.* Oakland: University of California Press.

Rojcewicz, Peter M. 1991. "Between One Eye Blink and the Next: Fairies, UFOs, and Problems of Knowledge." In *The Good People: New Fairylore Essays,* ed. Peter Narvaez, 479–514. New York: Garland Publishing.

Rose, Mark. 1993. *Authors and Owners: The Invention of Copyright.* Cambridge: Harvard University Press.

Rosenberg, Alexander. 1996. "Is There an Evolutionary Biology of Play?" In *Readings in Animal Cognition,* eds. Marck Beckoff and Dale Jamieson, 217–28. Cambridge: MIT Press.

Roy, William. 2002. "Aesthetic Identity, Race, and American Folk Music." *Qualitative Sociology* 25: 459–69.

Rubin, David. 1988. *Autobiographical Memory: Theoretical and Applied Perspectives.* Cambridge: Cambridge University Press.

Rubin, David. 1999. *Remembering Our Past: Studies in Autobiographical Memory.* Cambridge: Cambridge University Press.

Said, Edward. 1978. *Orientalism.* Vintage Books

Salisbusy, Joyce. 1994. *The Beast Within: Animals in the Middle Ages.* New York: Routledge.

Sardar, Ziauddin. 2010. "The Namesake: Futures; Futures Studies; Futurology; Futuristic; Foresight—What's in a Name?" *Futures* 42 (3): 177–84.

Savage-Rumbaugh, S., J. Murphy, J., R. Sevcik, K. Brakke, S. Williams, and R. Rumbaugh. 1993. *Language Comprehension in Ape and Child, Monographs of the Society for Research in Child Development,* serial no. 233, vol. 58. Hoboken: Blackwell.

Schmitt, Jean-Claude. 1998. *Ghosts in the Middle Ages: The Living and the Dead in Medieval Society.* Chicago: University of Chicago Press.

Schrempp, Gregory. 2009. "Taking the Dawkins Challenge, or, the Dark Side of the Meme." *Journal of Folklore Research* 46: 91–100.

Schrempp, Gregory. 2012. *The Ancient Mythology of Modern Science: A Mythologist Looks (Seriously) at Popular ScienceWriting*. Montreal: McGill-Queens University Press.

Schuetz, M., and B. F. Malle. 2017. "Moral Robots." In *Routledge Handbook of Neuroethics*, eds. K. Rommelfanger and S. Johnson. New York: Routledge/Taylor & Francis.

Schwartz, Bennett L., and Siân Evans. 2001. Review of *Episodic Memory in Primates*. *American Journal of Primatology* 55: 71–85.

Scott, Colin. 2006. "Spirit and Practical Knowledge in the Person of the Bear among Wemindji Cree Hunters." *Ethnos* 71 (1): 51–66.

Seeger, Anthony. 1992. "Ethnomusicology and Music Law." *Ethnomusicology* 36: 345–59.

Shankera Stuart G., and Barbara J. King. 2002. "The Emergence of a New Paradigm in Ape Language Research." *Behavioral and Brain Sciences* 25: 605–656.

Shimazaki, Satoko. 2016. *Edo Kabuki in Transition: From the Worlds of the Samurai to the Vengeful Female Ghost*. New York: Columbia University Press.

Silver, Carol. 1999. *Strange and Secret Peoples: Fairies and Victorian Consciousness*. New York: Oxford University Press.

Silverman, Carol. 1988. "Negotiating 'Gypsiness': Strategy in Context." *Journal of American Folklore* 101 (401): 261–75.

Singer, Peter. 1975. *Animal Liberation: A New Ethics for our Treatment of Animals*. New York: HarperCollins.

Simpson, Jacqueline. 1978. "The World Upside Down Shall Be: A Note on the Folklore of Doomsday." *Journal of American Folklore* 91 (359): 559–67.

Slabbekoorn, Hans, and Ardie den Boer-Visser. 2006. "Cities Change the Songs of Birds." *Current Biology* 16 (23): 2326–31.

Sliwinski, Sharon. 2011. "The Gaze Called Animal: Notes for a Study on Thinking." *CR: The New Centennial Review* 11: 61–81.

Slobodchikoff, C. N., and R. Coast. 1980. "Dialects in the Alarm Calls of Prairie Dogs." *Behavioral Ecology and Sociobiology* 7 (1): 49–53.

Smart, Alan. 2014. "Critical Perspectives on Multi Species Ethnography." *Critique of Anthropology* 34 (1): 3–7.

Smedly, Audry. 2005. "Race as Biology is Fiction, Racism as a Social Problem is Real: Anthropological and Historical Perspectives on the Social Construction of Race." *American Psychology* 60: 16–26.

Smuts, B. 2001. "Encounters with Animal Minds." *Journal of Consciousness Studies* 8: 293–309.

Smuts, B. B., and J. M. Watanabe. 1990. "Social Relationships and Ritualized Greeting in Adult Male Baboons (*Papio cynocephalus anubis*)." *International Journal of Primatololgy* 11 (1): 47–72.

Sober, Elliott. 2000. *Philosophy of Biology*. Boulder, CO: Westview Press.

Speth, J. D. 1989. "Early Hominid Hunting and Scavenging: The Role of Meat as an Energy Source." *Journal of Human Evolution* 18: 329–43.

Stivale, Charles. 2003. *Disenchanting Les Bons Temps: Identity and Authenticity in Cajun Music and Dance*. Durham: Duke University Press.

Stokes, Martin. 1994. "Introduction." In *Ethnicity, Identity and Music: The Musical Construction of Place*, ed. Martin Stokes. Oxford: Berg.

Stokoe, W. C. 2001. *Language in Hand: Why Sign Came before Speech*. Washington, DC: Gallaudet University Press.

Straub, Jürgen. 2005. *Narration, Identity and Historical Consciousness*. New York: Berghahn Books.

Suddendorf, T., and M. C. Corballis 2007. "The Evolution of Foresight: What is Mental Time Travel, and is it Unique to Humans?" *Behavioral and Brain Sciences* 30: 299–351.

Sugiyama, Michelle Scalise. 1996. "On The Origins of Narrative: Storyteller Bias as a Fitness-Enhancing Strategy." *Human Nature* 7: 403–425.

Sugiyama, Michelle Scalise. 2001. "Food, Foragers, and Folklore: The Role of Narrative in Human Subsistence." *Evolution and Human Behavior* 22: 221–40.

Sugiyama, Michelle Scalise. 2001. "Narrative Theory and Function: Why Evolution Matters." *Philosophy and Literature* 25: 233–50.

Sztybel, Daiv. 2008. Animals as Persons. In. *Animal Subjects: An Ethical Reader in a Posthuman World*, ed. Jodey Castricano. Waterloo, Canada: Wilfrid Laurier University Press.

Tager-Flusberg, H. 1995. "Once upon a Rabbit: Stories Narrated by Autistic Children." *British Jouranl of Developmental Psychology* 13: 45–59.

Tager-Flusberg, H., and K. Sullivan. 1995. "Attributing Mental States to Story Characters: A Comparison on Narratives Produced by Autistic and Mentally Tetarded Individuals." *Applied Psycholinguistics* 16: 241–56.

Talayesva, Don C., and Leo William Simmons. 1942. *Sun Chief: The Autobiography of a Hopi Indian*. New Haven: Yale University Press.

Tangherlini, Timothy. 2008. "'Where was I?': Personal Experience Narrative, Crystallization and Some Thoughts on Tradition Memory." *Cultural Analysis* 7: 21–37.

Tanner, J., and R. W. Byrne. 1999. "The Development of Spontaneous Gestural Communication in a Group of Zoo-Living Lowland Gorillas." In *The Mentalities of Gorillas and Orangutans*, eds. Sue Taylor Parker, Robert W. Mitchell, and H. Lyn Miles, 211–39. Cambridge: Cambridge University Press.

Thompson, Evan. 2007. *Mind in Life: Biology, Phenomenology, and the Sciences of Mind*. Cambridge, MA: Harvard University Press.

Thompson, Tok. 2004. "The Return of the Fairy Folk: A View from the Tourist Shops of Ireland." *Tautosakos Darbai (Folklore Studies)* 2: 198–208.

Thompson, Tok. 2007. "Something Fishy Going On: An Analysis of the Role of Fish in American Folkspeech." *Columbia Journal of American Studies* 8: 111–22.

Thompson, Tok. 2010. "The Ape that Captured Time: Folklore, Narrative, and the Human-Animal Divide." *Western Folklore* 69 (3/4): 395–420.

Thompson, Tok. 2011. "Beatboxing, Mashups, and Cyborg Identity: Folk Music for the Twenty-First Century." *Western Folklore* 70: 171–93.

Thompson, Tok. 2012. "Netizens, Revolutionaries, and the Inalienable Right to the Internet." In *Folk Culture in the Digital Age: The Emergent Dynamics of Human Interaction*, ed. Trevor J. Blank, 45–69. Logan: Utah State University Press.

Tonutti, Sabrina. 2011. "Anthropocentrism and the Definition of 'Culture' as a Marker of the Human/Animal Divide." In *Anthropocentrism: Humans, Animals, Environments*, ed. Rob Boddice, 183–99. Leiden, Netherlands: Brill.

Trewavas, Anthony. 2003. "Aspects of Plant Intelligence." *Annals of Botany* 92 (1): 1–20.

Tucker, Elizabeth. 2007. *Haunted Halls: Ghostlore of American College Campuses*. Jackson: University Press of Mississippi.

Tulving, E. 1972. "Episodic and Semantic Memory." In *Organization of Memory*, eds. E. Tulving and W. Donaldson, 382–402. New York, NY: Academic Press.

Tulving, E. 1983. *Elements of Episodic Memory.* New York: Oxford University Press.

Turkle, Sherry. 2011. *Alone Together: Why We Expect More From Technology and Less From Each Other.* New York, NY: Basic Books.

TyTe, Defenicial. 2009. "White Noise. The Real History of Beatboxing." http://www.human-beatbox.com/history (accessed May 2, 2009).

Usher, Abott Payson. 1959 (1929). *A History of Mechanical Inventions.* Boston: Beacon Hill.

Vaidhyanathan, Siva. 2001. *Copyrights and Copywrongs: The Rise of Intellectual Property and how it Threatens Creativity.* New York: NYU Press.

Valk, Ulo. 2006. "Ghostly Possession and Real Estate: The Dead in Contemporary Estonian Folklore." *Journal of Folklore Research* 43: 31–51.

Valk, Ulo. 2018. "Ontological Liminality of Ghosts: The Case of a Haunted Hospital." In *Storied and Supernatural Places: Studies in Spatial and Social Dimensions of Folklore and Sagas*, eds. Ülo Valk and Daniel Sävborg, 93–113. Helsinki: Suomalaisen Kirjallisuuden Seura.

Van Schaik, Carel, Laura Damerius, and Karin Isler. 2013. "Wild Orangutan Males Plan and Communicate their Travel Direction One Day in Advance." *PLoS ONE* 8: e74896. doi: 10.1371/journal.pone.0074896.

Varela, Francisco, Evan Thompson, and Eleanor Rosch. 1991. *The Embodied Mind.* Cambridge: MIT Press.

Vaz Da Silva, Francisco. 2007. "Folklore into Theory: Freud and Lévi-Straus on Incest and Marriage." *Journal of Folklore Research* 44: 1–19.

Voget, F. W. 1961. "Sex Life of the American Indians." In *The Encyclopaedia of Sexual Behavior*, volume 1, eds. A. Ellis and A. Abarbanel, 90–109. London: W. Heinemann.

von Frisch, K. 1967. *The Dance Language and Orientation of Bees.* Cambridge: Harvard University Press.

Warwick, Kevin. 2004. *I, Cyborg.* Champaign: University of Illinois Press.

Weil, Kari. 2010. "A Report on the Animal Turn." *Differences: A Journal of Feminist Cultural Studies* 21 (2): 1–23.

Welsch, Wolfgang. 2004. "Animal Aesthetics." *Contemporary Aesthetics* 2: n.p. http://hdl.handle.net/2027/spo.7523862.0002.015.

Wheeler, Brandon. 2009. "Monkeys Crying Wolf? Tufted Capuchin Monkeys Use Anti-Predator Calls to Usurp Resources from Conspecifics." *Proceedings: Biological Sciences* 276 (1669): 3013–18.

White, Hayden. 1987. *The Content of the Form: Narrative Discourse and Historical Representation.* Baltimore: Johns Hopkins University Press.

White, Lynn. 1967. "The Historical Roots of Our Ecologic Crisis." *Science* 155: 1203–207.

Wiener, Norbert. 1961. *Cybernetic: Or Control and Communication in the Animal and the Machine.* Cambridge: MIT Press.

Williams, Heather, Iris I. Levin, D. Ryan Norris, Amy E. M. Newman, and Nathaniel T. Wheelwright. 2013. "Three Decades of Cultural Evolution in Savannah Sparrow Songs." *Animal Behaviour* 85 (1): 213–33. https://doi.org/10.1016/j.anbehav.2012.10.028.

Wilson, William A. 1973. "Herder and Romantic Nationalism." *Journal of Popular Culture* 6: 819–35.

Wojcik, Daniel. 1997. *The End of the World as We Know It: Faith, Fatalism, and Apocalypse in America.* New York: NYU Press.

Wolfe, Cary. 2003. *Animal Rites: American Culture, the Discourse of Species, and Posthumanist Theory.* Chicago: University of Chicago Press.

Wright, Anthony, Jacqueline Rivera, Stewart Hulse, and Julie Neiworth. 2000. "Music Perception and Octave Generalization in Rhesus Monkeys." *Journal of Experimental Psychology* 129 (3): 291–307.

Ziegler, Charles A. 2003. "UFOs, Religion, and the Statistics of Belief." In *Encyclopedic Sourcebook of UFO Religions*, ed. James R. Lewis, 349–58. Amherst, NY: Prometheus.

INDEX

ABOUT THE AUTHOR

Photo Credit: Ling Luo

Tok Thompson is a folklorist with wide-ranging theoretical, topical, and geo-graphical interests, with a special interest in languages and ontology. He is currently an associate professor of anthropology and communications at the University of Southern California and has also taught in Ireland, Iceland, the United Kingdom, and Ethiopia. He has published over thirty articles on folk-loric topics ranging from the prehistoric to the cyborg and has authored four books. He cofounded the journal *Cultural Analysis: An Interdisciplinary Forum on Folklore and Popular Culture* in graduate school, which he continued to coedit for thirteen years. He has also served as editor of *Western Folklore* and is currently editing a book series of cases studies on world mythology with Gregory Schrempp for Oxford University Press.

www.ingramcontent.com/pod-product-compliance
Lightning Source LLC
Chambersburg PA
CBHW031133270326
41929CB00011B/1603